PRA
WITH ME ALL ALONG

"The mental and emotional aspects of health may have the largest single impact on you. This book helps you identify, navigate, and heal at a deeper level than genetics. After all, your emotions, and thoughts, trigger your genetic expression."

—DR. BEN LYNCH, best-selling author of
Dirty Genes and founder of Seeking Health

"Taking care of your mental and spiritual health should be at the forefront of healing any imbalance within the body. It's often the most overlooked aspect when it comes to true healing. This book takes you on a beautiful path of self-discovery and healing from the inside out."

—DR. KRYSTAL HOHN, co-author of *The Health Babes Guide to Balancing Hormones* and co-host of *Health Babes Podcast*

"A truly holistic approach to healing that addresses not only our physical needs but also often-neglected areas like connection, relationships, past experiences, self-care, and purpose. Katy has woven all of these topics together beautifully in this guide that belongs on the shelf of anyone experiencing chronic illness."

—MICKEY TRESCOTT, NTP, author of *The Autoimmune Paleo Cookbook* and *The Nutrient-Dense Kitchen*

WITH ME
All
ALONG

*Reclaim Your Innate Wisdom
to Get Well and Thrive*

WITH ME *All* ALONG

KATY BOSSO

RIVER GROVE
BOOKS

This book is intended as a reference volume only. It is sold with the understanding that the publisher and author are not engaged in rendering any professional services. The information given here is designed to help you make informed decisions. If you suspect that you have a problem that might require professional treatment or advice, you should seek competent help.

Published by River Grove Books
Austin, TX
www.rivergrovebooks.com

Distributed by River Grove Books

Design and composition by Greenleaf Book Group
Cover design by Greenleaf Book Group
Cover Images: Istockphoto/borchee and Unsplash/Jeremy Bezanger

Publisher's Cataloging-in-Publication data is available.

Print ISBN: 978-1-63299-603-9

eBook ISBN: 978-1-63299-604-6

First Edition

I dedicate this book to my brother, Robert Bosso. He had an enormous impact on my childhood, on my sense of feeling heard, of being fully seen, known, understood, accepted, loved, and cherished. May others be able to experience this type of bond and love in their relationships, for it is the most profound gift humans can receive. You are always with me, Bert.

CONTENTS

DISCLAIMER

This book includes the opinions and experiences of the author and is not intended to replace the advice of your medical care provider. The information is not intended to diagnose or treat and is not a substitute for professional and medical advice. Before beginning any program or treatment, you are advised to seek the guidance and advice of your physician or qualified health provider.

All names of clients and particular aspects of their cases have been changed to protect their privacy.

INTRODUCTION

We are not immune to the human condition. A brilliant professor from my doctoral program used this statement to refer to the fact that, regardless of any formal training we might have or how much we know (or think we know), life has a way of showing us our blind spots. This concept applies to all of us, not just therapists, coaches, or doctors. No person is immune to the human condition or human suffering. All are invited to the table, and at some point, in life, everyone becomes members of this club that no one wants to be part of. The suffering, the challenges, and the unpredictability become the underlying themes of life for a while. Yet what grows from the ashes is the most unpredictable of all.

I certainly was not immune, regardless of my training or experience. While working toward a degree in clinical mental health counseling, which focuses on serving those with a wide variety of emotional dysregulation, I ironically felt as dysregulated as one possibly could. Everywhere I turned, it seemed like I was slowly losing my mind. It felt as if I was trapped in a tornado, with no hope of finding the ground beneath me. My health had gone to hell in a handbasket, to be quite frank. The counseling program, along with family and friends, was one of the few things that kept me grounded and supported. During those years, I experienced a period of debilitating physical illness that, in turn, essentially ran over my mental health with a steam roller. If that wasn't enough, I also experienced a profound loss that forever rocked and altered my world, my family's world, and our entire reality moving forward.

For whatever reason, sometimes we need to be shaken awake. We need to learn how to grow deeper into ourselves than ever before. Sometimes that means a radical course correct or reroute of the GPS life path, depending on how lost or how far off track we are. No more autopilot for us. This book shares my personal and educational experiences and overall healing, from torment to triumph. It reflects what I learned and discovered along the path of the human condition we know as life. I offer tools and strategies to help address and combat mysterious and stubborn physical and mental health challenges by getting to the true core of these issues—not masking them, not covering them up, not ignoring them.

My journey to greater health began at age twenty-one. A type A problem solver, I was always reading, writing, and overanalyzing, trying desperately to crack the code. I knew there was something out there to help me, I just had to find it. Although I didn't know what it was or what it looked like, I heard a voice telling me to be relentless in my search for better health. I now know this relentless drive led to a wonderful ending—sharing my knowledge with those who need it most. What follows is everything I learned during my journey.

I learned that I had to bring my body
back to health to heal my mind.

And I had to heal my mind to
bring my body back to health.

Body and mind are beautifully intertwined. I share my findings in hopes that my journey awakens your faith in the limitless regenerative ability of the body, the mind, and the soul. Consider me your personal assistant, who researched, taste-tested, and tried countless healing approaches to get well. Each stop brought with it new information, new faces, and a passion for one of the deepest kinds of work a person can do—to heal thyself. I hope this book offers you a sense of compassion and hope, knowing that whatever you are struggling with, I have great empathy and love for your path to wellness.

This book will help you look at health from profound new perspectives. First, we'll examine emotional and psychological causes of mental and physical challenges, which are driven by chronic stress, our social environment, interpersonal relationships, traumatic experiences, and other difficult, painful past events. This part of the book includes a clinical lens and foundation from my education and work as a therapist.

Second, you will learn about a functional medicine approach to psychiatry and whole-body wellness. We'll look at the physical drivers of poor mental health, such as blood sugar, digestion, and the immune system, and explore simple lifestyle changes that can dramatically affect the brain's ability to function well. At the core of functional medicine is preventing or dramatically improving illness by addressing and focusing on physiological root causes and seeing the body as a whole with many parts that all interact and affect each other.

Lastly, we'll dive into significant, regenerating avenues through which you can finally feel connected to yourself again. These include spirituality, life purpose, connection, fun, and creativity. These elements were all important to me on my own wellness journey, and I find them powerful beyond words.

As humans, we have a mind, a body, and a soul. These components are not isolated. They intertwine in a beautiful combination, a unique symphony that creates each individual. When we do not fee well, each piece must be considered in its entirety, because there is a good chance that something (or some things) are off kilter. Allow the information in this book to sink in, increase your awareness, and create an opportunity for critical thinking. You'll be happy you did.

This information was gathered from my own experiences, brilliant doctors, healers and coaches, and my own clinical experience and education as a licensed therapist. To get the most out of this book, I recommend reading a small amount per sitting. There is no need to rush. In each chapter, you will find one or more reflections to pause and think about the material. I suggest you use a special journal or notebook designated for any answers and insights that come your way. The information that resonates most will jump out at you. Healing is not a rushed experience, so take your time. You are exactly where you need to be today, in this moment. Take a deep breath and congratulate yourself for taking a step forward toward better mental and physical health.

Finally, please remember, I am a trained counselor and a professor, but I am not a medical doctor. This book is my own understanding of how mental and physical health challenges occur. Since the body and mind are so incredibly intertwined, you may feel like certain sentences, chapters, or pieces of information are repetitive. Certain factors drive health challenges via a variety of overlapping pathways and mechanisms. Some key suggestions, such as diet and digestive health, affect several different systems of the body, brain, and wellness. This is exciting because it means there are several things you can do to feel better and recover your physical and emotional health. Some may be easy to implement. Others will be more challenging, perhaps because of your schedule, personal commitments, or because something is holding you back from moving forward, such as fear. The ideas and concepts in this book are by no means an exhaustive list. I encourage you to read through each chapter and find the concepts that truly stand out to you and to use those ideas to create an action plan for your own health.

Here is my story.

DEAR READER

DEAR READER,

This is a letter just for you. It is a way for me to share my healing process with you. I hope this letter helps you know how much I understand the struggle of the unknown and the brutal pains that come with renewal and ascension. And I hope you also come to know how much compassion I have for you and your own healing.

WHAT THE HELL JUST HAPPENED?

Ow. The burning. Ow. The stinging. Ow. The misery. I was terrified. My abdomen felt as swollen as a balloon and hard as a rock. My mom and my friends had seen my stomach like this before. I even showed a gastroenterologist, who was completely bewildered by it. My symptoms occurred after eating certain foods. Sometimes my stomach hurt, and sometimes it was just swollen. But on one such night, it was next-level pain. It was late summer of 2014 and I was twenty-two years old at the time. I had been experiencing inconvenient and confusing digestive pains for several months, but the struggle became debilitating that July. I was in such severe pain that I contemplated going to the emergency room. Clutching my stomach, I wondered what to do.

This time period, when the pain tripled, was the start of my healing journey. I didn't have the wisdom yet to know what I should reach for in order to feel better. I was simply scared and puzzled. I did have enough sense to know it was a severe reaction to something I had eaten. What I learned later was that my immune system was creating localized inflammation in my intestine to fight off a harmless food it thought was a serious danger to me. My immune system had gone rogue, in a sense. I didn't know it at the time, but I had acquired severe intestinal permeability, which I describe in depth in Chapter 14. I intuitively knew the emergency room staff would not be able to do much for me, since the several doctors I had visited in the weeks prior had labeled it as a sensitive stomach and irritable bowel syndrome (IBS)—and told me to take a probiotic. Although initially comforting, the vague information and suggestion did not take even a fraction of my symptoms away. So I rode out the pain that night, and my mother had to watch it all.

We have all had struggles and sufferings that are unique to each of us. I know what it is like to not know what to do, to be afraid, and to be in physical and emotional pain. What I can tell you is this: Keep going. Keep fighting for yourself and for your loved ones.

My story began in 2013 (well, truth be told, small, lingering symptoms began a lot earlier than that, but it really started hitting the fan around that time). I was twenty-one years old and was plagued by constant strep throat infections month after month after month. Sometimes I would sleep for several days and eat more vegetables, and it would resolve on its own. Other times I had to take rounds and rounds of antibiotics, along with steroids to get the swelling down so I could breathe normally. This vicious cycle became so severe that

I eventually had to get my tonsils removed, which required more medication. I became increasingly tired. In truth, my tiredness had started well before 2013, I just didn't notice it fully until then. Along with the fatigue came digestive issues, increasing and unwarranted anxiety, bouts of sadness and tearfulness that would come out of nowhere, and the immune system issues that were already clear and apparent. I experienced a lot of bloating, swelling, and inflammation in the gastrointestinal tract. My gut bacteria clearly did not like the antibiotics they were bombarded with regularly and could not recover before another round of medication arrived the following month. My gut microbiome was begging for mercy! And as if that wasn't enough, I also developed fungal and yeast issues from all of the antibiotic use.

BEGINNING THE CLIMB

As the doctors prescribed more and more medications, my symptoms mounted. I began looking into more holistic approaches to these issues, reading articles from mindbodygreen, and purchasing a few supplements here and there with hopes that I could really get myself back together quickly and easily. I had no intention of really changing much, of becoming a different person or growing and learning. At the time, I was completely unaware that this was a wake-up call from God. I didn't know that "growing from my experiences" was even a thing. I was twenty-one years old, and I loved parties, events, spending time with friends, goofing around, socializing, and staying as busy as humanly possible. So during my casual search for a quick fix, I came upon an obscure medication online that was supposed to completely fix systemic yeast and fungal issues and "balance everything out." This included fixing moderate digestive and skin issues, in addition to lack of energy, moodiness, and focus. If that claim had been accurate, this book would never have been written.

Here's what actually happened: I had a severe reaction to the medication a few days after ingesting it. It was the straw that broke the camel's back. The intestinal pain and digestive symptoms went from a five to a ten in severity nearly overnight. The aftermath of this medication ingestion, aside from the increasingly severe intestinal pain, also included chest tightening and severely shallowed breathing after eating. In addition, hives often popped up in random places on my neck, and I experienced overwhelming fatigue and brain fog after eating. I told close family members that it felt like something very heavy was being lowered onto my back, a physical sense of weakness. Every time—or almost every time—that I ate, this would happen. Over time, this made me afraid of something I had always enjoyed and celebrated my entire life—eating.

It didn't take long for this dramatic shift in health to impact my life. Just days after taking the medication, I became so dizzy and nauseated at work that I had to go home thirty minutes into my shift. I also began feeling lightheaded from many strong scents—from the smell of gasoline, cigarette smoke, and many other odors. I went to several doctors, and they all shook their heads, some with kindness and simple confusion, others with disbelief and disdain. I looked healthy, and I was young, so what could possibly be the matter? I would think to myself at each new visit "Trust me, doc, I'm just as confused as you are." One doctor even suggested that I was simply very stressed out and depressed, and maybe the very thing I needed was medication. My reality of suffering was completely invalidated, and it stung.

That following month, in August 2014, my schedule was consumed by going to so many medical professionals and still not getting the relief I wanted so badly, so desperately. I was SO tired of feeling like I just had to manage it, deal with it, and rally through it. SO. TIRED. OF. IT. I wanted to be able to authentically answer someone's polite "How are you?" inquiries with "Thanks for asking. I feel fantastic." But I couldn't! One day after a deep discussion about my health, I looked at my mother square in the eye and said, "Humans are completely capable of great health, of feeling energized and alive and well and feeling deeply at peace. I will not stop until I find that. I will not stop until I find the answer. My answer. No one will stop me." She replied, "And I will see you through it."

It was in that moment that I knew I was capable of finding the answer—because I had her support. I felt an inner knowing that said I would find the answer. I knew that at some point I would make it to the top of the climb, glowing with abundant health. I could feel it in my bones. I simply had to surrender and start the hike. It wouldn't always be easy. It would be tiresome and tedious at times. What I didn't realize is that the beginning breadcrumbs I needed to follow arrived more quickly than I expected.

YOU CAN GO YOUR OWN WAY

One special day in September 2014 my mom was talking to an acquaintance at the gym about my health. The woman gave my mom the name and number of a doctor she thought could help me. We made an appointment, and down south we drove. I didn't know it at the time, but this was the beginning of a beautiful and unexpected passion for holistic approaches, for naturopath work, and for functional medicine. It was also the beginning of an enduring, loving friendship with one of the most incredible, angelic, kind souls I have ever met.

Serena Bordes, a naturopathic doctor (N.D.) and acupuncturist, sat down with my mother and me. She listened to my story with eagerness and quickly handed me some supplements to start taking. She talked to me about my diet, about "energy" and "vibration." She talked to me about needing to "let go of things." Although at that time I didn't know what I needed to "let go of," somewhere deep down I felt very connected to her words. I can see plainly now, as I look back, that I had to let go of regrets, burdens, fears, and resentments that I had kept bottled up. I needed to forgive myself for all of those little "we are only human" mistakes and choices that so many of us hold onto for so long. The things I wish I had said, had done, and the could've, should've, would've plagued me, and I didn't even realize it. I needed to release my fear of the unknown and my fear of what people thought of me. I also needed to let go of my impatience in this healing process. In addition to her suggestion of "letting go," she also sensed that I had some form of pathogen or infection in my system that was complicating matters, such as a bacterial infection, virus, or parasite. I learned a great deal from her, and she opened up the floodgates for similar types of doctors and healers to enter my life. This was my start of letting go of things that did not help me and moving toward the things that resonated deeply with me. This is when I began following my own path.

The doctors I met during this time each had their own training and specialties and taught me unique things. I am happy to be able to share their knowledge, ideas, and understanding with you. Each chapter in this book is filled with the ideas and strategies taught to me by chiropractors, naturopaths, acupuncturists, coaches, healers, and many others. I have also included things I learned for myself through observation, personal experience, and in school. I mentioned in the introduction that during the most difficult parts of my health journey, including my mental health journey, I was trying to begin a master's degree in clinical mental health counseling (so you can bet that I learned a great deal about mental health from my professors, internships, and spending time with clients).

I spent five years searching, learning, meeting incredibly brilliant people, discovering, researching, and collecting (my own) data. And when I dug deep enough, I learned that it wasn't just ONE answer. God wanted me to learn all of the answers about what keeps the human body well, what keeps it radiant, resilient, and firing on all cylinders. I learned so many techniques that built me back up, that helped me find myself again and yet also for the first time.

When I look back at it all, I wonder whether my journey would have been shorter if I had found a more holistic approach to healing at the very beginning. Would I have healed more swiftly with less suffering? While the simple answer is yes, or probably, for healing to occur I would have needed to have complete commitment and buy-in regarding the big things that ultimately led me to the best emotional and physical health of my life. At twenty-one, I was looking for the quick fix. I was looking for that one-and-done, let's move on. I figured, *Just a couple months of this and I'll be back to my old self.* My OLD self. Looking back, I can say with certainty that I needed transformation. I did not need my old ways of thinking, the old ways that I had treated myself, the old habits and patterns, to heal. They would have done nothing to bring me deep and lasting healing.

Do you daydream of a quick fix too? I don't blame you one bit. I was on that train, first in line, ticket in hand. We're only human! We just want to get on with it, right? Do less work and get the most in return? The problem with these old ways of thinking and quick solutions is that they will never give you the enormous growth and personal healing that you so deeply deserve. You deserve a profound healing that makes you feel better and more joyful than you ever have in your entire life. YOUR ENTIRE LIFE. A healing that makes you love yourself to your very core. You will break patterns never before contemplated, and you will choose very different ways of being in the world through a transformative healing. This change takes TIME. It is not an overnight transformation, although some people certainly wake up with a renewed sense of self, brimming with motivation and readiness after doing the work. When you take an all-in approach to healing, know that it can take time and it can take patience. Sometimes successive waves of healing create a shift in attitude, and you realize that healing is a journey that will transform you in mind and body. It builds character, perseverance, motivation, and self-esteem. Is it painful sometimes? ABSOLUTELY.

Each discovery—finding a new doctor, a new therapy, a new diet, a new supplement, a new book, et cetera—brought with it renewed hope, excitement, and joy. That joy would soon wear off when the approach didn't completely heal me, and I was left with painful disappointment, frustration, and hopelessness. I was desperate and discouraged, and it dragged me down until I found the next thing that piqued my interest. Then the cycle would occur, again and again. I never recognized that each step along the way helped me—I gained additional knowledge (whether scientific or spiritual) and was propelled in the right direction. Sometimes it could be 5% better, or 10% better. I never noticed because I was so caught up on wanting to go from 0% to 100%.

How many times have you attempted to feel better, only to notice little change from whatever you tried? I have so much compassion for you, and I hold space for your disappointment, confusion, and frustration. What I want you to know is that if you don't give up, you will find it. If you don't give up, you will one day witness the miraculous capacity of the body and mind for healing. Things you have tried along the way have probably pushed you in a positive direction, even if you simply learned something, acquired information, conducted research, or achieved a real improvement in your mental and physical health. Have you ever felt worse from trying something? My hand is fully raised right now because I tried so many things that left me in bad shape.

It is my deepest and most sincere hope that this book helps you see things differently than you once did, that you become able to love others and yourself more deeply, with more compassion and less judgment, and that you develop a profound grace for humanity and all the mental and physical health issues that can arise. Every single person on this planet has a story and a unique series of events that have brought them to this point in their life. YOU have a unique series of events that have brought you to this present day. These things have shaped you, changed you, taught you lessons, and opened your mind to a greater awareness, if you allowed it to. There is so much suffering in silence, but that doesn't have to be the case. Information can be shared, changes can be made, and health can improve. It begins with each of us and what we choose to do about it.

Remember that growth and healing, whether physical or emotional, is not a linear process. It is an everyday process, a process that lasts a lifetime. As you learn and heal, things may arise that don't feel good and could bring you down momentarily. But by working through this struggle and healing whatever issues you face, you can reach newer and better levels of health than you thought possible. I hope you arrive at the best mental and physical health of your life, because you deserve it. Keep striving for more.

PART ONE

*Understanding Your
Mental Health*

1

WHAT IS MENTAL HEALTH?

The term "mental health" has escaped its dry, clinical origins and become a buzzword—and I couldn't be more thrilled. Mental health is now a regular topic in social media, is often discussed by celebrities, and is supported by structures and specialists in school systems and colleges. Prioritizing psychological wellness is no longer a taboo subject. Instead, it is openly talked about and societally supported.

When you consider your own mental health and your unique definition of it, you may begin by thinking about how you FEEL from day to day. Therapists often ask, "How have you been feeling this week?" to gauge your emotional temperature. Checking in with yourself about your mental health is vitally important. It increases your awareness about your current state and helps you identify when or where you feel better or worse. Ask yourself how you feel:

- Do you feel like your mood and energy are all over the place?

- Do you constantly feel anxious, stressed, or on edge?

- Is your ability to achieve your maximum potential being weighed down by your mood or thoughts?

- Are your relationships or work affected by symptoms associated with your emotional health?

- Do you feel you are making poor or unhelpful choices for yourself?

Did you answer yes to some or most of the preceding questions? You are not alone. Feeling off, overwhelmed, and dysregulated is very common and happens to all of us. Sometimes these feelings ebb and flow during certain seasons in our lives, and other times they feel like unwelcome visitors who forgot to go back home years ago.

WHAT IS "NORMAL" ANYWAY?

My father has always had a charming way to describe the human condition: "We are all just fruitcakes, and the cosmic baker took us out of the oven a little too soon." If you're like me, you may not pick up the song lyrics at play here. My dad is referring to Jimmy Buffett's song "Fruitcakes." I couldn't agree more with Mr. Buffet (and my dad). We all have our quirks and interesting ways of behaving, coping, and living.

Given the wide variety of human behavior, you may wonder how "normal" is defined or what constitutes "optimal" mental health. Those are excellent questions with complex answers. The *Diagnostic and Statistical Manual of Mental Disorders* (DSM-5) is a diagnostic book used by mental health professionals and will be referenced throughout this book. The DSM-5 defines a mental disorder as a "syndrome characterized by clinically significant disturbance in an individual's cognition, emotional regulation, or behavior that reflects a dysfunction in the psychological, biological, or developmental processes underlying mental functioning."[1] But optimal mental health is certainly not just the absence of dysfunction or disturbance.

Does good mental health simply mean having a positive demeanor and being upbeat most of the time? Does it only mean that we have good mental health when we are productive members of society who get our work done every day, take care of family members, and keep a clean home? Of course not. Our external portrayal is only part of the equation. What we show the world vs. what is going on inside can be entirely different. Mental health is about how you FEEL. Don't get me wrong—being productive, taking care of others, and keeping the home clean and organized are all great indicators that a person is functioning and not significantly impaired, as the DSM-5 describes it. But let's go deeper.

Mental health involves many categories: the wellbeing of a person socially, emotionally, and psychologically. It affects how we relate to friends, family, coworkers, and others. It affects our behaviors and choices in every aspect of our lives. When I observe optimal mental health in others and in myself, I see an ability to regulate emotions well. This includes the ability to feel anger, frustration, or sadness. In fact, being able to feel these emotions and express them without letting them control you or consume you is optimal. Good mental health is also about resiliency—an ability to tolerate stress without it becoming unbearable. Bouncing back from disappointments and perceiving stress as part of life is a component of optimal wellness. Good mental health also includes believing that the world is largely good, and believing that people generally mean well. Optimal mental health means feeling drive and purpose, and having healthy relationships.

We Are All Unique

Good mental health can mean something different for each of us. A dear friend of mine once shared a story she heard from another therapist: "Some of us are like the original eight-pack of Crayola crayons when it comes to our emotions. We have the basics and we use them when necessary. But some people are like me. I'm the value pack from Costco that has every shade under the sun, plus some. And those emotions are constantly coming out of the box, sometimes five at a time."

Raise your hand if you feel a whole lot of feelings. (I sure do.) We are all unique when it comes to emotions, sensitivity, and the degree to which we express emotion. Some people feel more deeply, have more thoughts, or need to process more extensively to understand their feelings and arrive at a conclusion. That is perfectly okay. Having good mental health means knowing what your needs are, knowing how to meet your needs, and actively doing so. You will learn more about your own emotions and needs as you work through the material in this book.

Mental Health Statistics

The statistics on mental wellbeing are staggering. Every year in the United States, 20% of adults experience mental illness,[2] ranging from very mild experiences to very severe. This statistic jumps to 70% for adolescents in juvenile detention.[3] Less than half of adults receive the mental health services they need; this includes clinical interventions involving psychologists and counselors.[4] According to research, results appear similar for children with mental health disorders that do not receive treatment.[5]

As you can see from the statistics, it is "normal" to need some help to have good mental health. If you have picked up this book for yourself, a loved one, or your clients, you should know that many people suffer from mental health issues every single day. Throughout this book, I will guide you through the many elements and factors that affect emotional wellbeing, including physiological, psychological, and spiritual concepts. These pages will have new, different, and fresh information that you can draw on to create a healing plan for yourself.

REFLECTIONS IN THIS BOOK

As mentioned in the introduction, each chapter of this book has a reflection to help you explore your own thoughts, feelings, and experiences and how they affect your life. Some of the reflections are journaling exercises, and a handful include tools and skills for you to try. I share these skills with my clients to help them with relaxation and mood, and I hope they help you, too.

Large portions of the reflections are questions that I ask clients in therapy sessions. These questions and concepts prompt insights, promote awareness of the self and body, and allow clients to get to know themselves on a deeper level. It is beautiful when people build genuine relationships with themselves, nurture those relationships, and honor their uniqueness—when they become truly comfortable being themselves. This experience is a sacred one, and I sincerely wish you experience it.

You may consider dedicating one notebook specifically to these reflections. The notebook will help you organize your thoughts as you make your way through this book and travel along your own healing journey.

Let's get started!

REFLECTION: DEFINING MENTAL HEALTH FOR YOURSELF

Take a moment and ask yourself right now: What is my own definition of mental health? If I, my child, or a friend had optimal mental health, what would that look like to me? Ponder the following questions and write your answers in your journal:

- Do you envision someone radiating joy or peace?
- Are they handling stress or setbacks with resiliency?
- Are they emotionally regulated?
- When you feel happy, what does this feel like in your body? Is there a sense of calm, or is the sensation difficult to feel or describe? Where in your body do you feel it, if anywhere?
- Are you able to feel uncomfortable emotions, such as anger or fear? What do those feel like in your body?

When our emotions are regulated well, we tend to be calmer, happier, more relaxed, and better able to move through and process stressful or hurtful situations. Anger is released in a variety of ways, such as through forms of art, moving the body, journaling, or doing therapeutic work, to name a few. When emotions are not regulated well, such as dysregulated anger, hurt, or pain, the result can be alcohol and drug abuse, domestic violence, behavioral outbursts, or verbal abuse.

A FEW WORDS ON THERAPY

This book outlines many concepts for you to consider and contemplate as you read, take notes, and complete the reflections in your own unique way. This is deeply personal work; it is solitary work that can be done only by you. Changes, choices, healing—all will be implemented by you. Doing this work will help you develop a more intimate and stronger relationship with yourself.

With that being said, there is never shame in needing help. Let me repeat that. **There is NEVER shame in needing and seeking help**. To be human is to need help from others. We are not meant to be isolated from one other. We are social beings, and our social relationships can be sources of tremendous healing. We can help one another navigate our struggles and celebrations as we journey through life. Having a skilled and knowledgeable person to talk to in a confidential and safe environment can be an enormous help. Therapists help us get out of our own heads. If you are an overthinker (yeah—me too), having someone sit with you as you sift through years of built-up thoughts, beliefs, memories, and perceptions can be powerful, and even transformative. Therapists can teach you about yourself and help you understand why you are suffering. It can help us with day-to-day struggles and pains and with memories and events marked by profound suffering. No one is immune to issues with mental health.

The thought of therapy can be scary for some people. If you are considering therapy to work through any type of problem or issue, know that this is a courageous step. If you were hurt in the past, it can be hard to turn toward people for assistance. But if you turn toward the right people, healing CAN happen. Part of healing is being able to safely connect with another person—trauma and pain can cause disconnection. We need "disconfirming" or corrective experiences to help us see the world, ourselves, and others in a clearer way.[6] We need new experiences that contradict our old, unhelpful beliefs about the world, other people, and ourselves. These corrective experiences give us new data about the world. With enough of these experiences, our beliefs, opinions, and perspectives begin to change. We may begin to believe that we really are worthwhile, that people show up for us, that we are supported, or that it is okay to show emotions or make mistakes.

In therapy, the individual or client talks about current issues, their goals, and how to move toward their goals. Issues can include something that happened last month or an intense, difficult situation that occurred years ago. The word "trauma" is often associated with very large, intense events of psychological or physical suffering. But less intense or less well-remembered experiences may also have affected us profoundly, and those experiences may need just as much processing as the larger, more prominent events in our lives.

Several different therapy modalities can help us process and move forward after trauma, including eye movement desensitization and reprocessing (EMDR) therapy, trauma-focused cognitive behavioral therapy (TF-CBT), somatic therapies, experiential therapy, transpersonal therapy, and psychodynamic therapy. It is important to address both the mind and the body when healing trauma because our bodies store and remember the specific stress hormones and energy released during the original experience(s). To find a verified practitioner in your area, visit Psychologytoday.com for someone who specializes in your unique needs.

Today, mental health is openly talked about, normalized, and (thankfully) more accessible. Therapy is for EVERYONE. We each get to define what good mental health means for us. Your joy and my joy may look very different, and your sadness could look like my anger.

In the next chapter, we will explore how mental health is intertwined with family matters.

2

FAMILY OF ORIGIN

"**W**hat do you remember from your childhood?" "What is the earliest memory you can recollect?" If you just pictured a large, comfortable couch with an inquisitive person sitting behind it, holding a notepad, wearing glasses, and scribbling away, I did too. The classic image of a shrink. All from two questions!

All joking aside, these are incredibly important questions to consider, contemplate, and unpack:

- Did you experience any painful or impactful events in your childhood growing up?
- As a child, were feelings of anxiety, sadness, or fear a common experience?
- Did you ever feel unseen, invalidated, or unheard?
- Was there a constant pressure to fit in or conform in order to feel safe?
- Do you sense that certain family patterns have not served you well?

In this chapter, you will learn about family of origin dynamics and how they may have impacted you (and how they keep impacting you). We will explore how our family of origin shapes our ways of being in the world, influences how well we do in other relationships, and what patterns we have brought into our current life from relationships we observed as a child. We will also look at attachment, generational trauma, and codependency as factors that affect mental health in relation to the family unit.

RETURNING TO YOUR ROOTS

The preceding questions are important because the family environment in which a person grew up taught them a lot of things. The family environment teaches children what behaviors and people are "safe" and what are not. Children experience and observe many events. With their young brains they create meaning from these events, even if their understanding is not the complete story or is out of proportion to the situation. Young children (even those of elementary-school age) do not have the capacity and tools to communicate emotions like we do.[1] This means if a child experienced something terribly frightening, hurtful, or confusing, and it was not processed or validated, this memory and emotion will stay with them and have an impact on their life and ability to relate to others and to the world. There may have been domestic violence or drug and alcohol abuse in the home, or a tragic loss that significantly altered the environment of the child.

A child may learn that trusting people is not safe. Maybe being seen, having needs, or existing is not safe for them. Now picture this child as a grown-up who still holds these beliefs. That the world isn't safe in one way or another. That life isn't fair, or that people leave and don't come back. Maybe they grew up believing that everything was their fault.

Events that occurred early in a person's childhood can continue to affect them deeply later on in life. These children grow up to be adults with their own lives, relationships, and families. They grow up to be people just like you and me. The Chinese proverb, *"Fish do not know it is water in which they swim"* illustrates the concept that whatever family context we grew up in is what we consider to be the norm. We don't know that life is or should be any different. If the water in which we swim is toxic, yet it's all we've ever known, how are we supposed to have that awareness?

ADVERSE CHILDHOOD EXPERIENCES

Traumatic, impactful experiences in childhood are sadly quite common. Adverse childhood experiences (ACEs) are traumatic events that occur between the ages of zero and seventeen years of age. They include violence, witnessing violence, abuse, and neglect. ACEs create toxic stress in the environment of a child who needs stability, safety, and healthy relationships for normal growth and development.

A study conducted in twenty-five states in the United States found that one in six people reported experiencing four or more ACEs, and 61% of adults answered that they had experienced at least one ACE.[2] We learn so much during our childhoods—how to love, how to express emotion, how to deal with frustrations, and more. These lessons are carried through the generations. Dysfunctional information remains until it is finally questioned, acknowledged, and worked through by someone in the lineage.

Sometimes individuals will look at the traumatic, violent, and unsafe dynamics that occurred in their childhood home and consciously choose a different path for their family and home life as an adult. I've seen this in adult children of alcoholic or drug-addicted parents. They want a different life for their kids than the unpredictability, instability, and neglect they grew up with. They choose a different path for themselves that includes abstaining from substances.

In less obvious situations, however, it can be very difficult to break free from the familiar interactions and patterns. Undercurrents of unhealthy patterning may not be so easily detected if it is a person's daily reality. Several clients have told me that they grew up in a household where screaming and yelling were the primary means of communication. They had thought this was the norm in every household—until they met their significant other. The partner was not a fan of this strategy and hoped for a change as they raised their new and growing family. Bringing awareness and attention to family patterns, such as ways of showing love, ways of asking for needs to be met, and types of communicating were eye-opening and helpful for the couples. They were then able to decide how to create their own dynamic, one that was healthier, calmer, and more assertive.

The following is an interesting parable on the topic of family patterns. I have heard a few different versions of the story, but the point remains the same: We often follow behavioral patterns for generations without really knowing why, even when those behaviors are no longer useful or needed.

One day, a woman was helping her mother prepare a turkey dinner. She watched as her mother cut the prepared turkey in half before placing it on a roasting pan and putting it in the oven. She asked, "Mom, why do you cut the turkey in half before baking it?" The mother replied, "Oh, because my mother always prepares turkey this way. I think it helps the turkey cook more evenly." The daughter, intrigued, called her grandmother later that evening and asked,

"Grandma, why do you cut the turkey in half before placing it in the oven?" The grandmother replied, "Oh, because my mother always prepares her turkey this way. I think it crisps up the skin a bit more." The granddaughter, even more invested in this family tradition, decided to visit her great-grandmother the next day. Upon arriving, she asked, "Great-grandma, why do you cut the turkey in half before putting it in the oven? Does it help the turkey cook evenly? Does it make the skin crispier?" The great-grandmother looked at her kindly, saying, "Now that is a good question, dear. I always cut the turkey in half when I prepared it because my oven was so small. The large bird never quite fit without some maneuvering." The great-granddaughter sat there, dumbfounded.

This is a classic illustration of how family patterns and behaviors, passed on through generations, most likely served a good purpose initially then lost their significance or value over time. A lot of these patterns are no longer relevant to us, yet we carry them out subconsciously.

Until you begin interacting with and having different types of relationships with healthy individuals, you may not be aware of the unhealthiness in your family relationships. Something may not feel quite right. Stubborn and relentless anxiety, fatigue, or depression can arise, but identifying the unhealthy behaviors of family or friends is more difficult to quantify.

Reflect on this deeply if you or your loved ones are struggling with mental and physical health issues. What is overwhelming you in your current environment? Check in and ask yourself, "What are the roles that I am currently playing in my life and the lives of others, and do they feel good to me?" The old saying "Love is blind" certainly holds true in romantic relationships, but it also can apply to relation-ships with family and friends if it's something you are just used to or dissociating from on a daily basis. Be honest with yourself in answering "Am I checked out?" And if the answer is yes, ask yourself "What am I checking out from? Is this really normal? Could this be a part of my anxiety, insomnia, et cetera?"

Only when we are surrounded by people who have different dynamics, different ways of being in relationships, and different ways of coping than our families did will our eyes open to the other ways of living and relating. I can't tell you how many times I have talked with clients about relationship dynamics that were in no way healthy, yet they did not have the slightest clue because they were in too deep to notice. They didn't have anything to compare it to.

ALWAYS A SOCIAL COMPONENT

When I work with children, teens, and families, it is often not difficult to see why some kids are having so many problems, whether academically, at home, or with peers. It is quite common to see on an intake form a long list of problematic behaviors and descriptions of a teen's attitudes and issues at school, with friends, and at home. But usually the problem is not just the behavior: it is the family and social environment. When I worked within schools or provided in-home care, I found understandable frustration coming from well-meaning adults and teachers regarding behavioral issues. But what didn't I see? The teen or child being asked about what was going on at home, or what was happening within their social circles (with their friends, peers, or teammates).

One client I worked with early on in my career, we'll call him Adrian, was always very polite and well-mannered during my home visits. We spent time painting, drawing, playing games, crafting, and discussing his weekly home and school behaviors. I felt compassion for Adrian's mother for the significant amount of back-talk he gave her. But it was sad and plain to see that he really just missed his dad, who was largely out of the picture due to drug and alcohol addiction. Adrian craved love from his father and the relationship they once had. On top of what I would call Adrian's grief reaction to the separation from his father, his stepfather was incredibly strict with him and at times flat-out mean, ignoring him and favoring his little brother. The stepfather even installed security cameras throughout the inside of the home to ensure that Adrian was "behaving himself."

It pained me when I finally left that job, because it meant saying goodbye to Adrian, who needed role models and relationships to help him model appropriate communication and behaviors. After all, children learn from their environment and adults. They learn how to get their needs met (if at all). They learn how to express their emotions, how to regulate anxiety or sadness, and how to problem solve. If the only way a child can get essential needs met is through being demanding and nagging a parent for attention, then that's what will happen. And if they are told over and over again how bad they are, do you really think they have a chance at believing otherwise? The family system in which a child is raised may instill belief systems that not only aren't helpful but are false.

For a child to get his or her needs met, they must communicate in some way to an adult caretaker what it is that they specifically want. Over time and as children mature, they watch and observe adults closely to see how they get their needs met so they can do the same. In the book, *Easy to Love, Difficult to Discipline*, Becky Bailey explains that in order to get children to behave or change, the parents and caregivers have to change. This is modeling and teaching at its finest. This is how we learn all things big and small regarding how to relate to the world and how to behave. If you're wondering why you act a certain way in some situations, blow up during conversations, or can't seem to speak up when you need to, I'd like to offer you a simple idea. Did either of your parents exhibit similar behaviors when you were growing up? How about an older sibling? A grandparent, aunt, uncle, or other adult caretaker? The answer may shock you.

Children learn from others, and they are like sponges, soaking things in, seeing what is "normal" behavior, "accepted" behavior, and "safe" behavior. Anything outside of these behaviors may be avoided, even if they are good, healthy, or desirable for optimal mental health. This includes healthy communication. We learn what types of communication are "right" and not right based on what our role models did. As adults, we may not be aware of this until we reflect on it. We know all too well the passive-aggressive style, passive style, and plain aggressive approaches to communicating, so it is a breath of fresh air when we come across someone who is assertive. They state their needs and goals plainly, and we can believe their word. It also may sound terrifying to those who only know the passive way. Just remember that you do not have to be defined by any of this. It is not who you are, it is how you grew up. It is not a reflection of you, it is a reflection of your past environments.

Looking back at the first two questions of this chapter, how would you answer them? Take a moment to read them out loud, then sit back and listen to your mind and body for about ten minutes.

"What do you remember from your childhood?"

"What was your earliest memory you can recollect?"

Have a journal or notebook nearby to jot down your answers. Think of this as a mini reflection. Some memories may surprise you, while others you may already be aware of. These can be fun events, special toys, and people. Experiences that were and are very difficult to process may also come up, and that's perfectly normal. This exercise is simply about increasing awareness and insight into what it was like to grow up as YOU.

Second, after jotting down some events or memories that come to mind, think about what these experiences may have taught you about life. It might be something like "my mother really loves me," or "it's always my fault." You may have felt like you had to take care of your parents' emotional needs constantly for fear that they would explode, break things, withdraw love, or even hurt you or another family member.

It may be strange to contemplate now, but you are no longer a child. You, friend, are all grown up. Some of those experiences and teachings, however, are still with you. Remind yourself that you are not that five-year-old or eight-year-old or twelve-year-old. You have outgrown your kid clothes and now have to decide whether you want to outgrow some of those limiting, false teachings about life and about who you are at your core.

ATTACHMENT

Put simply, attachment is an emotional connection between people. John Bowlby, who produced profound, novel research on attachment in the 1900s, said, "Thus, just as animals of many species, including man, are disposed to respond with fear to sudden movement or a marked change in level of sound or light because to do so has a survival value, so are many species, including man, disposed to respond to separation from a potentially caregiving figure and for the same reasons."[3] He believed, based on his clinical observations and research, that children's problems were "rooted in real relationships with real people."[4] He explained that attachments occur between caregiver and child during the first year and a half of the baby's life. At its core, attachment is part of how we evolved as humans and is part of how we feel safe and survive. Humans are social creatures and, in the past, strength in numbers protected our ancestors.

Attachment and its relationship to mental health fascinate me. It is a topic that has helped me better understand myself and others, including my clients. Knowing your attachment style means recognizing how you work in relationships and how you relate to others. We also have styles of attachment to things like money, our jobs, and God. The terms for different types of attachment vary, but my favorite version is discussed in Rachel Heller and Amir Levine's book, *Attached*. Attachment styles include secure, anxious, avoidant, and anxious-avoidant, sometimes referred to as a disorganized style.[5] Each style varies in its degree of dependence on others, how others are perceived, how the self is perceived, and the degree of avoidance.[6]

For example, anxious and securely attached people move toward others and see other people in a positive way. Avoidant and disorganized individuals may see others as unreliable, unsafe, or untrustworthy and move away from them. Anxious people and disorganized people think less of themselves, whereas securely attached people and avoidant individuals do not overly depend on others and they have a more positive self-concept. I have included some questions within the following reflection to help you better understand how your varying degrees of attachment affect your relationships and happiness.

Although Bowlby surmised that our initial attachment style came from our caregivers when we were very young, I suspect that our attachment tendencies as adults were also influenced by our experiences in elementary, middle, or high school, particularly with regard to our social environments, such as early romantic partnerships and friendships. Sometimes when I discuss attachment styles with my clients, we can work collaboratively and identify rather quickly how their early upbringing created a certain attachment style that they bring to their adult relationships. However, others report a very secure, supportive upbringing with little or no evidence to suggest that they were not nurtured as an infant. This is where I begin bringing up early friendships or first loves. Then we get to the heart of the issue.

Keep in mind that we don't have just one attachment style. We can have a different style based on each relationship we have. We can have a secure attachment to a partner, an avoidant attachment to a friend, and an anxious attachment to another friend. Maybe one relationship with a family member feels like a disorganized attachment. The possibilities are endless. What I find so interesting about attachment styles is that they can change. For example, if someone with secure attachment is in a relationship with someone from another style, it isn't uncommon to see this secure attachment style transfer to the other person.

What this tells us is that the environment has a HUGE impact on mental health. Can you imagine if every person we surrounded ourselves with gave us encouragement every day? If we felt supported, cheered on, and safe to express ourselves and move toward our goals and dreams? If we continuously experience what are called "disconfirming" experiences that are contrary to old, unhelpful thoughts and beliefs over time, those new experiences can be profoundly healing. In secure relationships, people aren't so afraid of someone leaving. People aren't terrified of being themselves. They feel supported, loved, and understood. Old coping mechanisms from the past can soften, for they no longer have so much to protect you from. So, how do YOU act and feel in your current relationships? What was or is your relationship like with your primary caregiver? What would a relationship with secure attachment be like for you? Let's turn our attention to the reflection for some answers and contemplation.

In the following reflection, I have provided you with questions to consider regarding the way you relate to others. I also want you to think specifically about secure attachment and what it means to you. I often ask clients these very same questions.

REFLECTION: EXPLORING YOUR ATTACHMENT STYLE

As previously mentioned, we have different attachment styles to different things and people. When answering the following questions, you may think of one specific person at a time and go through the exercise repeatedly for different people in your life, or you can answer them as they fit you overall. You may find that you have one attachment style for all of your relationships or that your relationships with different people have different attachment styles.

- How do you relate to others emotionally and socially? Do you tend to move toward people or away from them? Or both? Do you rely on others? Do you value your relationships? The answers can be yes, no, sometimes, or both.

- Do you believe that other people will meet your needs? To what degree do you rely on others? Too much? Never?

- How do you feel about your relationship(s)? Do they make you anxious? Do you feel supported? Relaxed? Do you think about your relationships constantly, rarely, or at all?

- Do you worry about others abandoning you or disapproving of you? If people leave, how do you feel? Is it a "Good riddance!" situation or a "Please don't leave me!" feeling?

- Can you speak your truth freely in a relationship without fear of retaliation?

- Can you remember what your relationship was like with your primary caregiver as a child? Did you feel close to them, or distant? Were your needs met sometimes, always, or never? Could you count on them?

- What does "secure" attachment mean to you? What would it be like to have a relationship that is secure, safe, and nurturing to your emotional health? List the characteristics of this relationship and how it would make you feel. Do you have any current relationships like this?

To learn more about attachment and your style, the book *Attached: The New Science of Adult Attachment and How it Can Help You Find—and Keep—Love* by Amir Levine and Rachel Heller is a great resource. We now continue this chapter by discussing generational trauma, followed by codependency.

GENERATIONAL TRAUMA

Generational trauma occurs when what was experienced by past generations is carried into the gene pool and expressed in family patterns and habits.[7] Physiologically, this is known as an epigenetic change, the result of an adaptation to one's environment. I first learned about generational trauma at a counseling conference in Tampa, Florida. The presenter described growing up as a child with depression and anxiety issues but being unable to identify a root cause. However, the family members in the previous generation had endured profound grief and loss. This personal experience sparked her desire to better understand this intriguing link. Thinking about what our ancestors went through and how the memory of their experiences has been passed down to us in our nervous systems is deeply moving. If we can better understand generational trauma and how family members were affected, we can begin to heal.

As I reflect on this concept, I think about my own relatives and what was passed down to me. Some events and traumas will never be uncovered if the experiences are many years old. Some are unveiled in time.

One day, I heard the phone ring at my parents' house. It was my grandmother. Virginia was calling to tell my mom that laundry detergent was on sale and that she better hurry to the store before they ran out. Later that week, I found out that my grandmother purchased enough detergent to fill a shelf in the garage. As I initially giggled at the hoarding behavior that we all tend to do in my family, my mother went on to tell me how my grandmother, who was part of a household of eleven growing up, stood in long food lines during the Great Depression. Although my grandmother felt a great deal of love and connection from her parents, grandmother, and siblings, there was an undercurrent of worry. Would there be enough food and supplies? What would happen if it dwindled down to nothing? A sense of the unknown. A sense of scarcity. Get what you can now, because it may not be there tomorrow. Grab as much as you can.

I felt a deep pain when I first heard the story. And I resonated with it so well. I never experienced anything like that growing up. And yet, the feeling was shockingly familiar.

If I am being radically honest, I see this behavior in my mother. I also see this constantly in myself. We are always worried that if we don't buy something now, it will disappear or discontinue. We overbuy things and then end up donating them or giving them to friends and family when we come to the realization that we really don't need that many of an item. It has taken work and insight to improve this pattern, and yet it still happens to both of us all the time.

If you have any information about your parents' upbringings, grandparents' lives, and great-grandparents' lives, consider writing down this information. Even guesses are helpful. As you review the information, reflect on how these behaviors may have affected them, their levels of stress, depression, and anxiety. Maybe these events sparked anger or frustration? What about trauma and behavioral patterns that kept them safe or protected them? Lastly, I would like you to take a moment to look at your own mental health, level of wellbeing, and behavioral patterns. Consider how any of these traumas may have trickled down into your life because of your family patterns.

This deeper understanding of your family can provide great insights and healing. When we have more information and understand what shaped us, we can be more compassionate with ourselves than if we didn't have this information. Were your relatives in wars? In poverty? What large historical events did they survive or live through? What losses did they experience? What deep emotional hardships? When I explored my family tree in greater depth, I found my heart brimming with compassion and my eyes filling with tears. I witnessed and held space for my past relatives and what they must have endured in those moments. I now hold an appreciation for their resiliency, a deeper mercy and grace for their mistakes, and an awareness that each successor who came after them (including me) was affected by their own trauma in some way.

REFLECTION: GENERATIONAL TRAUMA

Read each question carefully as you ponder your family tree and the events that have shaped your ancestors. It can be a very eye-opening and sometimes emotional exercise. Take all the time you need. It may be helpful to ask some of your relatives for this information. I found that just asking led to a lot of stories and information that I had never heard about before.

- What past hardships or historical events have your relatives gone through?

- How might these events have impacted the person's life? Their family's life?

- Reflecting on these events, how might you have been impacted by your relatives' past?

- What can you gain from reflecting on this? Forgiveness? Compassion? Inspiration? Mercy?

- What generational patterns can you identify that may have served family members in the past but do not serve you in the present?

I hope that this exercise gives you an expansive view of your lineage and of yourself. Every one of us has ancestors who experienced grueling, difficult times. The fact that we are here means that those great-great-great-grandparents embodied resiliency and had the strength to press on. They learned specific coping mechanisms to get them through adversity. Those coping mechanisms and behaviors may have helped them at the time, but after being passed down from generation to generation, they are no longer relevant to us. Asking relatives, such as grandparents, parents, aunts, or uncles about wars, abuse, and traumas can provide a great deal of insight into your family dynamics.

The final portion of this chapter focuses on family and relationships as they relate to codependent behaviors.

CODEPENDENCY

Codependency can be an exhausting situation that drains you of your energy and overall emotional wellbeing. With regard to family issues and relationship dynamics, codependency often does a number on a person's mental health. In her book, *Codependent No More,* author Melody Beattie describes codependency as "people, tormented by other people's behavior."[8] Codependency is categorized by taking responsibility for others, their mistakes, needs, and choices. Codependency can include low self-esteem, repressed feelings, having few or no boundaries, and unhelpful communication styles. Do you ever have a strong urge to just knock some sense into a person when they are not making smart choices and the behavior is relentless and prolonged? I have. Watching others make obviously bad decisions for themselves is exhausting over time. It's easy to see how someone can become codependent if they do not remove themselves from the situation, whether energetically or physically.

Codependent people are often seen as classic control freaks to those they are trying to control. However, this is driven by the fact that everything around them is completely out of control. You may have heard of the term codependency as it relates to addiction and relationships. If someone grew up around parents who were addicted to substances, there was likely an unpredictable feel to their day-to-day life. Some days were good at home, other days were bad. Maybe domestic violence also occurred. Maybe mom or dad were completely checked out and couldn't provide the necessary care for the child. The child may have grown up trying to be the parent, to take care of younger siblings and home duties. The child may even have acted as a caretaker to the parents themselves. The unpredictability of the atmosphere can cause anxiety and depression if there is a sense of feeling trapped, and inner rage or anger about the unfairness of it all. Such feelings of rage are often pressed inward.

Another classic example that can breed codependency is the spouse or partner who says that they need to quit alcohol or drug use but does not. There may be many consequences in plain sight, such as aggressive and risky behaviors when drinking, poor academic or work performance, and even financial or legal consequences. The other person in the relationship may become frustrated, irritable, and resentful if these behaviors continue. This can lead to depression, anxiety, panic, sleeplessness, and poor self-worth. The question observers have is often something like "Why stay? Why deal with that?" There can be many answers to this question, but Beattie explains in her book that sometimes it can be a fear of being alone or being on one's own. Sometimes taking care of others or being the savior in certain instances makes the sober partner feel better about themselves. Sometimes we feel responsible for others' happiness and try to take away their problems or consequences.

While codependency occurs frequently within families who struggle with addiction, codependency runs rampant in many families and relationships without any substance or drug abuse. It can take place in any instance where an individual is making choices or behaviors that another person is trying to (hopelessly) fix or control. The codependent person "knows" exactly what the other person should be doing and makes it their life mission to try to get it to happen. Codependent behaviors, as mentioned earlier, can be driven by the (sometimes justifiable) need for control. If things around a person are not predictable, such as a spouse's explosions of anger at the slightest things, gambling money away, or cheating repeatedly, it is easy to become codependent if you do not walk away from the situation and remind yourself what is and is not your responsibility.

In codependency, we become enablers and rescuers; we do not allow people to experience consequences for their actions and choices. For the codependent, this could mean tirelessly trying to help a partner stop gambling by attempting to manage their behaviors or giving them money over and over again if their choices have caused financial ruin. The helping individual blocks the other person from experiencing uncomfortable circumstances. It can look like a bailout of sorts. It can look like going to extreme lengths—undertaking the task of being around an individual 24/7 so that they can't have an affair—changing one's schedule and limiting one's life in the process. It may mean focusing on someone else's problems more than your own, and more than the other person does. It can mean being attracted to trying to mend "broken" people, because it makes us feel better about ourselves. We feel worthy and useful when we can fix someone, when we are needed. It often also occurs with health-related behaviors such as instances when a person isn't taking their prescribed medication or doing what was advised by a doctor, such as a diabetic, someone with high blood pressure, or other health conditions.

One remarkable statement about codependency comes to mind. Therapist Lee Ballard taught me that individuals are grown adults fully capable of self-preservation. This means that we are all capable of making good choices and taking care of ourselves. If we feel bad for someone and think that we need to jump in and rescue them out of complete pity, Ballard urges to think again. We may think, "They will never get this on their own. I need to take the reins and fix this for them!" We shouldn't want something for a person more than they do. It is their decision and their choice. We have to respect that they are in charge of the course of their lives. They have the capability. They will change only when they are ready to change, and we can't make them. Ballard is quite certain that the only people who need pity are the ones who are never going to get it or really figure it out. Otherwise, everyone else on the planet is fully capable of growing, maturing, and learning from mistakes and healing when they are ready.

Codependency is often present in families that are very enmeshed. Enmeshment means that the lines blur in families with regard to emotions, needs, wants, and problems. If I am in an enmeshed environment, I take on an inordinate amount of responsibility and weight in helping other family members solve their problems, because those problems feel like my own. If someone is angry or upset, then I am roped into being angry or upset. It feels like a life of limited choices, of suppressing your own needs, and of disempowerment. It can make it difficult for a person to know who they really are. If there are no lines dividing a sister from another sister, or a mother from a son, how are family members supposed to feel their own feelings and take responsibility for their own feelings, tasks, and choices? On the flip side, how can a person know what they feel, and what they aren't responsible for, without a boundary around themselves?

If, after reading this section, you resonate with codependency, here are some things to keep in mind in order to improve codependent behaviors (and keep your sanity and mental health in tip-top shape):

- Allow people to be responsible for their actions and leave it up to them to take the necessary steps to fix them.

- Allow others to feel their feelings, while feeling your own feelings. Feelings alone are not dangerous, and it is healthy to identify them, sit with them, and feel them.

- Instead of jumping in to save the day, ask someone about the next steps they are going to take to work on the problem. You can then ask them "What do you need from me?" Sometimes we think we can read other people's minds or know exactly what they need, but we may be shocked to find out what they actually need from us, such as a listening ear or a ride home.

- Learn to accept things as they are. You were not put here on this earth to try and help every single person out there who is hurting (themselves). You can provide information, support, and love, but if someone does not want help or is not ready for change, be respectful of their decision and their stage in life. This is one of the hardest things you can do if you really care about someone and know their highest potential. Honor their free will. I have had to learn acceptance over and over again when helping others and still have to remind myself of it.

Codependency is a very complex topic, one that has heavy roots in the substance abuse fields. And yet—it is often seen in friendships, as well as romantic, sibling, and parent relationships. It distorts and covers up a very real and true fact: You are your own person. You have needs, wants, and desires, and it is your job alone to fulfill them. We can help and aid others when they ask for assistance. We must respect when they choose not to change or work toward a healthier reality for themselves. In releasing this false sense of responsibility, we make our families healthier. In turn, we also free up space to focus more on ourselves and our own self-discovery.

Family of origin issues are always something I help clients uncover, as they can be at the root of unconscious patterns and programming. Understanding these behavioral patterns can promote awareness, understanding, and even forgiveness. If you are interested in healing from your past family dynamics, there are many different therapies available to help you, such as psychodynamic, Adlerian, EMDR, or family systems theory, to name a few. It is important to note that these life experiences within the family unit can be traumatic and even classified as abuse in many, many cases.

Whatever you have been through, I have much compassion for you. Whatever memories arise, whatever messages or limiting beliefs bubble to the surface, know that you are not alone in this. You are so much more than how these events made you feel. You are so much more than what these events made you think about yourself. You are a beautiful, divine creation. It may be hard to believe this statement right now because of all you've been through, but it will not take away my absolute certainty that this is true. Doing the work, learning about your attachment style, and uncovering generations of repeated programming can give you a sense of freedom in knowing, "I don't have to be my parents. I don't have to be my past. I choose to live life in the best way I see fit. I can take the wisdom while leaving behind the rest."

3

TRAUMATIC LIFE EXPERIENCES

We have ALL experienced trauma in our lives. In my initial meeting with a new client, I ask them about their trauma.

- How has the trauma you have experienced impacted your life?
- How has it prevented you from living the life that you long for and deserve?
- Have extremely difficult, stressful events in your life left you with emotional pain?
- Is trauma still impacting your relationships, your health, or your mental wellbeing?
- Are you unsure of how to untangle or heal the wounds of the past and move forward fully and freely?

If you answered yes to one or more of these questions, you are not alone. No one is immune to the potential dysregulation of mind, body, or spirit that can come from trauma. Trauma can be immobilizing and can also cause hypervigilance. It puts blinders on us that narrow our views and perceptions and make it difficult to see other possibilities, choices, or options. This chapter provides stories and information about trauma and tools to help you reflect on your own experiences.

FROZEN IN TIME

Traumatic experiences in our lives can have a monumental impact on how we see the world, on our feelings of safety, and whether we feel calm, focused, and confident throughout our day or anxious, depressed, and irritable. Dr. Stephen Porges, author of *The Polyvagal Theory*, provides one of the best descriptions of trauma as a "chronic disruption of connectedness."[1] This is such an incredible statement. When I recall some of the most stressful times in my life, they all involved an ongoing disruption of my ability to connect with other people in a meaningful, loving way.

Dr. Bessel van der Kolk provides a definition within his book *The Body Keeps the Score*. He explains that trauma is an illness of not being fully alive in the present moment.[2] Again, this makes a lot of sense given that people who experience trauma have problems with dissociation. They check out, go on autopilot, and remove themselves emotionally from the present moment because at one point, the present was too painful to accept.

Experiences such as sexual abuse, verbal abuse, domestic violence, physical violence, neglect, natural disasters, and war trauma are very serious, devastating, and painful examples of traumatic experiences. But trauma can also be the result of smaller insults that affected our nervous systems in such a way that it has a profound impact on our mental and physical wellbeing. Trauma can be prolonged and chronic, or it can occur from one single event.

Unpacking the descriptions in the preceding paragraph, you can see that trauma can come from something that may initially appear insignificant or be written off as harmless. When I ask clients the question, "Have you experienced something you would consider 'traumatic' in your life?" many say no. Not because they won't talk about it, but because they don't consider what they have been through as trauma. But if you have felt like you experienced a chronic disruption of connecting with others, or you feel that you are not fully alive in the present moment, there is more to uncover here. It does not matter whether your friends, family, partner, or others suggest or believe the event or experience was "not a big deal." What matters is YOUR perception of the event, how you processed it, and whether you were able to share your trauma or were shamed for it. That is what matters most of all. So, I ask you to gently consider the events in your life that have impacted you significantly, and what marks those events have left on you. Trauma and the body's built-in protective response can be impacted and triggered by things such as divorce, bullying, teasing, breakups, moving towns, changing houses, switching schools, taking new jobs, physical illness, and virtually any small or large event in which a person perceived that they were disconnected from others or not safe.

I felt terribly disconnected from others during those hard years when I was struggling with being unwell. Being ill was traumatizing. I went to doctors who did not know what was wrong with me or gave me a clean bill of health based on inconclusive blood work. People looked at me and thought I seemed healthy and "fine." At the time, I had no answers or explanations, so I told very few people the full story of what I was experiencing. People didn't know that my lungs and chest tightened when I ate. People didn't know how severe the fatigue or brain fog was while I was in class or trying to complete projects and assignments. I didn't share the pain I felt in my abdomen or the heart palpitations that woke me up in the middle of the night. I didn't express the anxiety I had around different foods or the reactions I was having to them.

I didn't talk about all these things because I didn't know what to say. When I did speak out, I was sometimes met with disbelief or apprehension. Those reactions were traumatizing, too. I became fearful of what people would think, of being disbelieved, made fun of, or ignored. It was downright depressing.

In contrast, when difficult experiences are shared and spoken about in an accepting, nonjudgmental environment, they create a smaller impact in our bodies. When trauma is safely shared and our truth is validated, the process helps us work ourselves free from the effects of trauma. But when trauma is not spoken about, or when it is shared and disregarded or disbelieved, then it leaves a thicker mark and a bigger scar. It's one of the biggest reasons why some people are less impacted by very hard things they have gone through, whereas others are burdened and plagued by their traumas for years on end.

In addition to my struggle to find health and wellness, I experienced trauma when I lost a very close family member. The loss was shocking and made it incredibly difficult for me to connect with others in a meaningful way during that time. I temporarily lost my ability to feel a sense of togetherness, belonging, and peace, and my mind was rarely in the present moment. I dissociated and was unable to share much or to use words to describe my struggles. We'll go into this more deeply in the next chapter, on grief. For many of us, traumas stack one on top of another throughout our life until the accumulated burden becomes too heavy to carry. In that moment, we know something has to be done because life has become too unmanageable, too unbearable, and too uncomfortable. That's when we realize we have work to do.

These difficult experiences and the powerful effects they have on the nervous system can make us see life differently and rewire our brains in an attempt to protect us from future danger. A mentor and friend, professor and psychologist Dr. Phil Henry, uses a great example to describe how a fearful situation gets embedded in our nervous systems and carried with us throughout life. Imagine that you are sleeping soundly and peacefully in the middle of the night. You awaken to use the bathroom, which is down the hall and just past a small linen closet. Groggily, you move toward the door, open it, and see a large black snake slithering down the hall just feet from the closet door. You swiftly retreat to your bedroom in fear and shock. You might even shout or scream in surprise. The next day, you muster up the courage to do what is needed to remove the snake from your home.

Now picture yourself waking up in the middle of the night to use the bathroom again, several nights later. As you open the door and begin walking down the hallway, you see something long and black on the floor coming out of the closet. Immediately you experience the same response of surprise and fear, and you shout, scream, and run back into the bedroom. But this time it is just the long black cord from the vacuum cleaner that has come unwound and slipped out under the closet door.

Even though the initial event with the snake is in the past, the conditioned response to the fearful situation is alive and well. Anything that looks similar sets off the snake alarm in the brain. Frightening events can affect us by distorting our perception of the world and changing our perception of reality. This is why many people have the same reaction to a harmless, everyday event as they do to a truly threatening or stressful situation, without even knowing where their reaction comes from. During a highly stressful or emotionally charged event, the brain creates memories to help avoid a similar situation in the future.

The body's survival mechanisms are truly marvelous. Our subconscious continually scans our environment to ensure our safety at all times. We store memories to ensure our safety in the future. Yet, these same helpful pathways can hold us back from truly thriving. These mechanisms can work against us when they create never-ending thoughts and maladaptive behaviors that do not serve us very well after the traumatic event.

REFLECTION: UNPACKING TRAUMA

In this exercise, we will focus on past traumas that cause you to have reactions in the present that are no longer relevant or no longer serve you. These can be triggers in interpersonal relationships or protective behaviors, such as avoidance, distrust of people, defensiveness, or lack of motivation. Please take your time with each question and feel free to revisit as needed. These can be hard questions to unpack and process, so be gentle with yourself.

Use your journal to answer these questions in any way that feels right. You might use bulleted lists; write descriptions of the experiences, words, and people associated with events; simply write freely; or draw pictures or use colors to help you describe and identify feelings and memories. The reflection questions may be difficult to work through all at once. That's perfectly normal and okay. You can always mark the page and come back to it when you feel ready. You can also pick one or two to answer at a time.

- What difficult experiences have left a mark on your life?
- How have they impacted you?
- In what areas of your life have they made things difficult, heavy, or burdensome? Make a list of ways that trauma has impacted your relationships, your mental health, your physical health, and your overall peace of mind.
- What did these experiences teach you about yourself and your world? Is this true now in the present moment?
- In what ways did these events disconnect you from yourself, God, and others?
- Have you spoken openly about these experiences to others and shared them? Did you when they occurred?
- Do you find yourself constantly on autopilot? Is it hard for you to stay in the present moment? Was there a time in your life that the present moment was dangerous or felt dangerous?
- Do you seem to have reactions to things in your life that are out of proportion to the event? Could these reactions be tied to a past event and an old way of coping? Is the protective response needed anymore?

Whether small or large, the events in our lives can have a monumental effect on our health. Author Michele Rosenthal said, "Trauma creates change you don't choose, healing creates change you do choose." Initial stages of healing include increasing your awareness of how painful past experiences have affected you in your present-day life. We all have triggers. When we explore the WHY, we can then begin figuring out what we need to give ourselves, as well as what we need from others. When we can connect pieces of our current patterns, behaviors, thought processes, and poor health to past events, our perception of the world becomes wider and more expansive.

Healing also includes having certain new experiences that rewire our brains and override the patterns formed in the aftermath of negative experiences. These include positive experiences with other people, ourselves, and life. The daily positive experiences show us over time that the world of possibilities is much grander, more loving, and fruitful than our trauma currently allows us to see. This is how the brain rewires—through time and with consistently positive experiences. We can give ourselves these experiences by implementing many of the techniques covered in this book, such as forming meaningful relationships, using meditation, and finding our life's purpose through deeply meaningful experiences and work. The remaining pieces of this chapter will review the limbic system, post-traumatic stress disorder (PTSD), and healing in daily life.

AN INTRODUCTION TO THE LIMBIC SYSTEM

This part of the brain affects every single system of the body. As you read through this section, I invite you to consider how your answers from the Unpacking Trauma Reflection are connected to the limbic system and how difficult, painful experiences affect this collection of structures. An old and primitive part of the brain, the limbic system is involved in our fight, freeze, or flight response.[3] The limbic system is located in the midbrain and is the nexus of our survival responses. When fight, flight, or freeze occurs within the body, we want to sprint away from the perceived danger, fight back in the moment, or freeze. The freeze response looks a lot like shutting down, dissociating, feeling immobilized, or playing dead. Our bodies have innate responses to perceived danger, and those responses prompt us to run very quickly or fight our best battle against the perceived threat. Notice the word "perceived." This magnificent mechanism does not always detect threats with 100% accuracy.

Think of the stress or panic you may feel when you are stuck in traffic and running late for a work meeting, fighting with a relative or partner, or when you are taking a hard test. Many events in our lives are not an immediate physical threat to safety, they are not life-or-death events. And yet, our bodies shoot us up with adrenaline, cortisol, or other stress hormones. Our limbic system shifts our temperature and blood flow to prepare us to mobilize. It moves glycogen into the bloodstream for quick energy and increases our heart rate.

The limbic system is responsible for interpreting the sensory and emotional input that we take in and storing it into categories and memories for future use. Interestingly, parts of the limbic system also regulate the parasympathetic and sympathetic nervous systems and has a large role in our emotions and relationships.[4] This includes love, socializing, and bonding with others. The limbic system defends us (or tries to) from any potential harm, much like a smoke alarm. It scans the environment and acts accordingly when it senses "smoke." Its main job is to keep us alive, to keep us safe. When the limbic system goes rogue as a consequence of traumatic experiences, this smoke alarm rings incessantly, in a never-ending state of emergency. This constant overfiring prioritizes safety and survival 24/7 and takes the focus off other body systems, such as healthy digestion, the ability to sleep deeply and rest, detoxification processes, and cell renewal and tissue healing. An overactive limbic system depletes and robs the other systems of energy and production.

Do you feel that you are always "on alert?" Is it difficult for you to relax or wind down most days? When I learned about the limbic system and how it can be impaired by trauma, my mind was blown. The brain's wiring can change and cause the traumatized individual to perceive the world only as dangerous. This can be caused by emotional or physical trauma such as concussions, bacterial infections, toxins in our environment, or viruses; and without question, it can be caused by emotional, psychological, or violent trauma.

The limbic system is very complex. If you are interested in additional information, there are many wonderful resources online and in books that discuss its structures and functions in detail. If you would like to learn more about trauma and how it deeply affects the brain, body, and mind, *The Body Keeps the Score* by Bessel van der Kolk and Peter Levine's book, *In an Unspoken Voice: How the Body Releases Trauma and Restores Goodness* are excellent sources. *Clinical Applications of the Polyvagal Theory* by Stephen Porges and Annie Hopper's book *Wired for Healing* are other sources that discuss trauma and the limbic system.

POST-TRAUMATIC STRESS DISORDER

A chapter on trauma wouldn't be complete without mentioning PTSD. Many people associate PTSD with war veterans who witnessed severely traumatizing death or violence. I held similar beliefs about PTSD for most of my life. I thought that PTSD related only to war or experiences of sexual abuse or severe violence. But PTSD can relate to many, many more events than just these. The DSM-5 lists the defining criteria of PTSD:

1. Directly experiencing the traumatic event(s), or
2. Witnessing, in person, the event(s) as it occurred to others, or 3. Learning that the traumatic event(s) occurred to a close family member or close friend. In cases of actual or threatened death of a family member or friend, the event(s) must have been violent or accidental, or 4. Experiencing repeated or extreme exposure to aversive details of the traumatic event(s).[5]

After reading the carefully curated criteria list of "who can have it," I was met with the shocking reality that I probably had PTSD and just hadn't known how to label it. The PTSD was caused by a life-altering and sudden loss in my life, which I will share with you in the following chapters.

The list in the DSM-5 cannot fully explain the vast and complex experiences that all of us go through. Trauma can occur anytime there is a disconnection between people that appears threatening or dangerous to those who are perceiving it. You don't have to experience traumatic loss, violence, or war to have PTSD or trauma. I hope knowing this allows you to give yourself grace and compassion. Many, many more people have PTSD than are diagnosed. And WE ALL HAVE TRAUMA. Functioning, productive members of society are walking around with it every single day, trying to manage it, cover it up, or stuff it down. In the Unpacking Trauma Reflection, we contemplated past experiences that could be considered hard or traumatic. Having that awareness is step one. I needed to become more aware of and develop insights into my own difficult circumstances in order to heal—and so do you. Here are some additional questions to think about as you move forward in doing your own work.

REFLECTION: HEALING FROM TRAUMA

Reflect on the following questions. Give yourself the time and permission you deserve and be honest with yourself. It doesn't matter whether other people in your life would define certain events as negative. What matters is YOUR perspective.

- What events have had a large, negative impact on your well-being that you have tried to brush off in the past? These can include any event that negatively impacted you and created a perceived sense of disconnection between you and others, you and yourself, or you and God.
- What type of (daily) support do you need to heal?
    - What do you consistently need from others? Is it a nonjudgmental listening ear? Support? Space to process? Understanding and compassion?
    - What do you need to give yourself on a consistent basis? Boundaries? More time off? Connections with people who make you feel happy? Working with a trauma-informed therapist? Participating in hobbies or activities that bring joy?

It can take time to figure out exactly what you need to grow and do the healing work. What you need is unique to you, and it is something that only you can decide. It is the same for therapies that are "trauma-informed." Many different modalities and types of therapy help a person move away from an overactive limbic system and the fight, flight, or freeze response and into a state of healing. Your inner compass will show you the way—you know what feels authentically good on a soul level and brings you joy. It may be letting go of or setting more boundaries. It may also be adding in more people, places, things, or activities (which can include rest) that light you up and help you to reconnect. Connecting with yourself and with positive, loving, healthy, and kind people is always the treatment, whether it is through therapy or other means. We heal by forming healthy relationships. We heal through telling our story and sharing. We heal through helping others understand us, and allowing them to help us understand ourselves even more.

HEALING BY RELEASING FEELINGS

Emotional expression in a safe context and witnessed by loving people is one of the most profound ways to heal intense emotional pain. By expressing emotion, the sensation decreases in intensity and lessens its power and control over us. We can see the pain as our inner child needing to be heard and seen. Think of the Disney movie *Inside Out*. If you have not seen it, it's worth watching. It is a story about a young girl named Riley who moves across the United States with her family and struggles to acclimate. It is told from the standpoint of her emotions within her brain, which are all distinct, humorous characters: Sadness, Anger, Joy, Fear, and Disgust. Joy always tries to manage Sadness and keep her from getting her hands all over things. But Sadness plays a pivotal role in allowing Riley and the other characters to heal and process their emotions. Once the sadness is felt, Riley begins to feel better and adapt to her new circumstances. The movie shows how necessary it is to express and experience the full range of emotions as a healthy, balanced part of living. These can be feelings of everyday living, or tucked away, long-hidden feelings from unresolved trauma.

You must feel your feelings. If you do not feel them, they will stay stuffed in the body and won't come out. You may have learned as a child that certain emotions were not appropriate. Feeling certain emotions such as rage, frustration, sadness, or disappointment may have (unintentionally) caused your parents to turn away from you, and this withdrawal did NOT feel good. I get it. If you learned that certain emotions are not "appropriate" or "lovable," how does that affect you in your adult life? It can cause anger and explosions for one. It can cause physical disease to manifest, as these repressed feelings can eat away at us. Louise Hay discusses this concept further in her book *You Can Heal Your Life*.

A very wise and absolutely incredible therapist once said to me, "All of your feelings are okay with me." Please read that again. That is a simple, yet deeply impactful, statement. Many of us need someone to say this to us, to release us from the stuffing, the hiding, the running away from our feelings. You can say this statement to yourself.

Have you ever heard the phrase "Don't feel that way" from a parent, other relative, or friend? How many times have you said something like "I just feel sad," only to be fed this line? We say it to other people too, out of habit. It's what we are taught, but unfortunately, it's not a validating statement. It's tempting to try to "fix" the situation or ignore it by getting the person to feel better. When we are with someone who is sad, discouraged, or angry, we often want to help by changing those feelings. It's hard to see loved ones suffering or regretful. It is hard to watch others become emotional and feel pain, disappointment, or sorrow.

I have said "don't feel that way," as an automatic response to someone who held remorse or shame so many times, and I still work on it to this day. I have a better phrase for you to use with loved ones and yourself instead. During the very first few months of dating my now-husband, Tim, I was in my second semester of doctoral work. I was having a difficult time balancing a part-time job that was not working for me and completing my assignments on time while planning out my research. I felt anxious, stressed, and worried some weeks. One day, I was talking on the phone with him about it, and saying things like "Oh, I shouldn't be feeling this way, I have a lot of good things going on" and "Why do I have to feel like this?"

Tim, who has no academic background in counseling whatsoever, said gently, "I'm never going to tell you how to feel, but I am here for you." No. Clinical. Background. None. Simply an intuition that I (like so many) needed permission to fully own my feelings. Utilize Tim's statement as you respect others in their emotional process while also encouraging and supporting them.

Many of my clients say the phrase, "I shouldn't feel this way." I often remind and teach clients in session to speak freely about how they are feeling about a given person or situation, and then I allow space to sit in silence afterward. No justification. No talking themselves out of the feeling (which NEVER works). No guilt. Just checking in with oneself and asking "How did that make me feel?" Again, this can be something that you feel stuck on from last week, or unresolved traumatic experiences that occurred years ago but were never validated or shared. Sometimes people have no idea how they are feeling because they've stuffed down the emotions for too long. In early childhood experiences, individuals may have been surrounded by people who had a difficult time helping them regulate their emotions or couldn't regulate their own in a healthy way. Sometimes our feelings were ignored completely, and we came to believe that having feelings didn't help us. But here's the thing—feelings are for YOU. They show you when boundaries have been broken. They are a guiding light regarding your needs. And often, they also show us who we feel safest around.

So, the next time you feel upset or you feel frazzled, fill in the blank out loud. "I feel _____." Then sit in the silence. You can even say the proclamation again. You can also say "I am mad/ angry/frustrated at _____." It can be a situation. It can be a person. It can be an experience. That's all you have to do. You don't have to fix it; you simply have to witness it. Time and time again, when people feel validated, when they can just admit how they are feeling and no one tries to fix it or make it different, that feeling goes from a high intensity level to a much more manageable level. Give yourself this gift. Let yourself FEEL.

RUNNING AWAY FROM THE PAIN

When we experience psychological pain and trauma, we learn ways to cope in order to feel better. Coping can include doing the healing work through various therapeutic modalities so that we are able to process the event better and create new meaning from it. It can look like letting ourselves feel and honor the emotions that arise without trying to change them. Coping can also include things like different forms of exercise, spending time with friends, being in nature, meditating or praying, and other stress relievers that regulate the nervous system.

Coping mechanisms and choices can be very healthy, but they can also become unhealthy. Drugs, alcohol, sex addiction, gambling, or excessive workaholic and shopaholic behaviors can be dissociating mechanisms to separate us from uncomfortable feelings or memories that come with trauma. If feelings are overwhelming or unmanageable, unhealthy coping strategies drown them out for a period of time. They are avoidance tactics and bandages over a large wound. Even behaviors like extreme busyness, binge watching TV, overexercising, overeating or undereating, or controlling behaviors are ways of coping that can become counterproductive. In a way, they are survival tactics. Michele Rosenthal said, "Survival mode is supposed to be a phase that helps save your life. It is not meant to be how you live."[6] These things can help us feel better in the short term by giving us a bit of a boost. These behaviors make us feel in control of something for once, since many things in life are out of our control. They can shift us into an alternative universe, a place where everything feels different, and it can feel like an escape. They can make us forget what happened for a little while. But these strategies won't work forever; we can't ever really forget what happened. We create coping mechanisms for ourselves to handle trauma, unhappiness, lack of purpose, grief, loss, and stress. While many coping mechanisms are okay in the short term, integrating deeper healing work is the best way to move forward.

I encourage you to reflect on your own toolbox of coping mechanisms, with honesty. You may have several healthy coping tools, but others are probably not so healthy. We all have these. We are human. Bringing awareness to these behaviors is the beginning of limiting them or letting go of them. The coping behaviors may feel like friends, something you rely on. They are predictable and ease the discomfort. But keep in mind that unhealthy coping measures can never take the pain away. They may mask the pain, put it to the side, or push it down. But it's still there. Only intentional healing work can help reframe and process loss or trauma. Sometimes this healing temporarily causes more pain. It can cause a lot of emotion. Making friends with your emotions and inviting them in might feel foreign. The "all are welcome" mindset can seem undoable. It can feel intensely scary. But it can also unlock you from the habits of depending on dissociating and avoidance mechanisms. I have so much compassion for you and all that you've endured. I have compassion for whatever behaviors you are using right now to manage trauma, abuse, sadness, disappointment, regret, fear, grief and loss, or painful memories. You are incredibly brave.

Disturbing, distressing experiences happen to all of us in life. They can appear as massive, violent, horrible events or small, overlooked occurrences that affected us enormously but flew under the radar. We become dysregulated and weighed down by these events, as they can narrow our view of reality and leave us emotionally and physically drained. Through witnessing, validating, and reconnecting, we can derive greater meaning from and understanding of these experiences. We can heal and move forward, lighter. Even with scars, we can live the life that we have always wanted; one that feels free, expansive, joyous, and purposeful. In the next chapter, we will discuss grief and loss. You may notice similar parallels in grief and the healing power of releasing feelings in a healthy, nonjudgmental way.

4

GRIEF AND
MENTAL HEALTH

rief is part of the human condition. We all experience it. We grieve for so many reasons, and often we do not realize that our pain or period of struggle is a grief reaction to something that is no longer in our lives. Some losses we will grieve for just a few weeks. Other losses will be mourned throughout our life. On some days, grief can feel quite light and unnoticeable, and on other days it can be heavy and immobilizing. Grief can knock you to the ground. It can feel suffocating and crippling. When you do get up from those moments, maybe simply rising only to your knees, you are a changed person. When you come to know the latter type of grief, you will never be the same again, and neither will your life.

Grief can shake you awake from a deep sleep, awaken you to a calling, to a deeper experience in life, to a deeper purpose and passion. Because you have now felt such a wide range of intense human emotions, you are now fully alive. You will learn things through the process that you never thought you would. You will become a stronger version of yourself than you ever thought possible. And you will carry a heavy backpack until slowly, over time, the contents in it will change and feel different, lighter. They will shape-shift into gifts. Into abundant blessings.

How do I know this? Because I lost one of my best friends: my brother. My brother passed away six years ago in a completely sudden, unexpected fashion, leaving behind a family that cared deeply for him. My eldest brother and I were robbed of our sibling, my parents of their son. I will share with you my own story and the ways that I have made meaning out of the unimaginable. I will share practical, useful information and skills to help you process and move through your own losses, in your own time. This section may help you if you have experienced any of the following:

- Have you lost a loved one?
- Have you experienced changes in living, work, health, abilities, or relationships that had a profound effect on your emotional or physical wellbeing?
- Do you often find yourself dwelling on what "could've been, should've been, or would've been"?

We all experience grief. It can be caused by death or a change in our lives. Periods of adjustment often include grief, yet that grief often goes unnoticed because we work through these life changes over the course of days, weeks, or months. Periods of adjustment can include changing jobs or schools, moving, a change in living situation, going to college, or becoming empty nesters. Other experiences of grief, however, rock our entire worlds and turn them upside down.

THE NEW NORMAL

"He's gone." The thought pierced my skull and numbed me. My arms, my legs, my face were all frozen in that moment, that morning in September 2015. The morning my father had to tell me my brother had been shot the night before. He could barely say the words; he was crying and in utter shock. At first, I had no idea what had happened or who it had happened to. I just knew it was bad, because I had never in my twenty-four years of life seen my dad like this. I felt like I had been hit with a semi-truck and was floating around my body in a stupor. My mother was in a similar state. We were each alone in our anguish, though we were together in the kitchen. I felt emotionally and physically separated from my family by thousands of miles, with no chance of finding them again. Friends and family visited in droves that day, and I received many hugs. Those embraces were warm but I felt none of them. Friends provided words of encouragement, advice, and loving guidance. I heard not a sound nor a word. My body had dissociated from reality.

In the months that followed, my emotional and physical state stayed much the same—feeling disconnected from reality and from those I love. As I began healing, the stupor and the shock slowly melting away, I faced the reality of a new, normal way of existing and a need for me to gradually accept and reframe this new normal. New traditions for family holidays and birthdays. A new dynamic within the family. A new normal for how to live my life. I couldn't simply stay the same. Everything around me and the world I once knew were now different. My brother was missing, and we were missing him. We were told that he was shot at his apartment complex after getting out of his car one evening. We were told it was an attempted robbery, but we were not there, so we cannot fully tell the tale and never will be able to. What I do know for certain is that I think of him every single day. I can say, without question, that the mind never forgets someone we love that much. And I can say with certainty that it is possible to heal after loss.

MANY WAYS TO GRIEVE

As I share this story with you, know that I am sharing my deeply personal and first-hand experience of grief combined with the academic and clinical training I learned in school. There are many types of grief, and not all are identified as such. Losing a loved one is the most common example we think of when we talk about grief. But we also grieve from the loss of relationships due to break ups, divorces, or moving. We grieve when our lives change, when our environment changes, when things simply aren't the same anymore. We grieve when children grow up, when WE grow up. We grieve for lost opportunities, or when we feel we don't belong anymore. We grieve for lost hopes, dreams, and aspirations. We grieve when loss is sudden, and we grieve when loss is foreseen and we have time to prepare and say goodbye. Grief and loss are incredibly common, and incredibly human. I sincerely hope this chapter on grief and the techniques for coping with loss and grief will help you feel understood, feel validated, and aid you in the healing process. And I am deeply sorry for everyone and everything you have lost.

Although grief is part of the human experience, and every individual on this planet will more likely than not experience loss in their lives, losing someone or something can be very traumatic. The DSM-5 has a small section on complicated bereavement. This can happen when a person is completely debilitated by grief and can't perform their typical everyday tasks. Most grief is at least somewhat complicated.

Humans grieve in complicated ways. John James and Russell

Friedman discuss in the *Grief Recovery Handbook* that when we are joyful and excited, we celebrate together, but when we grieve, we grieve alone.[1] Grief is unique to each individual, and the word "should" is never a helpful word to use in any sentence when discussing grief recovery. For example, well-meaning friends talking about you may say, "They should really be doing better by now; it has almost been a year." Or "They should get out there and start dating again; their partner has been gone for a while now." Every single person on this planet goes on their own grief journey, so please do not be shamed by these comments that well-meaning friends and relatives may say to you or about you.

Grief can promote intense feelings of anxiety or depression, irritability, guilt, difficulty concentrating, and insomnia. Grief can also cause feelings of ambiguity. For example, if a loved one passed away from an illness, the relief of no longer seeing them suffering battles with the pain of missing them. Group therapy for grief can be a wonderful asset for those who have lost a loved one. It may take some time before we are ready to share our grief with supportive strangers, but the process can be freeing and a healing way to work through struggles.

REFLECTION: USING BLESSINGS TO MOVE THROUGH GRIEF

When processing and moving through grief, it is essential to begin to think about the blessings you received from your loved one, your pet, or whomever you are grieving. This doesn't happen the first day, or even the second. But eventually you will be ready for this reflection. If the loss was an estranged person or someone abusive, you may not be able to come up with a list of blessings, learning lessons, or good memories. You are in charge of deciding whether or not this activity is relevant for you. The answers to the following prompts can be spoken aloud to a counselor or written in a journal. The choice is entirely yours. When you feel ready to move through your grief, here are some prompts:

- What did the relationship give you? What did the relationship teach you? How did it make you a stronger, better person?
- How was this person a gift to you in the time you had with them?
- What are some positive memories associated with the relationship?

Note that answering these questions may bring up bad memories, things you wish you had done or feel you should have said, things you may regret now, or even negative things the person said to you. This is completely normal and okay. No human is perfect (including you). No relationship is perfect. Most relationships will include some negative memories. When those thoughts arise, simply bring your attention back to these two questions: What blessings were given to you from the relationship? What are some positive memories associated with the relationship? Intentionally set aside time after this activity to journal about any negative feelings that arise. Grief includes overwhelming sadness, depression, sleepless nights, and anxiety. But when you look at the gifts you received from the deceased, the cherished memories, the lessons this person taught you, and what you loved about them your pain may ease. You will realize that, although there is loss, you received so many blessings from having this person in your life for as long as you did.

Sure, we all have a lot of could have beens, should have beens, lost dreams. I completely understand, trust me. But focus on all the things you did get to do with them; those experiences are worth more than priceless jewels. Shifting your attention to these simple, beautiful gifts might begin healing to your heart.

My memories about my brother include a sense of peace and childlike exploration. We made home movies together. We ran outside in the yard chasing down our flying Christmas toys. We were together on epic family trips, sometimes sitting on a mattress in the back of my dad's SUV during the drive to our destination. Always, there were feelings of deep connection, inner rest, acceptance, and togetherness. When my brother died, certain parts of me shriveled up and tried to die with him: the feeling of inner rest, the acceptance, the desire to connect with others. Yet through healing, with time to reflect on our relationship, these parts of me have emerged from hiding like a blooming flower. It is my hope that in time you trust yourself to do the same.

THE SPIRITUAL RELATIONSHIP WITH THE LOST

Your loved one will no longer be able to physically sit next to you or be able to grab a quick bite to eat with you at your favorite restaurant. They will be not be able to answer an iPhone for a chat. And yet, there is and can still be a relationship with your lost loved one. The relationship simply changes from a physical one to a spiritual one. This may be difficult at the beginning, but it can become easier over time. Taking moments on holidays and in your day-to-day life to acknowledge your loved one can build this new, different relationship. You can find a quiet space in your home, at the beach, or while driving alone in the car to say hello or tell them about your day out loud. You can write to them. Then sit back and think about what they would say back. The answers that come could surprise you. Our loved ones speak to us in unexpected ways, so be on the lookout for some interesting ways of your loved one saying "Hi, I'm here!"

I attended a spirituality conference for counselors a few summers ago in Colorado. A fantastic presentation was provided by two counselors who were presenting on strategies for working with grief. Their research focused specifically on those with a deceased family member. They found that when clients were able to connect to their loved ones and feel a sense of presence from them, a wave of peace overcame many of them, and much of the pain of grief dissolved. I can say with certainty that I have had similar experiences with my brother, and I have found unique ways of connecting with him that give me solace. The following reflection is intended to help you think about the topic of preserved connection as you process and gain insight into grief and loss. Question #5 is helpful when processing losses that do not relate to death.

REFLECTION: STAYING CONNECTED

Answering these important questions may not come easily. The questions may bring forth tears, sadness, and some "I don't know yet" responses. That is completely normal and okay. Deciding how to stay connected with someone we lost can take time. It may take a bit of trial and error to decide what feels right for you. I have every confidence that, in time, your intuition will show you how to honor the relationship.

- How can you find your new normal after loss?

- What are some ways that you can reconnect with a loved one who has passed?

- Which steps would you consider taking to talk about your grief and heal?

- What hopes or dreams were lost with the loved one, and how can you still honor or recreate those in a new way?

- If you are grieving a loss from estranged family, divorce, a job change, health issues, or changes in your living situation, similar themes will still hold true. The "could haves, should haves, would haves" often circulate in the mind. Write down your own "could haves" that circulate in your brain regarding your loss or change. What were you unable to say or express? You can write down any "I'm sorry for . . . " or "I forgive you for . . . " or "Thank you for . . . ."

A quote by blogger Jamie Anderson says it all. "Grief, I've learned, is really just love. It's all the love you want to give, but cannot. All the unspent love gathers up in the corners of your eyes, the lump in your throat, in that hollow part of your chest. Grief is just love with no place to go."[2] It is feelings of unresolve, energy, passion, love, and space that have nowhere to go. Grief is closely related to trauma in that oftentimes people do not feel seen, heard, or understood. It is a hallmark of disconnection, as grief means no longer having a physical relationship with someone lost.

In the following chapter, we will discuss a handful of promising strategies that not only help in healing from grief and loss but also improve the overall wellness of your mind and body.

5

REWIRING THE BRAIN, DNRS, AND EMOTIONAL PATTERNS

I n the midst of suffering, whether it be deeply emotional or physical suffering (or both), it can be really hard to get unstuck. Maybe you have been doing what others suggest, putting in the effort and doing your research, and yet the answers you find don't seem to unlock the healing you hoped for. You may feel impatient or unlucky or incredibly frustrated. "Do I just have to accept this? Do I just have to live with it?" We can each find the answer that provides the healing we always hoped for, on levels we never would have dreamed we could reach.

- Do you feel like you have tried everything to feel better?
- Are you doing all of the "right" things for your mental and physical health with few or no improvements?
- Do you feel "triggered" a lot, both emotionally and physically, by your environment?

- Do you have mystery symptoms that haven't been resolved with diet or healthy lifestyle efforts?

Suffering emotionally and physically can feel like you are on a stationary bike, unable to propel yourself forward. No matter how hard you pedal, you remain in the same spot that you began. You have an awful, constant feeling of stagnation. But there is help. One of the largest improvements I made in my own mental and physical health came from the concepts in this chapter. These strategies helped release me from a sense of immobility and gave me direction and motivation. In this chapter, we will explore the brain, the nervous system, and a specialized program known as the Dynamic Neural Retraining System (DNRS). You will learn how much the health of our brain impacts every other system, organ, and cell in our bodies. We will also discuss the different emotional patterns we might find ourselves in throughout our lives and what actions we can take to create healthy emotional patterns.

THE DISCOVERY

It can be challenging to keep going, to keep searching for answers, when you feel like you aren't finding the answers you need. I experienced this myself as I searched for my own answers. My determination was dwindling. But then one day, I found a pot of gold. During my period of illness, I frequently signed up for email and text notifications about functional medicine health webinars and eagerly attended many free online summits. I learned something new or helpful each time I listened in, and I always enjoyed hearing about the stories and successes of others. The seminars gave me hope and kept me on track mentally. They fueled my perseverance and gave my brain something to chew on. I was desperate to find someone, anyone, who could offer me more information or insight into my health.

Each day, while a summit was running, the hosts would release announcements about upcoming seminars. One particular day in early 2019, they announced a seminar for the following week: the Toxic Mold Summit, hosted by Margaret Christensen. I decided to sign up because I was curious about toxins and how environmental chemicals could harm mental health and physical health. The next week I tuned in and began eagerly choosing from the available inter-views. I listened to a talk by Annie Hopper, and I was completely in awe. Annie shared her deeply personal and painful struggle with chemical sensitivities and described a program that she created to heal her own suffering. This program is called the Dynamic Neural Retraining System (DNRS).[1] I was hesitant, yet curious (my typical initial response to encountering something new). Is this too good to be true? I had some fears and doubts, but an inkling of excitement rushed through me. It was as if all the pieces I had been searching for were coalescing energetically, and I was at the center.

Annie talked about how emotional and physical trauma, environ-mental chemicals, viruses, and bacteria can create dysfunction and damage within the brain and nervous system, in particular the limbic system. The limbic system is the primitive center of the brain that is responsible for our protective survival mechanisms, as discussed in Chapter 3. The limbic system can shift into a rogue response as a result of environmental stimuli. Rogue responses can drive the reac-tions of our immune system to even the simplest of foods, chemicals in household items such as laundry detergents and perfumes, and even sound and noise. Intense and painful emotional experiences, toxins, and pathogens can cause brain injuries? Seriously? SERIOUSLY. As Annie talked about the limbic system, I couldn't help but wonder:

"How could the limbic system possibly be involved in such illness? It's just an area of the brain!"

Annie had an intriguing name for this: limbic system impairment. The highlight of Annie's talk was when she explained that many mental health issues such as anxiety, depression, rage, pain, and suicidal ideation were common effects of limbic system impairment. So were many other things: Rampant negative self-talk. Whole-body issues. Food sensitivities. Exhaustion. An environmental, medication-related, or psychological trigger can cause the limbic system to go haywire and mount a massive threat response that does not match the initial stimulus. DNRS teaches that the brain is truly the control center of the body. It controls the immune system, along with many other systems and pathways. The brain, after all, is an organ. We often forget that.

That day, I learned how DNRS combines cognitive behavioral therapy (CBT), neurolinguistic programming, mindfulness, and mental imagery to shift the brain into a state of joy, euphoria, calm, and hopefulness. All of the wonderful neurotransmitters and hormones produced by our nervous systems, such as oxytocin, endorphins, serotonin, and dopamine, can stimulate deep healing and rewiring of the brain to create a different and more positive perception of the world around us.

Eager to dive in, I went to an intensive five-day DNRS seminar in May 2019. (Several DNRS seminars take place annually in the United States, Canada, and Europe.) It was truly a life-altering experience. If I had the choice, I would love to travel back in time and re-experience this remarkable opportunity again and again. I met some of the most loving and compassionate people I have ever encountered and still think of them often with joy in my heart.

I walked in the very first evening of my arrival, took a seat, and looked around the circle at thirty other people. For introductions, we went around the room and one by one shared what physical and emotional symptoms we had been experiencing, what we hoped to gain from the seminar, and something about ourselves. After hearing a few individuals share their stories, it dawned on me that many people are experiencing and have experienced what I was currently trying to understand and move through. I sat there dumbfounded and shocked. Someone finally understands? Then I realized: "Not just someone. This entire room knows what the last few years of my life have been like." I didn't feel the need to overexplain. I also didn't feel the need to hide things or sugarcoat symptoms anymore. I felt free. I felt authentic. The seminar had not even begun, and I felt like a light shone from deep within me in that moment. That inner guide said, "You are where you belong. This, this is it." My deep sense of connection to others around me produced great hopes, such a high. This concept—a sense of connection—will be discussed in greater depth in Chapter 18, "Meaningful Relationships and Connection."

I hope the information in this chapter provides you with much-needed hope and encouragement to continue on your own journey. Always remember: the answers are with you all along—you just need to keep searching until you uncover them.

DNRS AT A GLANCE

What exactly does DNRS look like? The program is multifaceted and complex, so I will not outline it fully in this book, though I will give an overview and provide you with information that will allow you to deepen your study, if you wish.

DNRS can take the form of an in-person seminar or DVDs (or both), weekly groups for those who would like more support, and coaching calls offered by specialists highly trained in DNRS. Part of the program consists of a daily minimum one-hour practice of specific visualizations and mental imagery paired with a version of mindfulness techniques. For those new to the term, mindfulness is an awareness of the present moment, including what thoughts are going through the mind and what emotions are present.[2] This is paired with a nonjudgmental approach to these thoughts, emotions, and sensations. DNRS focuses on gently monitoring your thoughts throughout the day and changing them if the theme begins shifting to negativity, focusing on symptoms, or worrying. Pillars of the DNRS program are practiced for at least six months or longer, with the end goal of rewiring the limbic system and brain.

DNRS can help with wide-ranging issues, from depression and anxiety to chemical and food sensitivities, to dizziness and beyond. For example, a young man who sat next to me in the seminar could not tolerate the smell of my morning tea. He very kindly asked that I throw it out because the fragrance was making him symptomatic. I felt deep compassion for him because I was dealing with my own bizarre symptoms. It felt like a gift to get up and throw my tea out for him, because I could genuinely understand how much it bothered him.

Although I found DNRS through the Toxic Mold Summit, I learned that my symptoms were actually not caused by mold or otherwise chemically induced (even though symptoms certainly can be). At the seminar, the experts asked me questions and reviewed my history. DNRS helped me narrow down the possible causes and see that other drivers, including viral, fungal, bacterial, psychological, and an immune reaction to medication, had triggered the limbic system impairment I was suffering with. DNRS also helped me realize just how much potential I had to heal. But it would take my time, effort, and unwavering patience.

RETURNING TO JOY

Our brains are absolutely capable of change, but that doesn't mean it isn't rough in the midst of the change. Neuroplasticity is the concept that the brain is able to "rewire" itself and create new connections between neurons, or brain cells. The wiring of our brain is based on our past and current experiences of everyday living. When we learn new things, the brain creates new synapses to support those pathways. It's like when we learn to ride a bike or walk or run. Those pathways are wired and pruned to support the skill. And that skill takes time.

When I first began the DNRS program, it took time to get the hang of it. In the early stages, I had a hard time catching those negative thought patterns. They simply flowed freely and went unnoticed until I began catching them like fish in a net. The rewiring process was very difficult because my brain had been following its own path for so long and had been shaped by the limbic system impairment, the health injury, and grief and loss. Sometimes these thought patterns are the result of years and years of experiences, so patience and grace are needed to allow the time required to change those patterns. It can feel like a struggle some days while in the DNRS process, almost like you are trapped in a wrestling match with your own mind. With diligence and consistency, old neurocircuits will have no choice but to give way to the pruning and reshaping. Change is absolutely possible and expected.

Training in a DNRS program is similar to training in any other skill-based program. If neural connections for being present, being joyful, or being grateful are weak in the brain, we have to go to the DNRS "gym" to strengthen them daily for a consistent period of time before the new pathways are created. We have to be committed. We have to WANT it badly enough. We have to be able to see past the (emotional) muscle soreness that sometimes comes with training. We have to muster up all we can to move past feelings of being unmotivated on certain days. And diligence really pays off. DNRS teaches that when you are in a triggered state or your symptoms have flared up, you are actually in a state of great neuroplasticity with the best opportunity for change. Isn't that incredible? This is such a fantastic way to reframe the experience of heightened symptoms. Instead of the dreaded doom feeling of "I'm not getting better," we can remind ourselves that our brain and health have the highest capacity for change during this time. The brain is more able to create new synaptic connections, which might mean feeling positive, happy, and calm more often.

Think of this as a silver lining to those triggering moments on those days when you find yourself stuck in a rut of negative thinking, of increased anxiety or depression, or of worsening physical symptoms. When you are in the midst of something you are trying to improve, if you can stop or halt the looping of negative thoughts, you will have an opportunity to create stronger synaptic connections than if you did the same practice when your symptoms were not activated. It is so challenging to do this. And yet, taking action can strengthen the prefrontal cortex and your ability to focus, help you think in a way that is more helpful to you, and help you feel physically and emotionally better. DNRS teaches that this focus away from symptoms over time resets the limbic system and brain, which affects our immune system, digestive system, and many other parts of the body. If you can take advantage of these times and choose the different reaction, choose the new, healthier behavior, and do a round of practice, you will reap the benefits.

When did I first begin noticing changes? At the seminar, I learned so much wonderful and helpful information. I practiced with the coaches and experienced a nearly immediate boost in my mood. After a week of two of consistent practice, I realized while driving one day how present-focused I was. My typical driving time was usually consumed by the thoughts racing around in my head: the to-do lists, predictions of the future, the overplanning and micromanaging of details. But not this time. This drive, my mind was quieter, so I could actually hear the radio, enjoy the weather, and admire the plants alongside the road. It was wild. When it came to physical changes, it is very hard to put my finger on how many weeks or months it took for my body to shift. I attended the initial training in May 2019, and I can remember trying, with success, to add back triggering foods (that I hadn't touched since the fall of 2014) in July and August 2019. When I reflect on my healing journey, I perceived the change as coming slowly, then all at once. I caught myself handling stressful situations much more easily. The internal dialogue in my head was more loving, encouraging, or hopeful, and it surprised me. I noticed my thought patterns shifting, reframing my life.

Some days, I was able to smell strong scents again without feeling lightheaded, and I took note of such occasions with surprise and excitement. As my healing progressed, I often forgot the old days of limitations. I found myself able to eat a wider variety of foods without having digestive or allergic reactions. My skin appeared clearer. I found myself in a more positive mood and was more patient with others. One evening, after spending a large part of the day working and being very busy, I realized that my energy levels were very stable, and I was HAPPY and upbeat. This was one of my many DNRS "aha" moments. I had completely mowed over and almost forgotten about my old way of living, my old status of health. My body was healing. My brain was healing. This is what normal feels like? It was like a long-lost friend embraced me in that moment. My health was being revived, and I was returning to joy.

NEVER GIVE UP ON YOURSELF

If I could give one message to my former self before I found DNRS and began to thrive, it would be this: Never give up.

You are worth so much. Your health, your wellbeing, your mood, your quality of life. There is a path to healing, and it may be different for every individual person. A large part of my healing journey was accomplished through DNRS, along with smaller contributions from other techniques I will be mentioning in the following pages of this book. I want you to know that you will find your answers if you search eagerly enough. If you want it and believe it, time and space will deliver the healing to you.

If I've piqued your interest about this beautiful brain-based, neuroplasticity program, you can learn more about it in greater detail at retrainingthebrain.com. Annie also has a lovely book specifically about the limbic system and chronic illness, named *Wired for Healing*. As mentioned earlier, DNRS offers a comprehensive program and a variety of modalities for support.

SHIFTING OUT OF UNHELPFUL PATTERNS

This type of modality and the suggestions that DNRS provides remind me of some crucial ideas by Louise Hay and Dr. Joe Dispenza, although the theoretical origins are somewhat different. Louise and Joe's teachings involve, to some degree or another, the law of attraction: what you focus on, what you think about, you get more of. Whether you believe in the law of attraction or not, no one would argue that focusing on frustration brings solace or comfort. Frustration builds and feeds off itself. Focusing on being resentful or angry with a person doesn't give you the warm fuzzies when you next see them.

This concept aligns with the principles of DNRS: the specific pathways and connections fired by a certain thought or action strengthen every time it is used. When we stop using those pathways, they shrivel up over time, like a grown-over path in the forest that is no longer being walked on or maintained. The new pathways become the road of choice and result in our new reactions.

But let me be clear: I am not advocating for numbing feelings, avoiding feelings, or pretending you don't have a problem if you do. Great power comes from acknowledging our emotions without trying to change them or wish them away. It is also a beautiful and healing experience when we can reflect on certain events to reframe or make greater meaning out of our experiences. I am a therapist, after all. I trust these processes, and I've seen them free people from pain. If you have ever participated in therapy, or plan to, a portion of the work includes connecting with your emotions and reflecting on what experiences you have not processed. Doing so can set you free from your pain and everything that you have tried forgetting about.

However, if an individual is stuck in a limbic system trauma loop, the same thought or very similar thoughts will circulate over and over and over again. No amount of talking about the problem, venting, or focusing on the feelings seem to do the trick. Does this sound familiar to you? If so, I challenge you to observe and write down (without judgment) for one day your common themes of thought or emotion. It is important to monitor your thoughts or check in and ask yourself, "What am I thinking right now? Is this a helpful thought?" That evening or the next morning, review the list and ask yourself, "Is this what I want more of?" "Is this a loving thought toward myself?"

Many times you will say no. Maybe there was a verbal altercation between you and your partner or roommate, or maybe your mother said something that stung. Someone with limbic system impairment may visit this scene and conversation hundreds or even thousands of times, with no movement toward resolution. That rumination over every word your partner said in the argument, the repeated feelings of pain or hurt, the consuming thought of, "Why me?" may repeat like a broken record. You may know people like this who have a hard time letting go of things. You may even be one of these people; and if you are, you may also be dumbfounded by people who can forgive and forget so easily. I am dumbfounded by them, too. They let go of harsh words spoken with such ease. The sting slides off them like water. They tend to sleep well at night, in silence and peace. People with limbic system impairment or those prone to it will be kept awake by the noise of their chattering thoughts—the replaying of painful events, the regrets, the overthinking. The self-criticism.

My reason for writing *With Me All Along* is to help you find resolutions, solutions, and direction. One solution is to stop the unproductive looping. By making this part of your practice, you will rewire your brain and feel more present, enjoy and experience life more, and feel not-so-stuck in your head.

To change, we must do something different than we have done before. Part of DNRS is completely stopping an unhelpful thought in its tracks by using awareness, observation, and distraction. What thoughts run through your mind? You can stop the thought by counting from one to ten, or counting backward, or walking into another room, or turning on a funny video clip, or putting on some music. You can focus on gratitude and make a gratitude list in your head. The key is to change the record player, tune in to a different radio station. We'll address this in more detail later in Chapter 7, "Finding

Mindfulness in Nature and Gratitude." The thoughts that we have can have a big impact on how we perceive life. They linger and leach into our behaviors. A lot of our thought patterns are affected by the synapse wiring of our past. As children and even adults, little and big events happen to us, and we adapt to survive. We create meaning from these events that in turn affect our thought processes. We may see people as dangerous after experiencing betrayal, for example. This can lead to defensiveness or an inability to trust. We may believe that we have to be perfect all the time to receive love, if, for example, we grew up in a home with unrealistically high expectations. Short term, the response typically protects us and is relevant. But over the long term, these behaviors, patterns, and thoughts are not useful or necessary. We don't need them anymore. If we hold on to them long after they are useful, the wired-in responses can keep us from accomplishing our passions and desires. It can even prevent us from reaching out for help. What protective, behavioral mechanisms do you have in place that do not serve you in the present day, but once did? This will be different for everyone, so it's important that you pay attention to your reactions. Another example relates to stress. If chaos or fear were familiar themes in your childhood, these can become unconscious, habitual patterns in adulthood. We are most comfortable with whatever is most familiar. It is our "norm." The brain can become used to the dose of adrenaline we get from stressful situations, arguments, or rushing around daily. And the brain wants to stay in equilibrium within the current chemical state.

What about constant thoughts of getting revenge or being a poor victim of life? Have you experienced these types of thoughts or ruminations before? Entertaining them enough can leave us seething with anger. I will reiterate this: these patterns are largely unconscious until we bring them to the forefront of our attention. Interestingly, these emotions, patterns, and states contain an energetic charge. Phrases like "good vibes only" nod to this concept of wanting only positive, loving feelings around. After all, we are made up of energy. Everything on this planet contains a unique energy, and even specific emotions have unique charges to them. Which emotions are constantly playing in the background of your life? The following questions may help you identify your own unique (unconscious) patterns and the energies associated with them. Let's unpack them in a reflection to wrap up the chapter.

REFLECTION: CHANGING BRAIN PATTERNS

We all have automatic patterns and pathways that our brains are accustomed to using. In order to change these pathways, we must first get in touch with what they are. Take some time to review the following questions. Answer each in a mindful way and write down your responses in your journal or notebook. This is the perfect time to get really honest with yourself because the more honest we are about our patterns, the more awareness we can develop and use in our change process.

- Do you tend to dwell on certain memories, events, or problems, over and over again? Are you the type to replay conversations?

- Do you feel a sense that you are in an endless loop of similar thoughts and emotions from day to day?

- What does this dwelling and thought looping result in? What are the consequences for you personally?

- Do you find that talking or "venting" makes it worse? Does talking about it cause the size and emotion to increase and build on itself?

After answering the preceding questions, review the following in-depth examples provided. The examples also include a concept related to the law of attraction—what you focus on you tend to get more of. Write down any thought themes that resonate with you in your journal. I have also included some phrases that may resonate with you. If they do, write them down so they can help you dissolve these emotional patterns.

- **PITY:** If you find yourself always wanting others to feel sorry for you, then what must happen in your life for you to receive pity? Put another way, for friends and family to "feel bad" for us or to pity us and our circumstances, something in our lives has to be going wrong, correct? Many people use pity to relate to and bond with others. It can be deeply ingrained as a past or present pattern. Pity and concern from others can feel good. It can make us feel cared for, protected, or safe. It can serve a social purpose and fill our need to connect, be validated, or bond. There are many other ways to relate to others though, such as celebrating life's wins and sharing passions and purpose. It is important to have balance.

Shows up as: "What about me?" "No one even cares!"

- **VICTIM:** If you find yourself always complaining to others, venting back and forth with friends about your problems, or connecting easily with those who have a negative outlook, what must happen in your life for this to occur? For you to be a victim of life or circumstance, it means unfortunate things have happened to you. Hard times happen to us all. It is important to take your power back and focus on the lesson instead of letting hard times rule you.

Shows up as: "It's not fair." "Why me?" "I'm all alone."

- **REVENGE:** If you find yourself constantly thinking about and wanting revenge on a person, what are you attracting into your outer landscape or environment? For someone to want revenge, what had to have already occurred to them? Wrongdoing toward them by another. Might holding on to thoughts of revenge prevent someone from moving forward?

Shows up as: "They should feel really guilty for what they did to me." "They should struggle because of this."

- **STRESS:** If you are operating from a place of constant adrenaline, busyness, and anxiety, what might happen in your life to create more of the same? Might it feel and look like constant chaos? Is it always having to rush? Are unexpected events, people, or news always popping up, uninvited, and derailing you from your larger goals?

Shows up as: "I have no time." "I am busy." "My time is limited." "There is so much to do."

- **PERFECTIONISM:** If you are constantly striving for (unobtainable) perfectionism, what does that feel like emotionally? Does it feel like a struggle? Like not feeling good enough? What will you be constantly searching for in your environment and in yourself? Might it be reassurance? A need to feel "enough?" A need for acceptance from other people? Does it involve low self-esteem?

Shows up as: "Everything needs to be perfect." "I need to be perfect." "Everyone needs to like me."

Below is a list of positive affirmations to combat unhelpful and limiting thought processes.

Positive Affirmations

Write any of these down in your journal that you connect with and relate to. You can also write them on paper and tape it to a door, mirror, or fridge, or even keep it in your wallet:

- "I get to decide exactly how I want to feel."
- "I choose health, wellbeing, and abundance."
- "I receive bountiful blessings and good things into my life with ease."
- "All of my needs are met with ease."
- "Life can be easy, lighthearted, and fun."
- "I am enough."
- "I love and approve of myself."
- "I am surrounded by people who love me, value me, and treat me well."
- "I have plenty of time to do all of the things I love, enjoy, and find meaningful."

Now that you have some affirmations on hand, you can expand them to create a visualization. An example of a visualization technique for the stress belief pattern follows. It will help you feel a sense of expansiveness, letting go, and relaxation in your body. You can utilize this example to create visualizations for the other negative patterns (pity, revenge, perfectionism, victim). The affirmations can be used as support within the visualization. When utilizing visualizations, it is important to think about and picture exactly what you DO WANT, and to identify the feelings of receiving those things. What would it be like for you to experience a situation like this?

Visualization Technique Example
for Stress and Lack of Time

Imagine for a moment what it would be like to have a whole two weeks off to do every single thing you WANT to do. Things that generate emotions of joy and excitement. A fabulous vacation of your choosing. You can stay home; you can go somewhere. Everything and anything that you would like to do. No responsibilities, no commitments. It is all on your terms and the entire experience is free. Each day and evening are filled with nothing but fun and relaxation. Describe this week in detail in a journal and read it out loud. Don't hold back. Immerse yourself in the feelings and emotions. Remember, this scenario is limitless. Then, write down how you feel in the present moment as you think about this magical opportunity. How does your body feel? The affirmation for this theme may include: "I have plenty of time to do all of the things I love, enjoy, and find meaningful."

You come back from this vacation, and your energy glass is full. Similar themes from the time off have followed you home. Even with your daily responsibilities, you still have all the time in the world to do things that you love. There is an abundance of time. Do you have a greater desire to help others or serve than you normally would? Can you relax and be more present in this changed reality? What would you do more of? Answer these questions in your journal.

These are simple, thought-provoking examples to ponder as you reflect on your energy and what you want to keep or change about your daily life. As you complete this activity, you may also reflect on how you may have acquired the specific thought processes in the first place. At one point in our lives, one or more of these patterns served a larger purpose. It offered protection from very real emotional or even physical threat. We discussed this complex and powerful information of patterning in Chapter 2, Family of Origin. I often share this information with my clients who ask me "Is it me? Is there something that I am doing to cause all of this chaos?" I am NEVER a fan of placing cruel blame on people for their difficult circumstances because the current state of affairs is influenced by past trauma and adaptation. I also want to empower people to change their lives by uncovering any blind spots perpetuating a problem. If the idea of shifting your thought patterns and raising your vibration resonates with you, you can learn more in Dr. Dispenza's book *Breaking the Habit of Being Yourself* or Louise Hay's *You Can Heal Your Life.* Many, many people do not realize that they have been swimming in these patterns daily, for years on end. And many do not know that there is a way to make changes.

In the next chapter, we will learn about meditation and several exercises to help you feel more grounded, at peace, and present.

6

MEDITATION

Acommon way to try meditation these days is through guided smartphone apps or videos. These activities can look and sound like this:

Sit quietly with deep inhales and exhales from the nose. Focus attention on the rise and fall of the chest, the wax and wane of the belly like a gentle wave breaking and ebbing on a beach shore. Marvel at the expansiveness of the lungs, the calm beat of your heart beneath your hand on the chest. Listen to the sounds of nature (cue rustling of trees and a flute playing in the background). Time seems to stand still in this moment. Everything is slowing down. Your thoughts are quieting. If you feel distracted, bring your focus back to your breathing. Your muscles are relaxed. Your jaw is relaxed. You have the gift of the present moment.

- Have you ever tried meditating but felt distracted or experienced a lot of thoughts?

- Do you wonder if you're "doing it right"?

- Do you wish you could get the hang of it because it's supposedly so good for you?

Focusing on the present moment can be really hard sometimes because our minds have so many thoughts running through them at full speed every day. Even if we happen to have the time, or the space, in our day to practice meditating, it can be tricky to get the hang of it. But I promise you, meditation can be for anyone. You do not have to have years of experience in order to benefit. In this chapter, you will learn useful meditation skills and techniques to put into practice.

PRACTICING MEDITATION

Meditation is a practice that focuses on the inner state of a person with the goal of stilling the mind. In a meditative state, the individual is awake but not focused on the external world. There are several different types of meditation, and most include some form of mindfulness. These include body scans or progressive muscle relaxation, Kundalini, breath-focused, loving-kindness meditation, and transcendental meditation. Mindfulness asks us to tune in to the present moment and pay attention to the mind and sensations of the body, such as the breath, what is heard, our thoughts, and our emotions, all with a curious, nonjudgmental attitude. If you have ever tried meditation before, you know how difficult the mind can be to train. It is like a small, rambunctious child, running around instead of staying seated and peaceful. However, with practice, meditative abilities can grow significantly along with the ability to quiet the mind. It is like any other activity or skill, such as learning to play a sport. It takes practice. It was through my experience with DNRS that I came to fully appreciate the value of meditation and similar practices.

Research has documented and supported the vast benefits of mindfulness. Mindfulness can be very helpful for improving mood, anxiety, stress levels,[1] and satisfaction in life[2] and has been incorporated into modalities such as mindfulness-based cognitive therapy, dialectical-behavior therapy, and mindful parenting. Why is mindfulness so helpful? Over time, meditation actually increases gray matter in the prefrontal cortex, the area in the brain that is important for decision making.[3] Meditation has been associated with a smaller and less reactive amygdala (which is a good thing).[4] When there is emotional, psychological, or physical trauma, amygdala function can be altered.[5] A smaller amygdala can mean more control over emotions.[6] And meditation is wonderful for improving memory, as it can thicken the hippocampus.[7]

My Own Mindfulness Practice

I was introduced to mindfulness concepts through DNRS and as part of research I conducted for my doctoral dissertation. I admired the science behind it, and I could see the improvements and impacts of practicing mindfulness in my own health and the health of my clients, and how it offered an incredible opportunity for joy and freedom. After all, most humans, at least to some degree, wrestle with thoughts that involve past pain and regrets or anxious, unknown futures. When we are freed from these thoughts, we can enjoy the present moment fully. We can be with the people around us and experience our surroundings in a more meaningful, more colorful, and more vibrant way.

Setting aside special moments for practicing visualizations and mindfulness can shift the mind into this lovely, resting state. It can be incredibly helpful and healing to schedule mindfulness practice into your daily routine, as repetition will strengthen the relevant neuropathways. But give it time. Even though I have made the conscious decision to invite mindfulness into my everyday life, I still get flooded by the brain noise sometimes. I forget my intentions, too. My practice will drop off for days or weeks. What matters is that we get back on the horse, every single time. I committed to the practice as a component of the DNRS program in early spring 2019. I always do my best to live by the program and its teachings, and I remind myself of this even in the busiest of times.

I was having a particularly busy week in the summer of 2020, and my schedule was congested by meetings and deadlines. I woke up one morning and decided to go for a walk along the beach. The beach is a twenty-minute drive away, and I was really looking forward to seeing the water. As I arrived at the beach and walked north, I noticed the all-too-familiar laundry list starting to pile up in my mind: "You have two meetings today." "You need to submit this proposal before July first." "You have a presentation to make next Tuesday, better prep for it." "I didn't bring my phone with me, I hope no one needs me right now." The endless chitter chatter wouldn't end.

Finally, it hit me. I needed to remind myself where I was and what I was doing. I thought, "I'm at the beach. Look at its spaciousness and this gorgeous water." I began focusing on how my feet felt in the wet, cool sand. I focused on the breeze on my face, the roar of the little waves making their way onto the seashore. During that hour-long walk, each and every time my mind started to wander, I would come back to these exact same thoughts. Over, and over, and over again. And a miracle occurred. By the end of the walk, I had so much energy that I decided to begin walking south. I simply didn't want the experience to end. I felt vibrant and present, and I shifted into positive thinking. I felt happy when I passed people, I enjoyed seeing little dogs as they followed their owners and melted at the sight of little children with their siblings running to meet the water. Typically, these things would never move me. I would notice them, but with my mind full of a hundred things to do, my body didn't even realize it was at the beach. Until I intentionally focused on my present environment and circumstance, I was on autopilot.

Mindfulness and Counseling

I began introducing mindfulness into my counseling sessions the semester before I graduated with my doctorate. One of my clients had a lot going on in her life (like most of us do). Alix felt depressed, anxious, couldn't sleep, and cried often from being overwhelmed. She couldn't see it for herself, but I always admired her incredible internal strength. Alix had a big heart and was always taking care of everyone else, leaving little time for herself.

Together, we decided that Alix needed a period of thirty minutes per day where she could be alone to enjoy a walk around the neighborhood—with no interruptions. Alix really enjoyed this time alone, and the exercise helped boost her feel-good neurotransmitters. I also taught her about meditation and visualizations. For some sessions, I led her through a head-to-toe body scan to bring awareness to tight spots in the body and how her body felt in the space. Alix also learned how to focus on her breath when she was stressed out. I would ask her to notice the rise and fall of her chest and to place her hands on her abdomen and collarbone to feel this shift. She also used the 4-4-4-4 technique, breathing in for four seconds, holding for four seconds, breathing out for four seconds, then pausing for four seconds to regulate her breathing and keep it from becoming shallow.

Lastly, I showed her how to use mental imagery and visualization.

During one of our sessions together, I had her close her eyes and picture herself walking through a beautiful scenic meadow. I then taught her how to use the technique to re-create old memories and make new ones. I stayed with her as she spoke aloud and visualized her ideal place and event. She was on the beach with her then-boyfriend, getting married to him. Her son was next to her wearing a suit and holding a bouquet of white roses. The image that she described was so magnificent and was filled with so much intensity I still remember it to this day. When she finished her visualization, she opened her eyes and cried tears of joy. She could not believe how ten or fifteen minutes of this simple activity could shift her mood so profoundly. What she didn't realize is that this practice, if done consistently over time, can heal the brain by boosting oxytocin, endorphins, and serotonin. Prior to her visualization, the usual anxiety that she endured had been eating her alive. Not today, anxiety cage, not today.

The Anxiety Cage

You may know how it feels to be in the anxiety cage. Since we live within the confines of our minds all the time, if it's filled with negative or overwhelming thoughts, it can feel much like a cage with no space to breathe. I've been there, too. It feels like a jail cell. It can rob you of your peace of mind, of your sanity, and of your joy.

Now, imagine what it feels like to be unlocked from the ball and chain of anxiety. I want you to paint a very clear picture for yourself about what this would look like. List every single thing that might be different. What would your life look like? What would you feel like? This might be difficult to envision. It might be surprisingly scary. But when you do envision it, WOW! Now that feels spacious. Feel the freedom from anxiety, depression, mood swings, and fatigue.

Do you feel exhausted by the day? Trust me friend, I have been there. When I first came to mindfulness meditation, I did not believe that one hour of practicing simple exercises in nature could free my body from the cage of a chattery mind and give me abundant energy. How was that possible? Can our thoughts really shut off our mitochondria or steal our energy stores? Without question. My thoughts typically consisted of the "to do" list, which drove up adrenaline production in the body on a daily (and most certainly an hourly) basis. As we'll discuss in the hormone chapter, adrenaline is released from the adrenal glands to supply energy to the host for fleeing or fighting. Adrenaline is also associated with activities such as skydiving or other activities that cause an adrenaline high. However, constant, persistent release of adrenaline in the body can cause less-than-pleasant things to occur and affect memory, focus, and a sense of calm.[8] The following reflection has some steps to get you started with mindfulness meditation. I share these exercises with my clients in private practice. You can start with as little as five minutes per day and work up to longer periods of time.

REFLECTION: MINDFULNESS EXERCISES

This reflection differs from others in this book—it doesn't involve much journaling. Instead, it presents several mindfulness and visualization exercises for you to try. If you'd like to use your journal during these exercises, you can write down how each exercise made you feel, which was your favorite, and what feelings or thoughts arose during the exercise. All experiences during these exercises are valid and normal, whether you feel a greater sense of peace, somewhat restless and frustrated, or flooded by a lot of thoughts. In my experience with clients, mindfulness does not always bring immediate peace or relaxation. It depends on the individual. Sometimes the brain fights back when engaging in a new activity. Simply notice your reactions and write them down.

Creativity serves a special role and place within these mental imagery exercises. The ultimate goal is to halt the looping in our minds.

MEDITATION FOR BEGINNERS

A list of simple, yet effective, tools for meditation follows. Each helps bring awareness to the present moment and promote a deeper connection with your body. Choose a space that is private and relaxing to begin. Find a comfortable seat. First, read through the list a handful of times. You can focus on each item in the list for a few minutes at a time. Close your eyes if you feel comfortable doing so.

- Bring awareness to the breath, how it flows in and out. Breathe in through the nose and out through the nose for now. You may decide to put one hand on the chest and one on the abdomen to feel the shift with each inhale and exhale.

- Notice the slight coolness of air flowing into the nostrils and the slight warmth of the air flowing out of the body.

- Take a moment to notice sounds around you, from outside the room or within it, such as the ticking of a clock or the gentle whir of the air conditioning.

- When breathing in and out, count the inner breath as one and the outer breath as two. Do this several times and take slow, deep breaths in through the nose and out through the mouth.

- When the mind becomes distracted, simply pause and notice it. Label whatever is coming up as a thought or emotion, and then bring your awareness back to the breath by counting one in, two out.

You can try mindfulness apps, such as Calm and Headspace, for guided versions of these exercises. Each have free trials that can help you lay a solid foundation for more in-depth practice.

PRACTICING MINDFULNESS MOMENT TO MOMENT

Bringing awareness to your surroundings is such a powerful, simple way to get grounded and connected, both to yourself and the present moment. If you start feeling overwhelmed with thoughts as you meditate, use these techniques.

- Ask yourself, "Where am I right now?" The mind is often somewhere in the past or the future, replaying events or anticipating stressors that might come in the next hour, day, or year. You may want to state out loud or in your head, "I am at home." "I am in my car." or "I am at the park." Let the statement sink in. Saying it several times can help.

- Look around and acknowledge your surroundings. Ground yourself in the present moment by observing different objects and naming three to five colors that you see.

- Touch something with your hands. This can be a pen or pencil, a bottle of water, or the softness of your shirt, to name a few.

- Ask yourself, "How does my current environment feel?" Really take it in. Describe with words, either aloud or in your mind, how the space feels. Is the space cold or warm? Does it feel open and spacious or crowded? Does it feel tranquil?

THE BODY SCAN

Body scan techniques bring awareness to each part of the body, such as areas of pain or discomfort, feelings of warmth or coolness, and sensations such as the expansiveness of the lungs or your heartbeat. These techniques can be helpful if you are looking for a quick pause and some stress reduction in the morning, during the day, or at night before bed. Sit comfortably. Then, starting at the very top of the head, slowly scan the body for places of pain or tightness. Include any and all parts of your body: the head, back of the eyes, nose, mouth, jaw, neck, shoulders, back, abdomen, hips, thighs, knees, calves, ankles, and toes. Focus on each body part for a period of time by pausing at each location, then slowly and gently move further down the body. You can roll the ankles or wrists, move the neck from side to side, and relax and move the jaw around when focusing on these parts. When you get to the feet, notice the contact point between the bottoms of the feet and the ground, the energy and friction between the two, gravity pulling your feet down.

CREATING A VISUALIZATION

Visualizations involve creating an image in the mind with the goal of promoting relaxation. Some can be short, while others can last up to twenty minutes. Visualizations can be simple, such as picturing your favorite beach spot complete with an umbrella and chair. They can also be a bit more complex, like going on a short journey. I have used guided imagery in both individual and groups sessions to take clients through forests and tropical landscapes. My favorite kinds use wonderful past memories and imagined future events to promote stress relief, joy, and peace. Sometimes this can help solve specific issues. Visualizations can be easier to hold than some of the previous exercises because it actively gives the brain something to do. Before you begin, it is important to ask yourself these questions:

- What is the location?

- Who is with me?

- What do I see?

- What do I feel with my senses?

- What do I hear?

- What do I smell?

- If this moment was a color, what would it be?

- If this moment had an adjective attached to it, what would it be?

- Be as descriptive as possible. It is best to describe this out loud.

These steps can be used for both past memories and imagined and hoped-for future events. These visualizations should be positive, joyful, and happy creations. I recommend choosing one past memory and one future event to review per day. Make sure you have a quiet space where you can speak aloud in private for ten to fifteen minutes.

VISUALIZATIONS FOR LETTING GO

We do not need what is not ours to be fulfilled. When we feel like we are pushing against a cement wall or trying to open a locked door, it's time to pause. If you find yourself struggling to release control, try the visualization exercises to help you decipher the two: to experience inner tension versus welcoming peace and synchronicity:

- Picture yourself playing tug-of-war with someone else, or something else over something you really want in your life right now. You are pulling so hard just to avoid losing ground.

Feel the tension, feel your deep inner fight, feel your muscles bulging. Then, picture yourself opening your hands gently and watching a rope fall to the floor at your feet. The rope does not go away, it simply falls at your feet. This is a powerful visualization. Reflect on the differences between the two actions, the pulling and the letting go. Think about the emotions they provoke and how the actions feel in your body. Do your reflections bring up any particular thoughts or memories?

- Visualize yourself holding on dearly to a branch of a tree. You are clinging for dear life. Feel your hands and fingers wrapped tightly around the branch as you hang there. Your legs swing in the air, and your heart races in terror. You look up at the branch and the top of the tree, which is very close to you. Then, open your hands and feel yourself touch the ground with your feet. The tree is only seven feet high, the branch is even closer to the ground. You reach the comfortable, soft ground in less than half a second. Once again, the hands fully open and release.

- Picture something you really love (and currently have) being placed in front of you. Consider something that is very easy for you to have or do that requires minimal effort from you. Maybe it is your dog walking over to you and sitting on your lap. Maybe it is a bottle of cold water or chilled fruit on a hot summer day. Whatever your specific vision is, tap into the emotion and ease of the visualization. Note the simplicity and effortless energy surrounding it.

- This visualization is for expansion. Often, when we are holding on to something or pushing against a wall in our lives, we feel restricted or we feel a shrinking in the chest. Picture a vast beach or forest. Nature stretches out on either side of you as far as the eye can see. The sky is blue and the world around you is open and inviting. Feel a breeze pushing your shoulders back. Open your arms out wide and close your eyes as you tilt your head back. Stay with your image of the large, open beach, mountain range, field of flowers, or whatever you have chosen.

These meditations and visualizations can calm the mind and body when practiced regularly. We will now shift our attention to mindfulness as it relates to nature, gratitude, and our thoughts.

7

FINDING MINDFULNESS
IN NATURE AND GRATITUDE

"Come to the woods for here is rest."
—John Muir

We seem to spend time indoors more now than ever. Maybe you go into work early or stay late, well before sunrise or after sunset. Maybe technology in a variety of forms is a temptation to remain indoors. Even schools seem to be slowly reducing recess in favor of other activities. When was the last time that you went outside? It may seem like a silly question, but prioritizing nature and fresh air was one of my healing components.

- Do you spend little or no time in nature?
- Is it hard to make time to get outside because of your schedule?
- When you do get outdoors, does your mind wander? Is it hard to remain present?

Nature has a profound impact on our mental health, and nature can help us heal. Research has shown that a camping trip in the woods among the trees and flowers can significantly modulate and improve immune function. This improvement can last over thirty days after returning from the trip. Spending time in nature also lowers adrenaline and stress.[1] So why is it that nature isn't one of the first things we turn to when we need to help the body heal?

CONNECTING TO NATURE

I had taken a trip to Colorado for a counseling conference one beautiful summer weekend in July of 2019. I walked along a beautiful trail one warm day, taking in the sun and landscape around me. The trail had invigorating inclines and calm, relaxing descents. The sky was an unforgettable bright blue, with not a single cloud passing near me. The view of the horizon was breathtaking. Magnificent mountains that felt within arm's reach stretched out in front of me, popping with bright greens and undertones of tan and gray. The vastness of the mountain range was incomprehensible. There was so much to explore, and I felt so free there. I felt like I had taken off a very heavy jacket and leapt into lightness. I almost felt like the air was blowing through me. I was one with the air.

Trips like this can have a deep and memorable impact on us and can even feel like a spiritual journey for the soul. Incorporating this type of experience into a daily routine can be great for our mental and physical health. One of my favorite self-care activities is to walk the beach on a peaceful morning, ride my bike along a trail near my neighborhood, or repeatedly walk along my driveway between my house and the mailbox. As I do these activities, I practice mindfulness by taking note of what I see and taking a moment to admire it.

Is it the incredibly intricate and uniquely shaped bark on a tree? Is it a colorful cardinal, blue jay, or woodpecker perched on the fence, eyeing me inquisitively? Is it the sparkle of the ocean at the beach, the sun dancing atop the surface and creating a spectacular light show for those who are present and privileged to see it?

We all have our own preferred spots in nature. Your job is to identify your favorite places and spend more time in them. Think about where you and your family can enjoy more time in nature. This may mean a walk in your neighborhood, a short drive to the beach, or even a planned vacation that requires travel arrangements. The important part is that you are getting outside. Vitamin D from the sun has enormous benefits for brain health. Sunlight helps regulate circadian rhythms and promotes deep, restorative sleep. For those who do not live in sunny areas, do not fret. Nature is incredibly healing even without the sun.

Benefits from spending time in nature include improved mental health and decreased levels of depression,[2] improved focus,[3] and decreases in rumination (that pesky looping we talked about in Chapter 5).[4] Have I convinced you to spend some time in nature yet? If a supplement could provide all of these fabulous side effects, who wouldn't want to take it? Yet, nature can be totally free, no prescription required. Trees purify everything around them and produce clean, fresh air for us to breathe in. Nature has so much intricate beauty that we hardly take the time to enjoy. Have you ever really looked at a flower? At each unique petal, the stem, the leaves, the center of the flower? We say, "Stop and smell the roses," and we should do so. Partaking in activities where we take time to really notice our surroundings can strengthen our memory and calm our minds.[5] It may be hard to find time to spend in nature given our work, school, or other obligations. Try making small changes to your schedule to incorporate more time in nature, such as walks around the neighbor-hood or in a local park.

REFLECTION: CONNECT TO NATURE

When you spend time in nature, be sure to complete these easy sug-gestions to immerse yourself and connect to nature in the present (and mindful) moment. You can write down your responses, experiences, and sensations if you choose to bring your journal along with you.

- Name at least three colors you see.

- Look for two or three animals.

- Concentrate on the air outside, such as the breeze blowing on your face and body. Feel the sun shining on you, or the invigo-rating chill of winter in the air.

- If there are flowers, smell one.

- If there are leaves, touch one.

These simple exercises improve mindfulness by using the mag-nificent tools our bodies have given us—the gift of sensation. Concentrating on the senses brings the body and mind into the pres-ent moment, reduces stress and anxiety levels, and helps us focus. In the final section of this chapter, we bring gratitude into our mindful-ness practice.

GRATITUDE

"Let gratitude be the pillow upon which you kneel
to say your nightly prayer."
—**Maya Angelou**

Many things happen to us that are completely out of our control. We cannot fix or change them. We can't change other people, and we can't always change what happens to them. When we are in the midst of difficult or stressful days, it can be hard or almost impossible to shift into a different mindset. A mindset and habit that produces one of the most radical shifts is gratitude. My family and I can't change our loss or the changes that came with it. However, after acknowledging the pain, the emotions, and the experience, we have talked about what we are thankful and grateful for in the healing process. It can be helpful to incorporate gratitude into your healing journey. It can be gratitude for the simplest things. It can be gratitude for time and memories. You can create a list on your phone, speak out loud during a drive, or make a tradition of a weekly gratitude discussion with your family or friends at dinner. Gratitude journals are another avenue as well.

Opening up a journal and taking time to intentionally connect with the lovely pleasures of daily living is one simple step to foster gratitude. We have many gifts in our lives, including simple luxuries. A cup of warm tea or coffee, the experience of oil in a bath, or savoring a piece of fruit are all part of the abundance that we enjoy in our lives and should take time to celebrate.

Using the practice of naming things you are grateful for can be part of a morning ritual for positive thinking and grounding. It is also a great way to rewire the brain from negative thinking.[6] Research has shown that gratitude can be a highly predictable variable of wellbeing[7] and an effective way to improve mental health. Practicing gratitude also creates sustained effects that last into the future.[8] Each breath we take is a gift, as is each day that we live. Life is precious, as are our experiences and the people in it. Deepak Chopra teaches that going "deeper" into gratitude means acknowledging things far beyond the material world. This includes family, good health, a sense of purpose, spirituality, and connection. Take time to look around you and notice all that you have. Sometimes it takes a temporary lack to prompt this process. Think about a time when your car wouldn't start or a storm knocked out your electricity. In those moments, did you really miss what you had just hours prior?

In 2018, I visited Haiti. It was a five-day school project and mission trip. I love traveling to new places and learning about different cultures. I also have deep respect and affection for the organization I went with; the people affiliated with it are some of the kindest, most positive, and generous people I know. During this trip, the organization I traveled and worked with was donating a school to a local village. Interestingly, what promoted a sense of gratitude for my life in the United States came the moment we landed at the airport and tried renting a car. It took four hours to receive our rental and proceed with the day. The roads in Haiti also made me thankful for our smooth, paved roads in the United States. The rocky journey around Haiti took far longer than the same distance would have on a normal road or highway near my home.

When I was in Haiti, I allowed myself to slow down and enjoy life: the beautiful array of stars in the sky as I slept soundly under them, the whole foods, flavorful cuisine, and the long drives. I had the time and headspace to acknowledge all of the beauty around me and the good works being carried out. I appreciated the generosity of those who hosted us and saw the joy in their eyes as they provided a meal for us. I soaked it all in because my world had stopped turning so quickly. I didn't have internet on my phone or computer. I simply had a book, a journal, and a set of ears and eyes to take it all in.

Have you experienced something similar? A period when you slowed down and appreciated life for what it is and appreciated the simple things that mean so much? As you complete the following reflection, I hope you find feelings of peace and gratitude.

REFLECTION: GRATITUDE IN ACTION

In your journal, answer each of the following questions. Take your time to carefully consider your answers. You can create lists, write paragraphs, and draw with markers or colored pencils, if desired.

- What are three physical things that you are grateful for today? This might be a piece of clothing that holds special meaning for you, a nourishing meal, a picture of something beautiful, or something else close to your heart.

- Who are three people you are grateful for today? What about them are you grateful for? You might feel their unwavering love and support, feelings of connectedness, feel able to really be yourself with them, hear the hearty and wholesome laughter of your child, or see a smile that lights up the room.

- What are three experiences you are grateful for today? You can acknowledge something that took place today, or a past memory of a deeply personal and special moment. This can include time in nature, time enjoying music and the arts, time with family, or time connecting to yourself or to God in a meaningful way.

I hope you enjoyed reflecting on who and what you are grateful for. I challenge you to incorporate these questions into your day and week and to pause and consider how you feel after reviewing and answering each question. Gratitude shifts our thoughts and helps us to feel more joyful.

MINDFULNESS AND THOUGHTS

While many neutral thoughts such as grocery lists or work tasks prevent the mind from staying present, negative thoughts create an added punch of exhaustion. DNRS coaches refer to relentless, consuming thoughts as a limbic system loop. When you're stuck in "the loop," there is constant negativity, fear, hesitation, and judgment. These relentless thoughts, whether they consist of never-ending self-criticism, lists of things that you have to get done today, or that fight you had last week with a family member, can drive anxiety and even depression. Think about it. If you lived with a radio on your right shoulder that played negative news, judgmental comments, and fearful stories sixteen hours per day, would you really feel good? This thing plays at work, while you are stuck in traffic, while you are spending time with friends, while you are making dinner, et cetera. Would you feel relaxed? No way in hell. You would probably want to smash the radio with a massive whack-a-mole hammer by the end of the day. So why do we think that all of the negative thoughts and beliefs we hold would be any different? With meditation, over time and through practice, we can become more mindful and more present in every moment. We can learn to slow those racing thoughts and observe them without judgment. When we do this, a separation occurs between these thoughts and our connection to them. In addition, after rewiring the brain, the looping fades away or lessens.

Why do our minds repeat thoughts like this? One hypothesis is that the brain is trying to get us to remember something, to protect us. Is it trying to remind us that something or someone isn't safe, because that's how the brain perceived or perceives the event. Several different areas of the brain are responsible for this, such as those that store memory and detect threats. When our limbic system, as was discussed in the DNRS chapter, is overactive, it may cause a lot of excessive worrying and overthinking. The limbic system's job is to detect threats and keep us alive. If we forgot about an argument, or about our mistakes, what might happen? The bad thing could happen again. Instead, our brain reminds us, "That person could hurt you again! You must remember this fight to protect yourself from them." Or our brain says, "If you forget this mistake, you'll surely make it again! And then you could get fired . . . or make someone angry." What an extreme alert system! And yet, the limbic system wants only to protect us. It is a surveillance camera. And when it is impaired, it makes little mistakes or uncomfortable fights feel like a nuclear explosion. It can come up with a worst-case scenario at the drop of a hat. I teach clients to thank their brains when a flood of warning thoughts come up, to acknowledge that they hear the warning and see it. This can help release and relax the loop over time when used repeatedly.

Another hypothesis is that looping of negative or intense memories produces adrenaline or the release of other stress hormones. This can feel good to some people—like riding on a roller coaster or bungee jumping. If your brain gets used to a certain neurochemistry of adrenaline release, it won't want to change so easily. Reliving uncomfortable memories or situations within your mind can maintain that adrenaline release.

A third hypothesis relates to control. If we are looping about every possible future outcome to a stressful situation in our lives, then we can try to predict and prepare for those outcomes. This can mean upcoming projects at work or school or difficult conversations we need to have with our spouse, family, or friends, to name a few. Control can also look like imagining a different outcome for a past event. "If only I had done . . . " or "If only she had said . . . . "

Here is a final hypothesis: With the mind going nonstop, it has enormous potential for problem solving and resolving issues. Flowing ideas and thoughts can promote creativity and generate a slew of new options and endless possibilities. We work through problems by wondering, "What if we approached the problem this way?" or "What if we tackled X first, then Y?" I am all for this type of brain chatter, especially if you set aside some time for it, notepad in hand, and label it as "my brainstorming hour."

The problem is, so much of this looping leads to no actual problem solving at all. It simply rehashes the same stuff over and over and over again. It replays the same fight that you had with that family member in an attempt to change what happened, to tweak it in some way that fixes it. The past is already over, though. We can't jump in and change the reality of a conversation we had five years ago. When your mind won't turn off (which inconveniently happens to me either early in the morning or right before bed) check in with yourself and ask whether your noisy mind comes up with any good solutions or simply keeps going in a circle with no clear road map. Therapist and educator Jon Connelly shares at his seminars that humans are the only animals on this planet that have this ruminative, reflective ability (which can lead to a great deal of anxiety). Here is his example:

Say there is a big hawk flying around, and he suddenly spots a snake. He swoops down and grabs the snake with his talons. As the hawk flies away with dinner in hand, he accidentally drops the snake. Now, do you think this hawk is saying to himself, "Dammit, how could you? Look how slow you are? Can't you do anything right?" No. This hawk is already looking for the next snake. He has completely forgotten about his little slip up and is moving productively toward his goal of capturing a snake for supper. I was blown away by this hilarious, yet simple example of how complicated we humans make things.

The most recent addition to our brains is the prefrontal cortex,

which provides us with the great gifts of problem solving, insightful-
ness, and reflection. But the fear centers in the brain can take over
and prevent the prefrontal cortex from shining its bright light of reasonable, balanced thoughts and realism on the situations we face.[9] If
we can strengthen and rewire the brain to favor these processes even
in stressful moments, we will feel all the better during it.

Think back to what it was like being a child and living in the
moment. Whether you were painting, playing with toys, or spending time in nature, you were beautifully present in the moment. We
were born into this world with minds that functioned in the present
moment. Think of a small baby. Six-month-old babies aren't thinking to themselves, "I wonder what Mom is going to mash up for me
for dinner tonight." That baby is fully absorbing everything around
them, wanting to touch things, feel things, and see things. They fully
embrace the present moment. They also embrace their emotions in
the present moment. They show us when they are scared, angry, or
happy, without overthinking any of it. It is real and authentic.

I want you to know that it is possible to feel better. Truly it is. We
don't have to revert back to our state of babyhood, but we can take
steps that help us shift back to a state of present-time, a time of peace.
My grandfather always said you need the right tool for the job. If you
can find the perfect tool for your specific, individual needs, things can
change. If you have tried many things before to improve your mental
and physical health but are still struggling, you are not alone. There
is an answer for you. And although the answer may be multifaceted,
mindfulness is almost certainly one of the components.

PART TWO

Understanding Your Physical Health

8

HONORING THE BODY'S INNATE WISDOM

Having a good mind-body connection is essential for good mental health. When your brain and body are out of whack, you don't feel like yourself at all. You may desperately want to connect with others, but depression or anxiety prevents you from fully showing up in the present with them. You may want to do really well at a task, but cannot reach your fullest potential. And you may be desperately trying to figure out how to feel better but cannot connect to that inner north star, that inner guide.

Dr. Rutherford is a wonderful doctor I met in Reno, Nevada. He explained to me that when your body is not healthy and aligned, you brain and mind aren't either: "You can't be spiritual. You can't be logical. You can't be intuitive." He had gained this wisdom as a result of working through his own health problems. You can't really have a healthy mind without a healthy body, and vice versa. The brain is part of your body. It is an organ. The health of your body is one determiner of how well your brain is going to function.

What exactly is optimal physical health? Physical wellness includes abundant energy levels that propel you toward your dreams and purpose. Physical health is digestive ease. Physical health is a well-functioning, balanced immune system. Physical health is being able to move however you wish—traveling, dancing, playing sports—without feeling hindered by pain. Physical health is when your body can take in and fully absorb nutrients and minerals. Physical health is feeling radiant and nourished from the inside out. What does it mean to you?

- Do you find yourself with little energy?
- Do you find that you have less endurance to tackle the day than you used to?
- Do you have digestive issues?
- Do you have immune issues?
- Do you complain of problems with your joints, skin, hair, or nails?
- Do you have a lot of pain in your body?

In this chapter and part of the book, you will learn what you can personally do to improve your overall wellness by improving your physical health. We'll focus on using food logs as a data collection tool to learn about and heal our own bodies.

THE ART OF THE FOOD LOG

"Out you go!" I thought to myself as I recently chucked one of my old food diaries into the trash in one piece. No shredding, no ripping out a few pages here and there to save. Nothing. Into the garbage can it went, never to return. This was the intense and somewhat comical but visceral reaction I had when I found my old journal full of food logs. When I initially found the logs, I thought they might give me helpful content to share in this book. Seeing them reminded me of how much insight they had given me and how far I had come in my journey to health and wellness. But the logs no longer served me since my immune system and digestive tract have healed so significantly. I do not suffer from many of the symptoms that used to plague me. Those reactions are long gone.

I have tried many "healthy" diets to improve my digestion and heal my immune system. The diets were supposed to provide anti-inflammatory benefits and were bursting with all of the nutrients in the world. I tried organic foods, 100% grass-fed beef, pasture-raised meat and poultry, raw foods, cooked foods, you name it. Most of these diets were suggested by practitioners that I, to this day, have the utmost respect for and am friends with. Yet none of these diets gave me a noticeable shift in wellbeing. None of them. I tried a paleo diet, the autoimmune protocol diet, a low FODMAP diet, whole 30, vegan, vegetarian, keto. I tried juicing. I tried bone broth fasts. I tried intermittent fasting. Each of these could be the golden key that unlocks abundant health for some people, which is why some swear their guidelines hold the answer for everyone. You may even know one of these people. I certainly do. I have seen lives transformed by choosing healing diets.

Yet, the perfect diet was not my key to better health. I did need to nourish my body with a healthy diet, but it became a secondary goal that complemented other work I desperately needed to do but was blind to at the time. Nevertheless, maintaining a healthy diet is something I prioritize because it supports every system of my body.

A healthy diet is probably one component of wellness for you, too.

This is where a food log can be a powerful tool, because if you try a certain diet or food, you will be able to identify how it makes you feel and what it does for you. We all have different emotional and physical needs, and I encourage you to identify YOUR needs through loving self-exploration.

When I used my food logs, I had no idea which foods were making me feel worse and which foods were making me feel better. I was a bit of an extreme case, since the anti-fungal medication I was taking had given me intestinal permeability, practically overnight. (I will dive into intestinal permeability later in the book, in Chapter 13, "Digestion and Immune Health.") My immune system was reacting to all of the foods that were leaking into my bloodstream. It built significant antibodies to whichever ones it found, because food particles are not supposed to circulate in our blood. When I had this "aha" moment, it became clear that my problem wasn't really the foods; it was something much, much bigger.

Nevertheless, the food logs helped me figure out which breakfast foods made me feel my best. I learned that I needed more carbs in the evening for better sleep and a consistent greens-packed lunch to help me power through the afternoon. I was able to identify the best diet unique to me, one with guidelines tailored to my body's needs. I was able to reclaim some control over the foods I ate instead of following someone else's plan, allowing them to "take away" food I liked eating, food that gave me joy and comfort in the moment. I learned what worked for my body by analyzing my detailed notes as well as by trial and error.

Food logs are a great tool for increasing mindfulness and tracking how certain meals or ingredients affect your mental and physical health. You can keep a log of what you eat for a few weeks or a few months—whatever feels doable and doesn't drive you too crazy.

Creating a useful food log requires diligence in writing down time of day, what foods were consumed, and how you felt before, during, immediately after, and a few hours after eating. You should include any digestive symptoms, your mood, energy levels, appearance of skin (clearness, blemishes, rashes, hives, et cetera), sleep quality, and any other health symptoms you are trying to improve.

I know that consistently keeping a list of what and when you eat isn't all that fun, and sometimes it's hard to stay on top of it. But you will learn a great deal about your body and what it has been trying to tell you for a long, long time. You may or may not have the severe food reactions that I experienced, but every single one of us has a unique constellation of what foods make us feel fantastic, the golden hours when eating will make us feel our best, what quantities of food we should eat and when, which foods really bog us down, and which foods cause inflammation in our bodies and brains. Our bodies often show us precisely what we should be eating, but we are too busy to pay attention. A food log can help you do just that—pay attention. If done correctly, the log will be a record of what you've eaten, when, and how you felt during various check-ins throughout the day. It is also a useful way to track the effects of removing a specific inflammatory food from your diet or bringing it back in.

Once you've collected data for a few weeks or so, you can start looking at patterns. The results and conclusions can sometimes be shocking—after you eat X, you may notice patterns of digestive problems the next day. After eating Y, you reported fatigue, joint pain, and irritability each afternoon on those specific days.

You can find printable food logs online. If it feels time consuming or inconvenient, know that this effort is going to a good cause and your efforts will be rewarded. You may identify patterns that change your health forever. But remember—food logs can serve us for a period of time, but we certainly don't need them forever.

The body and mind are joined together in many incredible ways. The health of one impacts the other in an interconnected relationship. Creating an optimal state of mind-body health includes giving yourself what you truly need. When we aren't exactly sure what we need, it is time to put on our research hat and collect some data. Using a food log for several weeks is an excellent way to collect the data needed to tailor your diet in a way that meets your unique, biochemical needs. It is your job to find the correct diet for you.

Know that as you learn more about your own body's needs, you might resist the proposed changes staring back at you. This is perfectly normal and to be expected. Letting go of that resistance will free up your energy to enjoy the journey toward wellness.

RESISTING THE BODY'S WISDOM

Resistant.

I can't think of many other words to describe my situation and attitude while I was in the process of trying different supplements, products, gadgets, and diets. When my health really started going downhill, I was resistant to the advice of my first holistic doctor, Dr. Serena Bordes, who prescribed an anti-inflammatory diet. This meant no more bread, no cheese, no pasta, no pastries, no donuts. No cake or ice cream. WHAT??? Her famous words were always "You're not having it!" I can still hear her voice ringing in my ear, saying those very words. Recalling those moments brings a big smile to my face because she is such a funny, lovely, PATIENT woman. I was incredibly resistant to the diet change she wanted me to try. I remember the day after her recommendations, I ate pizza and cupcakes at a friend's

Halloween party. I polished it off with some Milky Way minis. Talk about lack of compliance!

I have learned three important things about resistance. First, you will resist giving up some things that probably don't serve you anymore, but you will not be ready to let go of them yet. Second, you will resist trying some things that may actually be fantastic for you. And when I was farther along in my healing process, I experienced a third type of resistance. I told myself that the medical doctors were much wiser than I was or that the medical studies had all the answers I was looking for and I needed to just keep "pushing through" and do what I was told. I resisted listening to my own body.

My advice on resistance is simple. Listen to your body. Listen, listen, listen. Research may show that this diet or that supplement is incredible for you. But if it's making you feel terrible, your reaction may not be due to the detoxing process so many claim the symptoms are from. Sure, you may have a little discomfort when you shift from eating poorly to eating well. If you take a probiotic, you may have a change in digestive symptoms while the bacteria are rebalancing. What I am referring to is when you feel horrible from trying something new. Like on a scale from one to ten, it's a solid eleven.

My resistance often took the form of listening to medical advice instead of my own body. By 2015, if I was told to eat a certain way or try a certain supplement plan, you better believe that I did it. I was the dedicated patient, the perfect one who wanted a gold star for effort. Yet, a lot of these recommendations made me feel very, very sick. Whether it was fasting, the keto diet, juice fasts, bone broth fasts, or detox products, many things intensified my symptoms or did nothing at all. The same was true for moderate-intensity exercise. That would wipe me out in a not so good way. If I tried to sprint, forget it. My vision blurred and I became incredibly dizzy. It was clearly Not. For. Me. And yet, I was so determined to feel better that I thought I needed to push harder.

That is how a lot of research-backed strategies made me feel because my body could not take it. It could not take running, fasting, or any detox tincture products that had small amounts of alcohol in them. When I began respecting the wisdom of my body, I put carbs back in. I started walking and going on gentle bike rides instead of my intense daily gym workouts with heavy weights, squats, and the StairMaster. I never tried fasting again, and now I only drink green juice with a meal. I gave away and threw away the supplements that made my skin go crazy or gave me a headache. I gave up the power yoga and switched to the gentle, beginner's flow. Once I let go of the should-dos and connected with my personal and unique formula, things began to shift dramatically.

We each need to develop our own awareness, and with awareness comes growth, understanding, and a fresh perspective. I am confident that you will choose whatever serves your highest potential and that you will walk away from the rest. I know how the conundrum of "What should I try?" or "What changes should I make?" feels. Many times we end up trying A LOT of different things, only to feel more discouraged.

You can take the advice of a medical practitioner or try something that worked well for your friend. But if it does nothing for you, or if it makes you feel just awful, I suggest stopping and trying something else. Some of the well-regarded approaches did little for me because I was suffering from limbic system impairment, which was driving immune and nervous system dysregulation. For some people, fasting changes their life and helps them heal. Some swear by keto, or they feel revived from a juice fast. We all have different answers to our beautifully complex puzzles.

I assure you, there are probably at least one or two things in your life that you are resisting, whether it be an addition or a subtraction. It can be hard to identify this resistance, at least initially. When you are feeling resistant, the following reflection can help you determine your next steps.

REFLECTION: RESISTANCE ASSISTANCE

Take some time to look over each of these questions carefully. In a journal, answer them in any form you would like. You can write a list, write paragraphs, or draw images that come to mind.

- What overall changes are you currently resisting in your life?

- Make a list of things you suspect are no good for you or make you feel worse that you have not yet let go. Describe how they make you feel emotionally and physically.

- Next, make a list of wellness approaches that you have considered trying but have felt hesitant or reluctant to do so.

- Where are these blocks coming from? What do you tell yourself about each of these potential changes?

- What are the potential consequences of keeping things as they are?

Keep in mind that although I mostly talk about the effects of lifestyle changes on health and wellbeing, the same concepts can also affect your relationships and environment. Is there a relationship you need to let go? Is there a group or new hobby/activity to join that may be exactly what you need?

THE ALLURE OF ARTIFICIAL DEADLINES

In the midst of my baffling health problems, I had a tendency to set future-oriented goals for myself. "By the end of the summer, I'll be feeling much better!" "In three months, I'll have found the answer and be 'back to normal'" or "After completing this supplement and dietary protocol, I will have my life back." Hah! As if. I was only scratching the surface of my adventure. I would even ask my doctors "When is this going to be over?" My impatience was building and building with each new round of trial and error. Have you felt this way before? Wanting to feel better or different by a special occasion, a holiday, a wedding, et cetera? Clients ask me this, too: "When can I expect to feel better?" they say. Let me tell you a few reasons why this thought process should be jettisoned.

First, as human beings we are always striving for something greater, for improvement. Health, both mental and physical, is a long-term process that occurs over our entire lives. We will always keep striving for something that may be just out of our reach, until we achieve it. It is how we are wired. Second, the profound blessings and impacts of life's moments come not only in the "I hit my goal" events, but also in the journey, in the process that shifted you into your highest good, the best version of you. Third, setting health goals for yourself can often feel defeating if you don't meet them, despite your best efforts. If you did the protocol, or the exercises, or the diet, or the medication, or the therapy, and nothing has shifted yet, it can create a sense of hopelessness and feelings of being trapped in your current state. Reframing these efforts and events as a treasure hunt or as an accumulation of experience shifts the tone. It shifts the perspective, the energy of these endeavors. They are not a waste of time. They are data collection and research at its finest. Even the things that did not get me healthier provided gems of wisdom and insights. When

I look back at each strategy I tried, I can wholeheartedly say that it gave me new knowledge about myself. When your greatest efforts feel like a failed attempt, reflect on all that you have learned from the experience. Compare what you know now to what you knew before. A finding in research, even a negative result, is still a finding.

While goals and timelines can be great and effective, if you find yourself frustrated or hopeless it may be time to surrender the time limit or deadline for a bit and just let yourself be. Radical acceptance of the present moment as it is, while releasing yourself from the demand of a healing deadline, can impact your mind and body in many ways. Fighting a current reality can be so tiring, both physically and psychologically. If instead, we remind ourselves that the only timeline we are on is ours, we let go of the pushing, the pressures placed on ourselves and our bodies, and we let go of being cripplingly consumed by a full-time job of "getting better." When we do this, we may, miraculously, feel a bit better. When we release this heavy expectation of ourselves and our bodies, we welcome in joy, present-focus, mindfulness, and not wishing our lives away. We celebrate what we do have, and we celebrate the little wins along the way. We will get there in just the right amount of time.

FIND YOUR OWN PATH TO FEED YOUR BODY AND SOUL

I tried everything on this winding journey to better health. Something inside me kept pushing me, saying, "You are meant for much more than being sick. You are meant to thrive and LIVE." That little voice kept me going. It kept me exploring. It molded me into a researcher, with myself as the lone sample of one.

The information and concepts that I collected helped me to thrive in the end. Letting go of the artificial deadlines I mentioned was a huge "finding." Another big eye opener was a balanced mindset regarding my diet. Food is meant to be enjoyed. It is an experience and celebration of life, the transmission of energy from one life force to another. Food is meant to be flavorful and met with gratitude. There's a reason we get excited when we see the waiter coming with our table's tray. It's because we get enjoyment out of eating. I come from a very large Spanish, Italian, and Albanian family, and I have always had a passion for colorful and flavorful cuisine. Making so many limitations to my diet took a huge toll on me emotionally. You may be faced with the challenge of starting a dietary protocol to improve your mental and physical health. It may feel limiting at first. Creativity and trying new foods are absolutely fundamental in surviving the process. And many health-promoting foods are absolutely delicious and indulgent, so there is no need to feel deprived. You may even come to enjoy searching for new favorite snacks and ways to prepare them.

With that being said, if you try out a healing diet and it doesn't work for your body or you don't see results after a period of time, or if you find yourself anxious, overwhelmed, or compulsively controlling what you can and can't eat on your protocol, it's time to rethink your wellness paradigm and regimen. Results can show up in as little as a few days, or they can take a few months. Diet is only one piece of the puzzle. I'm not saying you should put this book down and drive to your nearest McDonald's to treat yourself. I'm simply saying that your sanity and peace of mind are worth more than obsessing over your food intake. That type of control can rob you of that carefree and light energy that I want you to have and exist in. So, no matter the suggestions in this book, always remember to check in with yourself and make sure that your lifestyle shifts add to your vitality and soul and don't take away from it.

I eat very healthy most of the time and always strive to choose quality ingredients. Most of my friends and family know this is a priority of mine. But I still enjoy and celebrate food. I will admit to you that recently over Christmas, I didn't just eat the organic, raw, 90% dark chocolate. I ate a Hershey's bar and other brands of chocolate that I ate as a kid on past holidays. Why? Because it made me feel like myself again. It helped me connect back to my childlike, carefree attitude of LIVING and ENJOYING life. It was nostalgia, joy, and most importantly—freedom. I didn't just have organic, low-sulfite wine, I had whatever was served at social gatherings. I let myself decide my limits, and that helped me feel limitless. When we hop on the health bandwagon, we don't always see the rigidity that often accompanies these lifestyle changes, which can be exhausting to follow in the long run and are not always sustainable. Letting yourself live a bit may not mean straying from your healthy diet. It may look like something else entirely, like staying up late once in a while because you are with a group of friends you absolutely adore spending time with. It could mean not always getting up so early to go to the gym, but instead having a sleep-in kind of morning. You get to decide what this freedom and ease of living looks like, and I am so excited for you.

The next chapter focuses on an extremely important, yet less focused on, aspect of mental and physical health. It is one of my favorites for many reasons: blood sugar.

9

BLOOD SUGAR

'm sure by now you have heard the word "hangry." It's what makes a Snickers commercial so great. This depiction of an individual who turns into an entirely different person when hungry is beyond comic. I know you've been there too; who hasn't?

We get hangry when blood sugar is unstable or drops too low. When this happens, we can become angry, frustrated, shaky, confused, panicked, defensive, impatient, dizzy, spacey, and say things we shouldn't. Blood sugar is by far one of the most overlooked reasons for mood swings and irritability, as well as one driver of inflammation in the body.

- Have you ever noticed that certain breakfasts or lunches keep you feeling focused for hours, while some leave you feeling exhausted or bored soon after?

- Have you had a bad mood disappear after eating?

- Have you ever felt shaky, dizzy, panicky, irritable, impatient, tired, or spacey from skipping a meal or waiting too long to eat?

- Just a few hours after a meal, have you ever experienced any of the symptoms listed in the previous bullet point? This is called reactive hypoglycemia. In this case, the body reacts to a high sugar meal by overproducing insulin, which makes blood sugar levels plummet.

- Do you have genetic predispositions to blood sugar dysregulation? Do you have any people with diabetes in the family?

If the issues in the preceding bullet list sound familiar, you may have an issue with blood sugar.

Balanced blood sugar has a profound influence on the brain's chemistry and functioning. This has been one of the hardest lessons I've had to learn thus far. I can say with confidence that anyone desperately trying to improve their overall health can benefit from taking a hard and honest look at their own blood sugar, learning more about it, and implementing an action plan. In this chapter, we will review vital information about the causes of blood sugar imbalance, review blood sugar symptoms, and discuss how to address them.

I'M SORRY FOR WHAT I SAID WHEN I WAS HUNGRY

You may have a genetic predisposition to blood sugar instability. I certainly do. Many family members on my father's side, including my father himself, have a form of insulin resistance. On my mother's side, my mom and grandfather have hypoglycemia (low blood sugar). However, we can do many things to manage, prevent, or even reverse these issues.

When I reflect on how severely my blood sugar affected my mood, quality of life, and peace of mind, it's almost overwhelming. I was mean, sensitive, and downright accusatory some days. I felt defensive a lot, because biochemically speaking—I was. The prefrontal cortex—the logical part of the brain that helps us see the world in a balanced, realistic way—goes on vacation. This creates a skewed, shrunken reality.

What else is affected by swings in your blood sugar? You know the answer to this one. Your relationships. When blood sugar drops too low, the brain can see this as a dangerous and threatening emergency. It needs a steady supply of fuel. Parts of the limbic system are wired to scan the horizon for the source of danger. And who does it find? A spouse, a parent, a child, or a sibling perhaps? Maybe it's a boss, a coworker, or the innocent cashier at the grocery store. The brain then may tag the environmental space as a threat to remember for next time and "save" you from harm.

Lots of stress hormones are released into the body if blood sugar drops, making you feel jittery, uncomfortable, and restless. What happens next? You unload unprovoked shortness, impatience, or anger on other people if you lack the insight to know what is happening in your body. I was very short with family members when my blood sugar dropped. I lacked empathy, patience, and kindness in those moments in a way that is extremely unlike my genuine nature and character. If you can learn to recognize these signs before you explode, you can keep impulsive, not-so-nice things from coming out of your mouth and avoid damaging consequences. You know what words I am referring to.

One of my absolute worst episodes was provoked by an unintentional fast. I had to fast prior to getting blood drawn for some lab work. I had to wrap up eating by midnight and wasn't allowed to touch a morsel of food until after the lab work. Although I arrived at the lab around seven, the line was incredibly long and the lab was short-staffed that day. I had a full breakfast packed in my fancy little cooler that I used daily. It sat on the passenger seat, waiting to be opened. As the clock ticked and ticked, I could feel it. The wave of shakiness. The wave of dizziness. The wave of fatigue. I thought to myself, "If I can just distract myself, I'll be fine." I cracked open my planned entertainment to pass the time—a book and a magazine. However, I couldn't think my way out of this one. The hit was coming, and I could feel it. It was like I was starting to go down an elevator. Time ticked on. My hands started to shake. At that point, I gave up all hope of getting a fasting blood draw and ran to the car. I tried opening the door, but my hands shook too much. Finally, I swung the door open and bit into a huge orange slice. I apparently ate several more, but I don't quite remember. By the time my mind refocused, I looked down to find seven or eight empty rinds. I sat there in my car alone in physical shock and emotional disbelief at this situation. I couldn't even delay or skip breakfast without turning into a ravenous beast? Seriously? Something had to be done.

You may wonder how and why blood sugar becomes dysregulated and how you can solve this problem for yourself. Although it seems obvious that eating balanced, regular meals is one way to maintain stable blood sugar levels, there is much more to it than that.

First, let's talk about what happens in the body. Insulin is a hormone released from the pancreas that removes sugar from the blood stream and ushers it into the cell after a meal. It also helps store sugar in the liver for future use as glycogen (extra sugar and fuel). If you eat a meal high in sugar and carbohydrates or full of processed foods, your blood glucose will surge. In response, the body will pump out large amounts of insulin in an attempt to maintain homeostasis and balance. However, too much insulin secretion can cause blood sugar to plummet just hours later (cue your hanger). The brain despises having fumes to run on, which may cause some form of agitation or dysfunction because it needs fuel in some form to run. In addition to glucose, fuel can also be made from protein and fats, if needed.

Over time this cycle of very high blood sugar can cause insulin resistance, where the cells no longer allow insulin to bring sugar inside. This means the sugar is circulating in the body instead of giving us the energy our cells need. Insulin resistance affects the brain, too. Symptoms of very high blood sugar can cause post-meal lethargy, lack of motivation, lack of concentration, cravings for sweets after meals, and weight gain.[1] Low blood glucose levels and very high levels not only affect waking hours but can also affect sleep. This will be discussed in more detail when we dive into rest and movement.

I've heard countless stories from friends and family members about feeling shaky from skipping a meal or blowing up on their spouse because they were hangry and needed dinner. Sound familiar? I've experienced this myself. In college, I would go from class to class on certain days without packing snacks or stopping to grab something to eat. If I did bring snacks, they were full of processed ingredients or sugar and lacked the nutrients I needed to maintain good blood sugar. I would grab a bagel in the early morning with orange juice and go all day long without much else. I remember attending the last class of the day from three to four in the afternoon: macroeconomics. Most of the time I felt spaced out, weary, and irritated in that class.

My blood sugar levels were swinging all over the place, especially when I was sick. Sometimes they were too high, but more often than not they were terribly low. My friends and family can attest to this. One afternoon, I was with a group of friends driving around town while visiting with each other. Several hours had passed since lunch, and I began feeling very dizzy and jittery. After a few minutes my vision started going in and out. Finally, I realized my blood sugar was low. I had to ask my friend to pull into the nearest store in order to grab something to bring my blood sugar up. My hands were shaking terribly (one of my rarer yet least subtle symptoms). We laugh about it now, but at the time it was a frightening experience for me.

In such cases, you may need fifteen grams of carbohydrates or more,[2] preferably in the form of a healthy natural sugar such as one to two servings of fruit, to bring your blood sugar up. Fruit was a quick fix when I was in such a direly uncomfortable situation, but I needed to do more on a daily basis. I now eat balanced meals on a more regular schedule. The mechanisms that regulate blood sugar have stabilized and allow me to go longer between meals now.

I've mentioned balanced meals, and you may wonder what those look like. You may want me to describe a diet plan for you, with perfectly selected portions, exact amounts of carbs in grams, and weighted amounts of specific foods. But I am not going to give that to you. I tried many different healthy diets that were supposed to be great for blood sugar regulation, but they left me in a tailspin. I had to figure out my own specific formulation, guided by what made me feel good. And you will have to do the same. I will, however, give you some basic guidelines to consider so that you can find the absolute best plan to support your own unique biochemistry.

Some people's bodies are superb at processing carbs and sugars, and other bodies don't do it as well. Your body will tell you everything you need to know. You should also know that your body's ability to process nutrients will change over time.

Rule number one is to eat as little processed food as possible. Shocking, right? I am well aware that you already know this one. But it's worth repeating. Why? Because processed foods almost always spike our blood sugar through the roof. They have very little fiber and very few nutrients to buffer the carbohydrates and sugar within them. Natural plant foods contain a lot more of these buffering agents. If you wish to indulge in something out of a box with a long list of ingredients, please include protein-rich and fiber-rich foods. Healthy fats are also an essential addition when balancing out a higher sugar, higher carb meal or snack. This will slow down the glucose surge. You can find lists of high fiber and high protein foods online. Check in with yourself regarding how you feel after meals. The reflection presents questions for you to consider. It may be a good idea to diligently keep a food journal over the course of two weeks or so to uncover what your body is trying to show you.

Rule number two is to be aware of the interconnectedness between the nervous system and limbic system. These two systems play a huge role in glucose regulation, which regulates mood. When our nervous system is overreacting and overfiring because it perceives something in our environment as a danger or a severe threat, it takes glucose from the liver and raises our blood sugar to give us fuel and strength to run like hell or punch something. It's how we are wired. It's our biology and how we are programmed to survive. Stress reduction in its many forms is essential to keep a balanced limbic system and regulated blood sugar. Here's a brief example of how blood sugar dysregulation affects someone with limbic system impairment:

- 7 AM The alarm goes off. The loud noise scares the bejesus out of you and spikes your blood sugar a bit.

- 8 AM You're in traffic and have to slam on your brakes several times. Your body raises your blood sugar.

- 9 AM A work meeting leaves you frazzled because someone had a differing opinion that provoked both anxiety and anger. Up goes the blood sugar.

- 10 AM You realize you never responded to an extremely important email that needed urgent attention by

YESTERDAY. And here comes some blood sugar so you can run (like hell) away from the computer or have strength to throw it across the room. You obviously do neither because you have social standards for yourself (and impulse control).

Even people without overfiring, overreactive limbic and nervous systems will have some type of physical and visceral reaction to each of the situations described. But if you are eating a clean and healthy diet and find your blood sugar is still out of control, you may need to look at your limbic system.

One of the most surprising lessons (rule number three) I learned about mood, blood sugar, and food is that if you are sensitive to a certain food or have an intolerance to it, it can cause your blood sugar to surge or drop even if it is not a notorious sugary, high carb, or processed food. It can make you moody, agitated, depressed, or even anxious. This is where being diligent about keeping a food journal comes in. It will help you figure out what foods you are sensitive to without needing to get excessive blood work done. If you are interested in further investments regarding food sensitivities, allergy panels are available through blood draw. I recommend the company Cyrex Laboratories.

Chris Kresser, a functional medicine practitioner, recommends checking blood glucose two hours after a meal with an easily accessible and low-cost glucometer found at any drug store.[3] Since we are all so different, what food works for one person does not get processed the same by another. Chris recommends that blood glucose be 120 ng/ml or lower about two hours after a meal.[4] Fasting blood sugar (a measurement after an eight-to twelve-hour fast) should be in the eighties or nineties, depending on age. If you find that your levels are not in these ranges, consider whether you might have a food intolerance or try adding protein- and fiber-rich foods to your diet. Chris has a wonderful website, chriskresser.com, which contains many other health and wellness resources.

Blood sugar problems are by far one of the biggest contributors to mental health problems.[5] You may feel shame or guilt from your mood swings or from snapping at friends and family. But if you understand the biochemical basis of these reactions, you may be able to give yourself grace and mercy and develop an awareness of what causes these behaviors. If you lean toward hanger tendencies, raise your hand high and proud. I am right there with you. In the following reflection, you will find actionable steps for learning more about your unique blood sugar patterns and how certain foods or meals are affecting you. You will be your own researcher and investigator.

REFLECTION: HARNESSING HUNGER ACTION STEPS

Use your food log to keep track of exercises one and two and use your journal as a place to reflect on your findings about your blood sugar. You may be surprised by your results.

1. Make your food log your best friend. For one to two weeks, diligently write down your meals and meal times. Include how you feel between meals emotionally and physically—your mood, ability to focus, energy level, and irritability level. If desired, you can also write down your sleep quality and any other health symptoms (headaches, joint pain, digestive distress, et cetera). Rate these on a scale from one to ten (one being very low and ten being very high). This will give you a more complete picture of your habits and the specific foods that help or hurt you.

Write down:

- Meal composition and meal time

- How you felt right before the meal

- How you felt right after the meal

- How you felt in between meals

2. If you want to learn even more about how food (or lack thereof) affects your body, purchase a glucometer and strips at a drugstore. Two hours after meals, check your blood sugar and write the result in your food log. When you do so, rate each of the following: mood, ability to focus, energy level, irritability level on a scale of one through ten. You will then be able to look for correlations between your physiology, moods, and meals.

3. Even when you don't have your food log or glucometer handy, it's a good idea to get into the habit of monitoring your mood throughout the day. That way you can practice identifying your unique hanger symptoms. In moments of irritation or fatigue, ask yourself:

- When was the last time I ate?

- What did I eat?

- How much did I eat?

It takes practice to make this thought process and action a habit. Sometimes your blood sugar will have nothing to do with your mood in that moment, and you can write it off. However, you will be pleasantly surprised by how many times the answer will be "I didn't eat breakfast today," "I skipped lunch," or "I ate something that affects my blood sugar." Getting mindful and pausing more may keep you from saying things you wish you hadn't to friends or family. You can take a little time and space for yourself in these moments to have a snack before continuing an important or heated conversation. You will reenter it with a calmer, clearer head.

4. Ask parents, siblings, or other relatives about your family lineage and examples of hypoglycemia (low blood sugar), prediabetes, or diabetes (high blood sugar). In your journal, write down the names of your family members and their relevant medical interventions, such as insulin or oral diabetic medication.

Balanced blood sugar, without a doubt, can be one of the most profound influencers of good mental and physical health. When blood sugar levels are off, they can rob us of our vibrance, energy, and positive mindset. Our next chapter describes how good nutrition and food choices are crucial to our health and wellness. As with many other chapters in Part Two, blood sugar and a healthy diet go hand in hand.

10

NUTRITION, VITAMINS, AND MINERALS

Good nutrition is at the foundation of health for many reasons. We need adequate fuel for our bodies and minds to work. When the body is running low on the necessary materials to build and repair itself, things begin to break down.

Nutrients are the main building blocks and fuel for cells and come in two types: macronutrients and micronutrients. Macronutrients include proteins, fats, and starches. Micronutrients comprise essential vitamins and minerals. But how do we get enough nutrients? It begins with what you are putting in your mouth. Meals full of whole-food ingredients, vibrant colors, plenty of vegetables and fruits, and adequate protein fuel our bodies and minds and provide necessary materials for our bones, muscles, skin, brain, immune system, and the rest of the body. The many chemical reactions that take place in the brain rely on ample supplies of these nutrients.

- Do you find yourself feeling worn down constantly?
- Do you have certain dietary restrictions or choices that cause you to cut out or avoid certain foods?
- Do you dislike vegetables or rarely eat them?
- Are many of your meals eaten on the go?
- Do you have problems with your skin, hair, or nails?

Put simply, we need a variety of sources of vitamins and minerals to thrive. If you answered yes to some or all of the preceding questions, you may be lacking in this department. Deficiencies are actually much more common than we could ever imagine. For example, 95% of American adults have inadequate vitamin D intake. Sixty-one percent of American adults have an inadequate intake of magnesium, and 32% do not consume enough vitamin B6.[1] Deficiencies can lead to immune dysfunction, impaired cell regeneration, fatigue, and mental health issues, to name a few.[2]

Vitamins and minerals are vitally important for good health, and I encourage you to do some research to help you decide what you may need more of based on your own symptoms. I have included some websites and book recommendations in the Resources section. In this chapter, we'll discuss how to provide your brain and body with the fuel they need. This includes using supplements, choosing unprocessed foods, and listening to your body to fight inflammation and give yourself a sharp brain and body capable of experiencing abundant joy, energy, vitality, happiness, and peace.

USING SUPPLEMENTS

When it comes to using supplements, I heed an Ayurvedic saying: "When diet is wrong, medicine is of no use; when diet is correct, medicine is of no need." Supplements can be effective if you take high-quality ones that provide you with the specific nutritional support you need. However, supplementing should never replace dietary changes. They are called "supplements" for a reason—they provide an extra boost to the body during specific times. It's important to focus on diet first as you contemplate adding nutrients or even medications for mental and physical health issues.

Before supplementing, write down your goals and incorporate the supplement into a comprehensive wellness plan that includes a healthy diet, adequate sleep, movement of the body, learning, and other health-promoting activities mentioned in this book. I urge you to first modify your diet to incorporate more vitamins and minerals in your daily intake and limit or completely remove processed foods and refined sugars from your cabinets. Using a food log during this time can help you keep track of which foods you are consuming. After improving your diet for thirty days or so, you can then consider which vitamins and minerals to supplement with based on your goals. Dosages should be tailored to your unique needs, although the recommended dosages on the backs of the bottles can be a good place to start.

Before beginning any supplementation, please consult with a health-care provider. Your physician or health-care provider can order a blood test to check for adequate levels of vitamins and minerals. For example, I supplement with B-12 because my levels are often low in my yearly blood workup if I do not take it regularly. Excessive levels of vitamins from supplementation can have their own side effects. I often ask clients and parents about their diets and recommend visiting their physician to explore their levels of iron, B-12, folate, and vitamin D.

When I was sick, I was throwing everything but the kitchen sink at my symptoms, to no avail. I had no idea which things might be helping; even worse, I didn't know whether some things were exacerbating my symptoms. Throughout my health journey, many high-quality supplements recommended by well-educated individuals often gave me the worst, most severe symptoms of all, even though I precisely followed all directions and guidance. They were not my solution, and my body did not want or need them.

If you have intestinal permeability (discussed and defined in the immune chapter) or limbic system impairment, oftentimes less is best with supplements while you are healing. In either of these conditions, the immune system is often hyperactive and can mount a response to the most basic supplements. In addition, these conditions can involve a weakened ability to detoxify, creating symptoms if the body is overloaded. Even supplements have to pass through our livers, everything does.

This is a trial-and-error experiment. You have hypotheses, collect data, and learn whether your hypothesis is right, wrong, or somewhere in between. It took me more than three years to find my own answers, and I know you will find yours, too. Your answer may include a cluster of supplements in combination with other lifestyle changes, or it may have nothing to do with supplements at all. Select supplements have helped me in specific moments and periods of life.

SUPPLEMENTS RUN IN THE FAMILY

My mom's side of the family has a lot of people who find it difficult to wind down, to put it mildly. We are incredibly passionate about certain topics and tend to get a little heated. A lot of these tendencies probably tie in to genetics and the slow speed at which our stress hormones clear our systems, but those are topics for the next chapter.

One of the first efforts I made to improve my health began with researching supplements. I remember standing in the vitamin aisle at Whole Foods in Orlando with my brother, Bert. It was spring of 2014. He knew a lot more about supplements than I did at the time, and he was attempting to educate me and motivate me to learn more. I began taking specific supplements to support my body's natural processes and relax my mind. One consisted of a relaxation support supplement, which contained B-6, magnesium, zinc, other minerals, amino acids such as L-theanine, and calming herbs such as valerian and passionflower. The supplement was designed to increase GABA in the brain, which is a neurotransmitter we all produce to promote a sense of calm.

This GABA support was fantastic, and I could clearly see how it promoted a calmer, more relaxed mind. I was falling asleep quicker, experiencing fewer restless thoughts, and could focus on one thing at a time without rushing. My mother, impressed by my results, started taking them too. My mother and I have a running joke that any time we experience or anticipate experiencing a stressor in the near future, we'll just grab a bottle of GABA support. We have even roped my high-spirited Albanian grandmother into our fun and games. At eighty-nine years old, she's open to taking GABA support. It's a miracle.

The supplement has a cream version available as well, and my Aunt Susan has taken full advantage of this by rubbing the cream on my grandmother during stressful periods. My grandmother will continue discussing the upsetting event without noticing the particular cream Aunt Susan is using until the end of the discussion when she concludes with "Hey, I'm feeling better." Imagine that!

Now you may be thinking about going out and purchasing every vitamin bottle from your local health food store, particularly the GABA-promoting supplements. Just remember my rules: (1) first decide on the goals that the supplement may help you with and (2) incorporate the supplement into a larger wellness plan for maximum results. Go slow.

Based on my experience trying many different supplements (I used to take handfuls of them every day in an attempt to feel better), I recommend a gentle approach to supplementing that includes time on and time off supplements. This type of method is focused on an "as needed" basis and not ongoing supplementation with no foreseeable end. Researching which foods contain vitamins and minerals you are deficient in can be a way around supplementing. And our needs vary markedly. Some individuals have genetic variations in their ability to absorb and synthesize specific vitamins such as B12, vitamin A, and folate (to name a few) and need to supplement.[3] Compromised digestion will also impact the amount of nutrients you absorb from your food and can create deficiencies. Having allergies to certain foods or choosing a diet that cuts out specific food groups (vegans, vegetarians) can also cause deficiencies, which can be addressed by supplementing.

ESSENTIAL FOOD FACTS

I know how busy life can be, trust me, and sometimes schedules can get so full that it is simpler and easier to grab convenience food, fast food, or even no food (skipping breakfast or lunch because of a crazy day at work). However, our bodies need high-quality food and nutrients to function at our very best. Think about your car. You probably use it to drive around every day, and most days it works just fine. But what would happen if it didn't have enough gas? Or if you decided to put something in it that wouldn't be useful to it? It wouldn't move. We are much the same. We can't expect to put complete garbage in day after day and have our health and energy be fantastic. My nutrition recommendations are summarized in the following paragraphs.

You already know you should eat healthier, less processed foods, right? Those boxes of food with long lists of ingredients with names you can hardly pronounce typically aren't filled with many vitamins and minerals. They hardly resemble the original product that they were made from. Do they taste good? Of course! But you are smart, do your research, and know what is healthy and what isn't. You know that fruits and vegetables are a better choice than something that's packaged up with questionable, unpronounceable contents.

Many cuisines have unhealthy components. I have been a fan of carb-laden food since the day I was born. The more pasta, bread, and pizza mixed with a variety of cheeses, salt, and oil, the better. I am also obsessed with any type of dessert. I am deeply aware of how delicious those unhealthy foods taste. They can remind us of childhood or bring comfort or energy on bad days. And they are often easy and convenient to prepare. My family and friends know that I am a seasoned, passionate foodie, and I have a deep and personal relationship with my meals. My essential food facts follow and come from a place of love for you and your health and from a place of compassion and empathy for your love of (junk) food.

Eat the rainbow.

Food that is naturally bright and rich in color contains polyphenols and antioxidants, which fight off inflammation in the body and support the immune system. This means a much healthier brain. You absolutely need some of these fruits and vegetables to feel your best and get these compounds into the body.

Less is more (literally).

Foods that have a very short list of ingredients and are whole have significantly more of these nutrients than do boxed foods. Heavily processed foods are not recommended.

Don't forget your blood sugar.

Processed foods spike your blood sugar, which you learned in the last chapter. This is a gentle reminder that your blood sugar balance is immensely important for your brain, mood, and ability to focus. Don't forget it! Hypoglycemia can create cravings for these types of foods as a way to quickly bring up your blood sugar. If you receive a burst of energy after eating, it may be because you waited far too long to eat.

Junk foods jerk you around.

Junk foods are highly inflammatory. The ingredients may be synthetic, contain chemicals, or trigger the immune system. Do you want to know what an inflamed brain and body look like? Depression, anxiety, fatigue, joint pain, digestive distress, brain fog, irritability, poor memory, low motivation, apathy, the list goes on and on.

Additives are addictive.

Some junk food ingredients are actually as addicting as cocaine. Studies have found that sugar is one of these.[4] Other potentially addictive ingredients include white flour. Refined carbohydrates like white flour are more processed and tend to have a higher glycemic load than other food choices.[5]

PRIORITIZING PORTION CONTROL

Do you find yourself overeating certain foods like bread or dairy? If you somehow consume a block of cheese with your favorite crackers in one sitting, no judgment here. I know what it's like to be hypnotized by sizzling pizza, fluffy warm rolls with butter, or cheesy pasta. How about those salty kettle chips or your favorite cookies? Some hypothesize that we love these foods because they are high fat and calorie-dense. Meaning, from an ancestral, evolutionary perspective we are wired to prize foods that give us more energy to stay alive. However, I'm not sure I completely buy that. You don't see people consuming absurd amounts of avocados, which are relatively high in fat, unless they are made into guacamole and accompanied by processed tortilla chips. Likewise, I've never experienced an inability to stop myself from eating tons of fatty fish, eggs, steak, or coconut milk. If you find yourself unable to stop eating certain types of foods, take note. This is your body relaying a message to you that these foods are affecting your hunger-full hormones in a negative way. Sure, you can have cravings for healthy foods too. But feeling out of control is a different story entirely. Promoting good health means keeping high-craving foods to a reasonable portion (if you can).

Sometimes you have to get really honest with yourself when it comes to food and nutrition. Some people find any type of sugar addicting. Food that has sugar in it tastes delicious. Period. Whether it's the Häagen-Dazs caramel cone ice cream or a dairy-free organic frozen dessert made with "only natural" ingredients, sugar and processed food can be addictive and bad for us in excess. I definitely understand enjoying and indulging in an occasional dessert wonderland of creamy, chocolatey goodness. I will never take that away from you. What I want you to know is that sugar and processed foods can be slippery slopes for people, and before you know it, they can become more of a habit than a treat for a special occasion. Foods with higher sugar contents start sneaking into your diet. Even healthier options can include high amounts of sugar that keep you hooked. Smoothies can be a culprit. Granola is a culprit. Yogurt is a culprit. Maple syrup, honey, dried fruit, coconut sugar, alternative baking flours. These are all thought of as healthy, but they can get you hooked and keep you craving. They can also drive skin issues such as cystic acne on the face or body. Excess sugar can also cause digestive imbalances. It can overwhelm the liver. It can drive hormonal imbalances, and it certainly affects the blood sugar balance. People who are particularly stressed out, have limbic system impairments, or are genetically predisposed to blood sugar dysregulation are less able to handle and process higher sugar loads efficiently (and are more prone to mental and physical health problems due to high sugar intake).

I didn't create this list to make you feel deflated. On the contrary, I'm sharing it because I want to help you increase your awareness of good nutrition. I also have some encouragement for you. You can find new favorite foods. I know the thought of cutting out some of your favorite chips, cookies, desserts, and easy breakfast items makes you feel deflated and depressed. But you can find new favorites and new alternatives that may taste very different but will make you feel very different in a good way while still being delicious. This is one of my greatest passions—exploring and discovering new foods and recipes that support the body and mind and help us thrive. The following reflection will help you review how different foods make YOU feel.

REFLECTION: FOOD LOG

This reflection contains some questions relevant to your food log and prompts for examining the emotions driving your food choices.

Use your food log to keep track of these crucial points:

- How do certain foods make you feel after ingesting them? It can be helpful to rate your level of emotional and physical wellbeing after meals to discover which foods are working for you and which are not. Refer to the last chapter for an outline on what to write down in a food log.

- Pay particular attention to foods that come from a box, foods with long lists of ingredients on the label, and foods high in sugar. Use a highlighter for these food log meal entries.

Use your journal to ponder these questions about emotions:

- Reflect on the memories that certain foods bring to mind. What emotions do they invoke? Do they make you think of home? Of family?

- What do certain foods do for you emotionally? Are they numbing? Comforting? Addicting? Make sure you list the foods and how each makes you feel.

- What "healthy" foods are you consuming that still make you feel less than vibrant? What does the ingredient list look like? What is the sugar content?

- Is food used as a coping behavior when you are anxious, bored, or depressed? We've all been there on this one.

- What food cravings may be caused by low blood sugar or a way to improve energy levels?

If you are looking for recommendations on nutrition, look in the Resources section for a list of recommended snacks, foods, and supplement brands.

Food choices and nutritional intake are incredibly important for our bodies and our minds. We need these raw materials as building blocks to keep our bodies feeling strong and energized. Nutrients are the building blocks for our neurotransmitters in our brains, and they also help keep our blood sugar and hormones in balance. In the next chapter, we will uncover the role our genes play in wellbeing and how we are not as constrained by our genetics as was once thought.

11

GENETICS

Genetics are heritable traits. They play a huge role in what we look like on the outside. Things like height, natural hair and eye color, body type, and skin color are influenced by our genetic makeup. Genetics also influence how we feel on the inside—our emotional and physical wellbeing. We can feel limited by our genetics, feel empowered and grateful for them, or a combination of both.

- Have you been told by family members that your problem is probably genetic?

- Do you feel like your health and happiness are limited by what was genetically handed down to you?

- Do you worry that there isn't much you can do to feel better, and that you may have to just "live" with it?

- Do you notice particular mental and physical health patterns that run in your family?

In this chapter, you will learn about how genetics are one piece—but only one piece—of the puzzle of health and wellness. Both nature AND nurture influence our health. We will see how variations within our DNA can impact both our mental and physical dispositions. And you will have the opportunity to organize information about your own genetic inheritance and take action to achieve the body and mind you've always dreamed of.

DIVING INTO YOUR GENE POOL

Many people blame their genes for the issues they face. These may be valid complaints since our genes affect our mental and physical health. One of the most common genetic variations in genes are SNPs, or single-nucleotide polymorphisms. Many SNPs have been identified by researchers,[1] but not all of them influence our mental or physical health. Some do influence behavior, affect, and emotional responses, and through modern technology we can discover which genes we have.

It is important to note that, while the genes we were born with can predispose us to a multitude of different conditions, epigenetics can be a source of hope. Epigenetics means that our genes take different expressions based on a multitude of factors. Genetic expression is partly affected by our environment and by how we live our lives. If lifestyle factors are in alignment with the individual, such as diet, relationships, and stress management, the body and mind can and will function at their best. In order to be expressed in the ways that give us the most benefit, genes need a healthy environment. Have you been told that mental illness runs in your family? That your physical illness is the result of the genetic patterning you were handed? That you just have to live with the cards you were dealt? You don't have to feel stuck without options. You don't have to accept your health as it is or believe that there is no possibility of much improvement. Epigenetics brings hope and empowerment; know that ultimately you can be in control of your own health.

"You have the genetics." This is what I hear often from my dad when I have one of those days. You know the kind I am referring to—a day that is just a little harder or more tiring than the rest.

You. Have. The. Genetics.

This is a simple, yet powerful statement of encouragement and strength every time I hear it. It reminds me of resiliency. It reminds me of what my grandparents and parents have overcome, both physically and emotionally, and it allows me to imagine what my earlier ancestors experienced, too. This very phrase was spoken to me on my sickest days as well—around the ages of twenty-three and twenty-four when I did not know how to heal my body or mind. I was told that I had the genetics to not only get through it, but the determination and wit to figure it out. It was one of the most inspiring things I could have held onto in those moments. My mom has her own version of the phrase that she mentions to family members who encounter difficulty. "Remember that you are the daughter/son/granddaughter/grandson of James Sandy." My grandfather is one of the most resilient people I have ever met in my entire life, both physically and mentally. You can find pride and strength from looking at your genetics and what your family members have endured. Our ancestors can inspire awe and share wisdom and motivate us to continue on. You may have some genetic variations that have held you back in the past, but each of us also has many, many genetic strengths, too. Remember, most genes are adaptive over time and are shaped and molded by our environment.

THE EMPATHY GENE: BORN TO BE A THERAPIST?

Our genes can influence how we relate to and experience other people. Some genetic SNPs and variations influence our knee-jerk anger, stress, or compassion in certain situations. SNPs can also influence our empathy. Empathy is the ability to put yourself in another person's shoes, sense another person's feelings, and feel compassion for others. There happens to be an intriguing mental health SNP that affects empathy—a particular variation known as rs53576. It is tied to the empathy level a person exhibits.[2] Someone can be GG (homozygous), AA, or AG (heterozygous), depending on what they received from each parent. Those with the GG allele tend to have more sensitive parenting styles, show an increase in optimism, and are more empathic responders to others. Know anyone who is incredibly sensitive to others' feelings or says things like "I really feel that person's pain"? They may have this SNP.

I have the GG allele for rs53576, and it explains a great deal of my life and probably a large portion of why I am so sensitive and why I became a therapist. My mother has the GG allele (to a fault), and my grandmother is a walking billboard for it. Just hearing a story about someone's shortcomings produces a noticeable change in my grandmother's mood, and she demands immediate solace and restitution for the person involved. This is the part where someone might ask whether this is nature or nurture. Are these behaviors from a specific gene someone holds, or is it because they grew up surrounded by people with certain personalities and ways of being? If we think about identical twins, separated at birth, who ended up with different personalities, we can see the environmental factor at play. If I had not been around my mother or grandmother all of my life, maybe the expression of the rs53576 SNP would look different, and maybe I would not have chosen to become a therapist. Yet, here we are. I want you to understand that genetics are one piece of the puzzle, and the environment around us affects how the genes are expressed. Our social relationships, upbringing, nutrition status, food choices, exercise, rest, play, et cetera all shape what genes are turned on or off. You can embrace this fact while also understanding that, regardless of your genetic health predispositions, you can choose how to live and who you surround yourself with.

MY EXPERIENCES WITH GENETIC TESTING

Our wonderful world of modern technology and advancements has given us the privilege of learning more about ourselves, which provides the potential for deeper levels of healing. Did you know that there is now a genetic test that can be run on saliva to assess our ability to synthesize certain antidepressants? No blood draw or needles necessary. Not only that, but it can also tell us specific vitamins that can improve our mental health. This is a huge leap for the world of mental health and leads us to a greater understanding of why some people do so well on antidepressants while others feel no different and can even feel worse. It also opens up an additional source of information on how we can take better care of ourselves.

I was introduced to genetic testing by functional medicine practitioners when I was in a period of health discovery and exploration. Although genetic testing is not a common protocol run in many psychiatry offices or wellness clinics, I recommend seeking this out through your current physician or a new health-care provider if you suspect genetics have a role in any immunological, psychological, or other health impairments that run in your family. I myself was fascinated by how much information this testing can tell you about yourself, from what foods your body will process the best, to how the liver handles medications. Some of the information was relevant to other family members and provided answers to previously puzzling questions.

For example, my grandmother has had bizarre reactions to many, many things over the years. From bandage adhesives to lemons, my Puerto Rican grandmother has a wealth of stories that trace back to a gene variant involved with histamine. You may associate the word histamine with itchiness or hives, and be familiar with the well-known antihistamine, Benadryl. Seasonal allergy medications are also common antihistamines. Having higher levels of histamine in the body can be due to a variant in the DAO gene, which causes a slower breakdown of histamines.[3] Aside from being itchy, high histamine levels also cause irritability, headaches, or an inability to wind down. My grandmother has always taken a high dose of vitamin C most of her life because it makes her "feel better." This is probably no coincidence, as vitamin C has been shown in research to be a natural antihistamine.[4] You may have similar family stories, or intuitively know that certain vitamins, foods, or ways of living make you feel really good. It may be because those particular foods or actions interact with your genetic blueprint in an ideal way, and your body responds by saying "Hey, thanks!"

Here is another example of an SNP that can affect the entire body and all of its systems. I have mutations in the MTHFR gene; potentially, up to 40% of the population[5] has MTHFR mutations. Could this be you, too? MTHFR is involved in many processes in our body, from supporting hormones and immune system cells to detoxifying the body. MTHFR can also affect brain function; a poorly functioning MTHFR can be involved in anxiety, depression, irritability, and ADHD.[6] Other mental health concerns that relate to a poorly functioning MTHFR gene include bipolar disorder, Alzheimer's disease, chronic fatigue, and schizophrenia.[7] If you are struggling with physical or mental health issues, testing for this genetic SNP may give you some insight into your genetic makeup and help you learn how to accommodate it. Maybe some of your lifestyle factors are not adequately supporting specific SNPs. The MTHFR gene variant needs ample amounts of folate (vitamin B-9) in the body to function correctly, so I do my best to eat a ton of leafy green vegetables and salad. Maybe it's a placebo effect, but I love salad and feel my absolute best when I eat a big one every day. Other lifestyle factors for MTHFR SNPs include supporting detoxification pathways and taking supplemental activated folate. Stress from various forms of trauma absolutely have an effect on what genes are turned on and off, so painful past experiences and the limbic system (discussed in Part One) are important to address.

In practice, if a client is considering medication for a period of time, I will mention genetic testing to help determine which will work best with their body and medication processing abilities. They can then bring this information to their psychiatrist. I also recommend genetic testing to clients to determine the status of MTHFR if depression or anxiety are present. These tests provide valuable information that answer the question "Why?" and can even lead to better results than just therapy alone. It can highlight targeted supplemental support and lifestyle factor changes necessary to support the brain. I also find that talking about mental health and gene patterns with clients is an avenue of lessening shame and guilt over a person's state of emotional wellbeing. Some individuals have gene patterns that prevent them from quickly clearing adrenaline and other stress hormones, so it is harder to wind down. Others have gene patterns that predispose them to having feelings of low motivation or difficulty concentrating. When you know your makeup, you can better support your body and mind without feeling like it's just who you are.

Genes are important, but they are by no means the only avenue for good health. Lifestyle factors and genes, as described earlier, go hand in hand. We have the power to influence our genetics through many adjustments in the way we live, eat, and move. Factors like stress, poor sleep, or lack of nutrients affect many genes and prevent us from supporting our genetic makeup favorably. We do not necessarily need a genetic test in order to improve the expression of our genes. Nutrition, stress reduction, and better sleep are often discussed in this book. Know that each of these affects whether genes turn on or off. Each factor is information to the body.

If you would like to learn more about genetics and mental health, I recommend Dr. Ben Lynch's book *Dirty Genes*.[8] He provides many organized lists of common symptoms as they relate to SNPs along with how to address each of them. In addition, Genomind is one company that offers testing to determine a wide variety of genetic mental health and wellness factors. Specific testing through Genomind can also be used to assess your ability to process medications based on your genetic makeup. Working with a functional medicine practitioner can provide tailored genetic test suggestions, helpful result readings, and lifestyle changes.

REFLECTION: YOUR GENETIC MAKEUP

In your journal, take some time to review each of the following prompts. You may not be able to complete each question in one sitting if you have information to collect from relatives. Honor the value that this knowledge and awareness brings to your own health journey. The genetic patterning of our ancestors can provide a road map for our own health by telling us where to look and how to support our bodies in disease prevention.

- If you are biologically related to your parents and relatives, create a list of hereditary traits that family members have mentioned over the years. What have you been told about your genetic makeup and family tree regarding mental and physical health? For example, your parents could have shared that your family has a history of heart disease, mental health issues, or diabetes. Comments such as "Your grandfather always needs a B12 shot because his levels are low," "We are prone to low blood sugar in this family," or "Your grandmother lives on vitamin C, it helps with her allergies" are some examples. In addition to physical traits, personality traits or emotional temperaments also apply. Here are additional examples: "We blow up easily, it runs in the family," "Everyone on that side of the family has anxiety," or "We are resilient and built strong."

- Has this information limited your beliefs regarding the degree of healing that is possible for you, or has it empowered you? If it has discouraged you, how can you use the information in this chapter to shift these beliefs? Remember, your genetic blueprint does not have to be your destiny.

- What are the positive aspects of your genetic makeup? Dr. Ben Lynch teaches that each genetic SNP served a purpose for our ancestors at some point in time. Each gene SNP has an adaptive component to it.

- If you don't know a whole lot about the health of your relatives, ask genetically related family members to find out more information about mental and physical genetic traits that could run in the family. Write down what you learn in your journal.

Action steps:

- Learn more about genetics from great resources such as Ben Lynch's book, *Dirty Genes.*

- Work with a functional medicine practitioner. They can recommend genetic testing based on your current and past health history.

- Utilize genetic reports, especially if you are not in contact with biological relatives.

Genomind's Mental Health Map is a great place to get started if a mental health focus is one of your health goals. This specific test requires a saliva sample and can be purchased online without a medical practitioner. Your genetic blueprint may be just the "aha!" moment that you've always wanted as you explore your individual health. It can provide both eye opening and insightful information into your health and the health of your relatives. What is even more interesting is the fact that our lifestyle and attitudes toward life deeply affect our genetic expression. When you learn about your genetics, you also learn how to best give the body what it needs. In the next chapter we will look at ways in which several different hormones impact how we feel.

12

HORMONES

I t is profoundly evident that hormones of all kinds have an intricate part to play in our moods and wellbeing. We need sufficient amounts of hormones to thrive. Hormone levels can be too low or high and cause mental health and physical problems, so we strive for balance. The body is always trying to return to homeostasis, so we simply need to give it what it needs.

Hormones include commonly known ones, such as the sex hormones estrogen and testosterone, but there are many others, such as thyroid hormones and stress hormones. Uncomfortable symptoms, like feeling depressed, anxious, tired, or irritable, are all information from your body and should prompt you to make changes to aspects of your life that are not serving you. When hormone levels go awry or are severely depleted, some of the following symptoms may appear.

- Do you feel tired all of the time, have a difficult time concentrating, or feel depressed?

- Are you constantly feeling frazzled, sensitive to loud noises, overreacting to situations, or in a constant state of anxiety or fear?

- Have you taken birth control before or other hormonal contraception? How did your body respond to it?

- Do you suffer with uncomfortable symptoms related to your menstrual cycle? Do you have painful cramps, hot flashes, mood instability, heavy periods, or irregular periods?

This chapter includes sections on the major groups of hormones that affect vitality, mental health, and wellbeing. When these hormones are out of balance, they can create symptoms that rob us of good health. Hormonal imbalances can be a driver of poor health, and at the same time can be an underlying symptom of larger problems such as limbic system impairment, extreme stress, trauma, nutritional deficiencies, blood sugar imbalances, and even an imbalanced immune system.

Hormones are substances that are released in the body to regulate or stimulate cells and tissues.[1] The name is derived from the word *hormao*, which is Greek for "I excite."[2] We have over two thousand hormones in the human body, and they are all made in the various endocrine glands. You may be experiencing elevated or low levels of hormones in the body and really struggling through your day. Let's dive into some of the major hormones and groups of hormones and the reasons why hormones can be out of whack and what you can do to befriend and balance them.

THYROID HORMONES

At one point in my search for answers to my health issues, I turned my attention to the thyroid. My blood work showed that my thyroid antibody levels were slightly above functional medicine standards. I was feeling exhausted at the time and had severe brain fog. My thinking was very fuzzy, and my short-term memory was subpar at best. I also suffered from anxiety, and my feet felt like icicles. The thyroid controls a wide array of functions in the body, and low levels of the thyroid hormone (hypothyroidism) affect the state of the brain and energy levels, as well as how strong your digestion is.[3] A poorly functioning thyroid can mean depression, fatigue, brain fog, and a sea of physical issues.[4] Sadly, these issues are rampant in our modern world. An estimated twenty million Americans have some form of thyroid disease.[5] Thyroid problems are often caused by autoimmune thyroid conditions wherein the thyroid gland is broken down slowly over time.[6]

I have worked with several clients, both teen and adult, who uncovered a thyroid problem as a driving factor in their mental and physical health complaints. Each came to see me because they were experiencing relentless anxiety, rumination, and depression. Regard-less of the amount of emotional processing, coping skills learned, and types of therapies used, their symptoms remained mostly unchanged. Oftentimes they also experienced weight changes, low libido, and made statements such as "I am always exhausted. This is just my normal." I was surprised and my clients were surprised when they found out that they were actually suffering from a thyroid condition, which was often an autoimmune issue (Hashimoto's thyroiditis or Graves' disease). When clients have made an effort to improve their mental health and physical health with little to show for it, it is now routine for me to mention their thyroid as a possible contributor.

The health of your thyroid affects your mental health. There is no question about it. Some common physical side effects of a low thyroid include cold hands and feet, thinning hair, pregnancy difficulties, and stubborn weight issues.[7] On the flip side, hyperthyroidism (or too-high levels of thyroid hormone production) can include sleeplessness, anxiety, and heart palpitations, as the excess thyroid hormone wildly ramps up energy production.[8]

What exactly is the thyroid? It is a butterfly-shaped gland located at the front of the neck and is responsible for a myriad of processes in the body. It controls energy production and temperature and helps the body grow and develop, among other things.

While the thyroid can be a large driving force for some, I learned that the main problem was farther upstream. The thyroid, along with many other glands, can take a hit when other things are awry. It was my nervous system and limbic system impairment ramping up my immune system and stress hormones, which then negatively impacted my thyroid. Prior to learning this, I took tailored thyroid nutrients and ate a thyroid-friendly diet. The thyroid-focused methods did not work because I was not using the right tool for the job. A lot of people end up in this position. Good supplements and a healthy diet certainly did not hurt me and did support me during that time, but when you uncover the key to your issues, you will see things change. My brother Bert used to tell me to give any product or protocol a few weeks to work. If nothing noticeable shifts in two weeks, well, you're barking up the wrong tree. Bert, you were spot on!

Your thyroid may, in fact, be the main factor causing you issues. If it is, you should love and support your organs and glands with lifestyle interventions. Review the preceding information and symptoms and consider whether the thyroid could be an essential piece of your puzzle. If you internally scream, "This sounds like me!" more information will be of great help to you. First, check with your doctor and ask to have your blood tested to find out how well your thyroid is functioning. Insist on having your thyroid antibodies tested (a TPO test), along with the usual TSH that they run. Many doctors will not evaluate thyroid antibodies as part of a general lab workup, so it is important to ask for and request this. In addition, looking at the T3 and T4 markers can help determine whether your thyroid is affecting your overall wellness. For detailed information about the thyroid, which blood markers are essential to run, and tailored lifestyle interventions to promote good thyroid health, I recommend Dr. Datis Kharrazian's book, *Why Do I Still Have Thyroid Symptoms When My Lab Tests Are Normal?* and *Hashimoto's Food Pharmacology* by Dr. Izabella Wentz.

STRESS HORMONES

Ideally the body releases stress hormones to equip us with a surge of energy to execute the fight or flight response. DNRS and meditation helped me directly address my stress hormones and bring them back into balance using specific types of visualizations. Stress hormones are released by the adrenal glands, which sit right atop the kidneys. The brain releases these hormones when it detects a threat. When does this become a problem? When our nervous system, specifically the limbic system, is oversensitive to danger, our brain will cause our stress hormones to be constantly pumped into our system.

You may or may not be familiar with cortisol as it relates to stress. Cortisol, along with the other stress hormones, is damaging in excess. In chronically high amounts, cortisol breaks down the body and suppresses the immune system. Prolonged secretion of cortisol can also reduce the size of the prefrontal cortex (the control center of the brain) and interrupt the regulation of synapses, which are signals between brain cells.[9] This causes difficulties with learning.[10] Do you feel like you overreact to stressful situations, or are constantly on high alert? Do you have sound sensitivities, high degrees of fear, or generalized anxiety? You are likely pumping out large amounts of stress hormones around the clock. No wonder you can't sleep or think straight! I have been there, too.

Don't get me wrong, some stress hormones are just fine. For one, adequate amounts of cortisol are used to regulate blood sugar in the body for quick energy when needed.[11] And cortisol is actually a steroid hormone. Ever heard of the steroid cream hydrocortisone? Same thing. It is used to reduce inflammation in the body by dampening the inflammatory response. As you can see, having sufficient amounts of cortisol is necessary for a healthy body and mind. When the body is functioning optimally, cortisone levels are highest in the morning upon waking, as cortisol gives us energy to get up and go, and lowest in the evening, when it is time to rest. However, when these hormones are out of sync, fatigue upon waking or insomnia at night may occur. I remember when this was my reality. It was next to impossible to get out of bed in the morning. I described my experience to friends and family as either being hit by a truck or carrying a large piano on my back. At my sickest, around age twenty-three or so, I remember mindfully checking in with my body to see whether I felt as if I had been run over by a small scooter (a good day) or a Mack truck (a bad day). My question to you is this: Is your morning fatigue a small scooter or a Mack truck?

In situations such as these, it is important to address the rogue limbic system that is signaling to your body to release stress hormones. Various techniques can help with this: meditation, DNRS (discussed in Chapter 5), exercise changes (reviewed in Chapter 16), and mindset changes (shared in Chapters 5 and 7). Happily, most of my mornings now are a far cry from my old reality. I have energy to get up and get motivated. I learned how to regulate my cortisol rhythms and keep stress hormones in check.

SEX HORMONES

I once worked with an eighteen-year-old in her senior year of high school who suffered from exhaustion, depression, anxiety, and difficulty concentrating. It was confusing to both herself and her dad because it came and went. The symptoms were not constant. She would come into sessions on some days with so much to talk about. She would be upbeat, positive, and excited to share about plans with friends. But on other days, she would barely speak. Her exhaustion was so bad, she could hardly keep her head up. She felt too anxious to finish homework or spend time with her friends. It was debilitating for her. After asking about bullies at school, friendships, and family issues without any leads, I decided the best and only course of action would be for her and her dad to write down and document for as long as necessary these waves of exhaustion and dysphoria followed by periods of feeling "normal." The results that came back shocked me: the symptoms were during the week before her period.

As therapists, we often don't jump to a diagnosis of severe hormone dysregulation as the driver of a teen's anxiety, depression, or lack of focus. Sometimes we chalk it up to self-esteem issues, trauma, or school problems. However, my client was actually suffering from premenstrual dysphoric disorder (PMDD), which is different from premenstrual syndrome (PMS) in level of severity. PMDD symptoms include debilitating insomnia, fatigue, significant increase in dysphoric mood, and impaired cognitive performance during the late luteal phase of the menstrual cycle.[12] This phase takes place after ovulation and just before menstruation. Once the client recognized this, she actively pursued regulating her hormones with prescription and natural methods and saw positive results.

Hormonal imbalances are no joke. Although only 3% to 8% of women of child-bearing age meet criteria for PMDD, roughly 13%

to 18% have PMS. In my experience, PMS has always felt like a common issue that many women struggle with and talk about among themselves. However, during my own health journey, I uncovered the shocking reality that all women don't have to battle this common experience, as I once thought. Aggressive fluctuations of sex hormones that lead to irritability, insomnia, nausea, dizziness, severe cramps, tearfulness, feeling sensitive, or crippling fatigue do not have to happen. They are not something we have to just accept and live with. Yes, you read that right. These awful symptoms don't have to happen. Chiropractor and practitioner of functional medicine Michelle Narson once shared something profound with me. She said, "Katy, while PMS symptoms are common, they are not normal." What exactly does this mean? It means that while many of us suffer from hormonal imbalances and fluctuations, a well-balanced body has few symptoms of PMS prior to the beginning of a menstrual cycle.

You may be wondering how to go from common PMS symptoms to feeling normal, balanced, and aligned, like Dr. Narson explained. First, let's talk about stress. Sure, we all know stress is bad and causes problems for us in many ways. But did you know that stress can wreak havoc on your hormones? Chronic, prolonged stress alone can cause many different hormonal imbalances, and can even make PMS symptoms worse.[13] Stress lowers the hormone progesterone significantly and can lead to estrogen levels becoming too high, which can cause depression, irritability, insomnia, and cognitive issues. Incorporate more stress-reduction activities into your day, such as your favorite exercise, meditation, getting adequate sleep, and spending time in nature. If you're looking for ideas and inspiration, refer to the reflections throughout this book.

It is ideal to remove overloads of stress from your life as an act of prevention. You can do this by establishing relationship boundaries, knowing how much you can handle and honoring that, meditation, and other techniques. However, we also need mechanisms to lower stress levels within the body once they have already occurred. Moving the body in a way that feels good to you is fantastic because it releases and efficiently processes all of those stress hormones circulating in the body, helping us reduce feelings of stress. And remember—stress hormones are released to get us to move or take action so we can either fight or get to safety quickly. When we have all of these hormones circulating but don't move enough to efficiently remove and release them, they break down the body and mind and make us incredibly uncomfortable.

Second, we can look to genetics for more answers. For those of you who have tried birth control and felt wonderful on it, kudos to you. For your friends, family members, and others who felt just plain awful while on birth control, we can turn to genetics as an explanatory factor for these different reactions. Some gene mutations affect the ability of the body to clear out or dispose of extra estrogen that the body does not need. So, if I pour lots of estrogen into a body that does not clear and dispose of excess estrogen well, it creates an overload of estrogen. When female clients in their childbearing years come in complaining of depression, anxiety, fatigue, irritability, or overall sensitivity, I often ask about periods, PMS, and birth control use for this very reason.

A third hidden cause of hormonal imbalances is found in our treasured beauty and bath products. What an unsuspected culprit! Thankfully, we are in the midst of a paradigm shift in beauty. Look at all of the companies touting "clean beauty" and a more natural approach in makeup, lotions, hair care, and other products. Online stores are fully committed to and stocked with these products. And even big-name brands are creating lines of products that contain fewer chemicals.

But what should you look for or buy? Look for personal care products that do not contain "parfum" or "fragrance" in the ingredients label unless they are marked as naturally derived and phthalate free. Chemicals such as phthalates and parabens are endocrine (hormone) disruptors and can cause dysregulation in both men and women. Candles, laundry detergent, and cleaning supplies also often contain phthalates and parabens.[14] Sulfate-free is also a must-have when avoiding chemicals in personal care products. You can feel good about lotions, shampoos, and soaps that are free from these chemicals. How ironic that we use these products to improve ourselves in one way or another, but many are actually toxic to us. I know you want to look your best and feel your best, and by choosing better personal care products, you can do both. The Resources section lists some specific suggestions for hair care, body care, makeup, and dental care brands that I find quite effective. (And they also smell lovely.)

FOOD CONTAINER CHOICES

Sadly, hormone disruptors are not just in your favorite body wash—they leach into our food and water too. Thankfully, just like with clean beauty products, we have seen a recent paradigm shift promoting glass water bottles and stainless steel jugs. They are trendy and fun, but they are also much better for our health. Do you drink from plastic water bottles often? Before arriving at your nearest grocery or convenience store, cases of your favorite brand of bottled water—in plastic bottles—often travel from hot warehouses on hot trucks. Plastic that is heated can leach into the water, contaminating it with hormone disruptors such as bisphenol A (BPA), bisphenol S (BPS), and other hormone-disrupting chemicals harmful to our health. This includes heated plastics used in food consumption, such as the plastic lids on your hot coffee and reheating leftovers or other foods in plastic. BPA is commonly found in many everyday products.[15] Heated plastic is all around us. You may never look at a plastic water bottle from a vending machine the same way again. I am not at all sorry for informing you about this important issue. Instead, use healthier food container alternatives. Glass containers and glass bottles are excellent choices, in addition to reusable silicone bags, beeswax wraps, and stainless steel containers and steel tumblers. Stainless steel pans and cast-iron skillets are also great for cooking food.

Unfortunately, I have to add another offender to the list—many nonstick pans are coated with materials that flake off and can become ingested in the food if scratched or can produce toxic fumes when heated. Some of my favorite nontoxic food containers are listed in the Resources section.

DIET AND HORMONE BALANCE

This is where all the information we've been discussing begins to come together. The nutrition and dietary changes suggested in the previous chapters also help you balance all your hormones, including your thyroid, stress hormones, and sex hormones. Dr. Sara Gottfried recommends a pound per day of vegetables, as fiber can bind to excess hormones, such as estrogen, and carry them out of the body.[16] In her book, *The Hormone Cure*, she also recommends seafood and eggs over red meat for women with hormonal imbalances because red meat has the effect of promoting estrogen production.

Blood sugar stability (discussed in Chapter 9) is another suggestion for keeping hormones balanced. Dr. Datis Kharrazian says that blood sugar imbalances are often one of the biggest causes of hormonal imbalances.[17] When women have high blood sugar issues, this can increase testosterone levels. On the flip side, high blood sugar in men can increase their estrogen production. Interesting, right? Women with high blood sugar are prone to polycystic ovarian syndrome, a condition that causes acne, excess hair growth, weight gain, and irregular periods.[18] Men with high blood sugar can develop extra fatty tissue around the breast area, loss of body hair, loss of muscle, and sexual issues.[19] The following reflection will help you discover more about your own hormonal levels, sex hormones included, and what steps you may decide to take first.

REFLECTION: HORMONE BALANCING

Take some time to ponder each question before writing your response in your journal. Reflect on your current mental and physical health. Compare your symptoms to those mentioned in this chapter and set goals for taking action.

- Do the most common thyroid, stress hormone, or sex hormone symptoms apply to you?
- What is ONE step you can make today to move toward improving your hormone levels?
  - What small changes could you make to use cleaner personal care products?
  - What tweaks can you make to make better food container choices?
  - Do you have a favorite stress reliever that you can do more of?
- What changes had you already made to increase your use of clean beauty products and food containers before reading this book?

- Is there a hormone in this chapter that you would like to learn more about?

- What diet tweaks might you consider based on your hormone symptoms?

When I consider all the hormones in the body, I always focus on the crucial need for balance. Hormones, even cortisol, are not bad. They, just like food, water, and air, are essential and healthy in the correct amounts. However, just as excessive amounts of food or air are not good things, so it is the same with hormone levels. The mind and body are connected and intertwined, not separate and isolated from each other. In the next chapter, you will see how digestive and immune health are impacted by certain lifestyle, psychological, and emotional factors and the bidirectional relationship between all of these issues.

13

DIGESTION AND IMMUNE HEALTH

My research (case study of one) into my health issues tore down my old belief systems and paradigms of the body and wellness. In my introductory letter to you, I shared my story about how I took many rounds of antibiotics consecutively in an attempt to get rid of a severe case of strep throat at the age of twenty-one. Not only did the antibiotics not get rid of the strep, but they left me with a lot of painful and confusing digestive problems as well as emotional and cognitive problems. This is when my research began in earnest, and the gut microbiome was the focus of my first attempt at addressing my health issues.

- Do YOU have digestive problems?
- Do you feel constantly uncomfortable or bloated?
- Do you have a very unpredictable digestive system?

- Do you suffer from frequent heartburn, trips to the bathroom, or constipation?

- Do you experience pain in your abdomen, whether higher up or lower down?

In this chapter, we will review information about digestive symptoms, the gut microbiome, and how the two relate to each other. I will also share some personal stories and experiences about my own digestive health and several ways it can become compromised. Lastly, we will review how digestive health and mental health are intertwined.

YOUR GUT MICROBIOME: WHAT IS YOUR GUT TELLING YOU?

Healthy digestion is necessary for us to absorb all of the good things we get from our foods. Healthy digestion also fuels brain health.

Our digestive tracts house some pretty incredible features that break down foods and help us assimilate nutrients. Residing within the confines of the large intestine (and partly our small intestine) are one hundred trillion microbes (yes, you read that right).[1] One hundred trillion! This is astounding. What is even more astounding is how much these little creatures do for us every single day. They help us break down and digest our food, release anti-inflammatory agents for our intestinal lining, and even make vitamins like folate, which are essential for brain health.[2] In addition, gut bacteria help make about 95% of the body's serotonin.[3] Serotonin is a neurotransmitter released in the brain that allows us to feel connected to things we enjoy, helps us feel motivated, and enables us to feel happy. Serotonin demonstrates the intricate and complex relationship between our mental health and the state of our gut microbiome.

"I can totally figure this out," I thought to myself as I sat at my desk one day in fall 2013. I stared intently at my laptop screen, reading several pages of information on the internet about eating habits that would improve digestion. As I scrolled through page after googled page, I identified the common (bogus) themes about eating more fiber, eating more fruits and vegetables, and staying active. No doubt, you have heard this simplistic advice over and over and over again in health magazines, at your doctor's office, and on TV. Venturing further down the rabbit hole, I learned about "food combining," eating for your blood type, and taking a digestive enzyme to efficiently break down the foods we eat. I needed to slow down, chew the food many times, and eat in a relaxed, calm atmosphere (apparently).

It seemed simple enough. I was convinced this could be the shift I needed. Rumor had it that a lot of my family members were lactose intolerant, so I was hopeful that taking a lactase enzyme was the miracle key. I'm sure you've been there too, hopping on Google hoping to uncover some tips to feel better. I seemed to think this would do the trick quickly and simply, and I'd be feeling like myself again in no time! What planet was I on? I had so much going on inside me, issues that had been subtly present for years. I laugh when I look back at this time in my life. I was naive, yet open-minded, as most college kids are. I also read about the paleo diet for the first time that day and contemplated eliminating grains from my diet altogether. I knew something had to be done. I couldn't bear the pain any longer, the unpredictability of my stomach, and the imbalance that had occurred from the antibiotics. I also had fatigue, low motivation, and anxiety. I would sit at my desk for hours, trying to answer essay questions and to assimilate large quantities of information from my textbook while bogged down by brain fog. Prior to all of the antibiotics, my brain had been quite sharp. In elementary, middle school, and high school,

I could sit for hours at a time, even in a moving vehicle, reading, writing, and studying after a long day. Yet, something had changed once I reached my junior and senior years of college. What I didn't yet know was the significant connection between digestive health and the brain.

This chapter is dense with the results of my research. I was astounded when I first learned this information from books and functional medicine doctors. They don't teach this stuff in most schools, so you're in for a fun ride. I hope this knowledge will motivate you to change your own habits.

The Gut Microbiome and Antibiotics

When I first learned about the gut microbiome, I found out how severely antibiotic overuse can impact digestive health. Don't get me wrong, antibiotics are lifesaving and essential at times. However, when used repeatedly and excessively, they can bomb the gut microbiome. The gut has a delicate ecosystem, and if certain types of good bacteria are wiped out, this means the "bad" bacteria have room to grow and proliferate.[4] Cue the digestive symptoms. Gut issues can include abdominal pain, bloating, swelling, diarrhea, constipation, nausea, indigestion, delayed stomach emptying, heartburn, and gas. These symptoms can come from eating certain foods, or sometimes just any foods.

Antibiotics also allow fungi such as yeast and *Candida* to overgrow in our intestines because the good bacteria that once kept them in check are now largely diminished for a period of time.[5] This perfect storm happened to me. After taking high doses of antibiotics, some with doses that were far too strong for my system, my gut microbiome was devastated. The microbes that usually break down my foods were in scarce supply. I had only limited numbers of the microbes that usually release anti-inflammatory compounds. And the friendly bugs that kept the bad bacteria and fungi in their place were few.

It's interesting to note that when bad bacteria and yeast overgrowth take place in the intestines, the process produces chemicals from the yeast and bacteria that can be very harmful to our overall health, including our brains. Many bacteria in the gut contain a substance on their outer membrane known as lipopolysaccharide (LPS). LPS serves as a shield to the bacteria and protects it against things such as our own bile salts. But LPS is extremely destructive if it gets beyond the inside of the intestines, into our bloodstream. LPS in the bloodstream can produce a large cascade of inflammation throughout the body. Here's where it really gets interesting: Research has associated LPS with depression.[6] LPS in the bloodstream is also associated with anxiety disorders.[7] When the intestinal lining is intact, LPS cannot gain access to the circulatory system. This is an important consideration in the mind-body connection and maintaining mental health. We will discuss the integrity of the gut wall in much greater detail in the next chapter, and I hope it will paint a more complete picture of the gut, the immune system, and our mental health.

Gut issues can come out of nowhere and leave you feeling confused and uncomfortable. I often encountered these annoyingly inconvenient problems after a lovely dinner out, a holiday party with friends, or just a lunch at home. The persistent digestive problems were also accompanied by a heightened level of generalized anxiety, sad moods that came out of nowhere, taking more and more time to complete school assignments, dragging myself to classes or social events because of fatigue, and irritability at the little things in life. Does this sound like you, too? You may need to take a closer look at your gut microbiome.

Research has documented the intricate relationship between gut microbes and mood. In 2018, one study looked at a sample of individuals diagnosed with generalized anxiety disorder and a sample of those without the diagnosis, comparing their gut microbiomes.[8] Those with high anxiety actually had lower degrees of diversity and lower amounts of bacteria that produce anti-inflammatory short-chain fatty acids. In addition, bacterial overgrowth of the "bad" strains was observed in the high anxiety group. In my particular case, this all made a lot of sense. The antibiotics I took had reduced the diversity of my gut microbiome. As I took more antibiotics, I felt worse with each round as the effects accumulated.

The process of building up a healthy gut microbiome may be different for every person. It includes basic health tenets such as exercising and eating more fruits and vegetables. It can also include utilizing herbs for a period of time to kill bad bacteria and yeasts, as well as using probiotics or probiotic-rich foods. Great resources with specific food lists or supplement protocols to improve the gut are available, such as those found on draxe.com or books by functional medicine doctors such as Dr. Datis Kharrazian. Yet, healing the gut oftentimes also means a radical shift in mindset and perspective on life. It can mean having to look at the limbic system and brain in order to bring about more pronounced digestive changes.

THE LIMBIC SYSTEM

We learned about the limbic system earlier in the book. Put simply, it is a collection of structures in the brain responsible for survival mechanisms, among other things. When we are really stressed out, and loads of stress hormones are circulating in our body, this mechanism changes the microbial composition within our guts.[9] As you now know, we need the balance of bacteria to help us digest efficiently and fully. Furthermore, bacterial suppression in the intestines lead to yeast overgrowth and dysbiosis, which is an imbalance in microbiota of the digestive tract. Clearly, prolonged stress will have a significant impact on the gut.

Overly sensitive and overfiring limbic pathways mean that the prefrontal cortex is suppressed by the limbic system. The prefrontal cortex is in charge of muscle coordination, including the movement of food through our intestines and the opening and closing of valves.[10] If our intestines are not swept clean of food and bacteria, these bacteria can overgrow in places they are not meant to be, which can cause digestive problems from the compounds released from the overgrowth. My digestive symptoms were exacerbated by the diminished functioning of my prefrontal cortex. The muscular tone of my digestive tract was not at its peak level, and thus valves stayed open when they needed to be closed, food particles and bacteria were not being swept cleanly through, and so forth. Here's the story about how I came to learn this obscure information.

GUT HEALTH AND TRAUMA

It was just another day. I was sitting with my laptop and phone, googling and researching, hoping that I could unravel the mystery of my digestive and emotional symptoms. I felt so broken. It all felt incredibly wrong. In spring 2017, I was only twenty-five years old. For the last few years, I had been suffering through things that my friends and family had never even heard of, and I had no idea why.

I started googling "causes of digestive problems" and came across a video that changed my life. It was hosted by Dr. Randall Gates and Dr. Martin Rutherford. This video link can be found in the Resources section of this book. These two functional medicine doctors from Reno, Nevada, were discussing the need to look to the brain for solutions in order to improve the health and functioning of the digestive tract. By this time, I had tried all of the healing diets. I had tried a lot of supplements. I had tried cleanses. I needed something different, and this could be it. I was extremely curious. The brain? I need to look to the brain to heal? The doctors talked about all of the stress hormones and how the fight or flight response could go "rogue." I now know this intimately as limbic system impairment, as Annie Hopper calls it. Near the end of the video, Dr. Rutherford gave examples of patients whose health problems began when they encountered severely stressful problems, such as a divorce, parental divorce, or sexual abuse.

In reviewing these patient conversations, he walked the audience through responses he received when he asked patients when their gut problems started. "Well, it happened when I was eleven years old." When he asked what happened when the patient was eleven years old, he received a very interesting response: "Oh nothing. Ummm, my parents got divorced. It was divisive." Then he uttered the words that I consider a sign from God. Continuing the list of statements from patients, he said, "My brother got shot." My entire body went numb. What are the chances, that on this day and time, I would find a brief video that led to this conclusion? That with two minutes left of the video, I would stay to the end to hear these words? My brother. My beloved friend. I had pushed away the pain and the suffering of losing him because I did not want to process or contemplate the intense impact his death had on my body, my mind, my nervous system, and my health. I had to address the limbic system. This was a massive breakthrough, and one that I want you to remember. Traumatic experiences can become a huge burden to every system in our bodies.

Every. Single. System. Think about what you have personally been through—your experiences and those moments you've held close to your heart and not shared. How have they affected your health? How have they changed your gut microbiome? In the following reflection, you will have the opportunity to review how your intestinal microbiome is doing, and whether the information in this section could be your golden key to health and wellness.

REFLECTION: HOW IS YOUR DIGESTION?

Write your responses to the following questions in your journal. You may answer with "I don't know," and that is completely okay. The prompts are here to help you build greater awareness and mindfulness about your digestive health and the impacts to it.

- How often do you suffer from digestive issues? Is it a rare occurrence? Is it every day?

- Reflect on any medications you have taken recently. Have you taken any antibiotics? Do they give you digestive side effects?

- Contemplate your current and past stress levels in addition to any ACEs. (A link to the ACE assessment can be found in the Resources section.) Keep in mind that the assessment does not include an exhaustive list of what you may define as trauma or painful experiences from your own past. You can write down any experiences in your journal that you would categorize as such. Do you notice a connection between your gut and emotional states? Do you see any connection between when your digestive issues began and events that occurred during that time?

As you can see, the gut microbiome has an underrated impact on your overall emotional and physical wellness. Many wonderful lifestyle changes can improve gut health and help heal your nervous system. It may be time to shift to a more healing diet, or diligently utilize a special supplement for your gut. It may also be time to honestly reflect on what you have been through in your life, how it has affected your mind and body, and whether you are in serious need of a nervous system-limbic system revamp. In the next chapter, we will look at how the intestinal microbiome relates to our immune system.

14

THE GUT MICROBIOME
AND THE IMMUNE SYSTEM

Abalanced immune system is critical for good health. We need our immune system to protect us from bodily invaders that could otherwise harm us. The immune system fights and deactivates bacterial, viral, and fungal threats. It is essential for the immune system to know the difference between invader and friend to ensure that our own tissues, organs, the healthy foods we eat, or household and personal care items are not marked as invaders or pathogens. These include items like traditional laundry detergents, fragrances from candles, or ingredients in our personal care products. The immune system can become suppressed by a multitude of factors and can also go into an overdrive of hypervigilance. In the latter instance, it shifts into an overactivated, overzealous militant erroneously hell-bent on targeting what it perceives as dangerous. This can lead to body-wide symptoms that may or may not seem to be related to one another.

- Do you have unexplained fatigue, dizziness, pain in your body, depression, or anxiety?

- Have doctors given you a clean bill of health, but you still feel terrible?

- Do you lack the energy and drive for life that you once had?

- Do you have symptoms within multiple systems or organs of the body, such as the skin, joints, digestive track, or brain?

Our immune systems can absolutely be responsible for more than just responding to cold and flu symptoms and healing wounds. We may experience uncomfortable, seemingly unrelated symptoms because of the immune system. That daily malaise, brain fog, fatigue, severe joint pain, or digestive issue may be deeply rooted in something you would have never expected. In this chapter, I am going to describe how the health of the immune system is deeply intertwined with our digestive tract, gut microbiome, and intestinal lining. These systems are not separate; they work together and influence each other. Understanding and improving how these aspects of your body work together can be the difference between the wellness that you are searching for and the fatigue, anxiety, or low mood you are experiencing. We will also review autoimmunity, which is often overlooked as a health issue.

THE IMMUNE SYSTEM: OUR FRIEND AND DEFENDER

Working with a handful of functional medicine practitioners, I learned that a lot of the issues I suffered with were caused by the immune system. In retrospect, it was profoundly clear that my immune system was completely out of whack. This was discovered through my self-reports of symptom clusters and in-depth blood work. This was one of my first "aha" moments, because a lot of my doctors' visits prior to this point did not identify an immune problem for me at all. I had visited a gastroenterologist, an immunologist, and even an infectious disease specialist and left each appointment with no insights or helpful information.

When I learned that my fatigue, restlessness, irritability, and pain had a biological origin, I felt my shame and confusion melt away. I was finally uncovering answers and explanations for why I felt the way I did. I was finally beginning to get some clarity. Although in the end the immune system was not my ultimate "aha" moment, it fostered the beginning of self-compassion, of grace, and a connection to science and research. A connection to my body and how to listen to it.

The immune system and how well it is functioning can be the difference between abundant wellness, a balanced mood, and abundant energy or a head-to-toe breakdown of the body. Initially, our immune system is provided by our mothers; it is then strengthened via multiple mechanisms.[1] When delivered via the birth canal, newborns receive a lot of beneficial bacteria. Breastfeeding gives newborns many immune-modulating compounds in addition to a prebiotic that is food for the microbiome in the baby's gut. This helps develop the gut microbiome that will be with them for years to come. Those who were not delivered vaginally (such as myself) or breastfed have been shown to have more allergies and immune-related issues later in life.[2] Other factors that stimulate the immune system include exposure to pets, consumption of foods other than breastmilk, and exposure to other pathogens.

Before learning about the intestinal microbiome and the health of the immune system, I always thought of the immune system as something that helped us during cold and flu season, or a part of the body that got stronger when we had enough vitamin C. Unless I was sick, I rarely thought about it. When I was sick, I knew it needed rest, vitamins, and healthier food. Our immune system is SO much more than this, though. Immune health relates to environmental, food, and psychological factors. We have an immune system all over our skin. We have an immune system in our gut.

The gut is a significant barrier between the outside world and our insides. When we consume food, it travels along a tube that stretches from the mouth all the way down to our bottoms. The food particles are broken down by bile acid, stomach acid, and digestive enzymes from the pancreas into very small particles to be absorbed. The small intestine absorbs the majority of those lovely vitamins that we consume, but under strict circumstances. The intestinal walls keep out the larger particles (or should, under healthy conditions). The wall of the intestines is only one cell thick. Is that not incredible? Just one little cell that allows us to absorb only what we need through it. These cells are called enterocytes. Nutrients are absorbed through the gut's epithelial cells as well as between them. The connection from one gut epithelial cell to the next is called a tight junction. These junctions act as a protective barrier between the rest of our bodies and the large food particles we have ingested, along with bacteria and other larger particles. Immediately inside the enterocyte wall are some very important immune cells that protect the body from incoming invaders. Between these cells and the gut microbiome, it may come as no surprise that about 80% of our immune system resides in the gut.[3] Gut bacteria have been shown to regulate and influence the immune system.[4] Interestingly, imbalances in gut bacteria—something we reviewed earlier in this book, can actually weaken this wall over time.[5] When this barrier is compromised, intestinal permeability develops;

this is also known as "leaky gut syndrome," and it can trigger a systemic inflammatory cascade of the body, including the brain.

I can say with confidence that I had a severe case of this at one point, and it profoundly affected my brain health. It created debilitating fatigue some days, anxiety, sadness, irritability, a difficult and frustrating inability to concentrate, and defensiveness. Who would ever think that a problem in your immune system and gut could have such a jarring impact on the brain, on your joy, peace, and happiness? Who would guess that it could affect your ability to read a book with ease or give a presentation in a clear, calm, meaningful way? To relate lovingly to your family and friends? People are experiencing mental health problems that are directly related to their malfunctioning immune system EVERY SINGLE DAY without knowing it.

FOOD ALLERGIES/INTOLERANCES AND BRAIN INFLAMMATION

As you can now see, a leaky gut allows large particles to make their way from the intestines into the bloodstream. These can include pathogens, LPS, other toxic substances, or even undigested food particles. When the body detects something in the blood that should not be there, it mounts an immune response. The tagged invader could simply be a bite of your lunch. Say you ate a green pepper but it wasn't broken down well. Because of intestinal permeability, it gets into the bloodstream. Your body will attack that pepper and target it as "dangerous." At this point, what do you think happens every time you eat a green pepper? Your immune cells are going to blow it to smithereens!

For those with a severely leaky gut, your immune system will have a long list of targeted foods. With enough time away from the food and a restored integrity of the gut wall, the body may become much less sensitive to the food(s). These are the mechanisms behind being immune-sensitive to certain foods and the way the immune system reacts to those foods. If we inspect the mental health aspect of these reactions, they can create brain fog, difficulties concentrating, low mood, fatigue, and irritability.[6]

When I was at my worst, this happened to me every single day. Scratch that. It was happening every single meal. After eating I would often retreat to my bed and lie there wondering when the symptoms would go away. It felt as if something very heavy was being lifted onto my body, and the fatigue was debilitating. To make matters worse, sometimes my lungs would tighten up, and I became extremely disoriented. Other times I would be incredibly irritable, which turned into guilt and shame for having these emotions. I could not describe them, I was too embarrassed to share them, and I didn't know where they were coming from. It was a downward spiral of hopelessness, fear, and confusion.

The gut and brain are intimately involved with one another through the mechanisms of the gut-brain axis. If you think back to a time when you felt nervous, maybe nausea set in or you felt butterflies. Some people can feel their stomachs tighten up when stressed. If you imagine yourself smelling a big, juicy lemon, and biting into that lemon, what do you feel in your body? Most notice a sensation of the mouth watering or lips puckering.

This simple observation illustrates the power of the mind-body connection. The enteric nervous system (ENS) is located along the digestive tract and can be referred to as the "second brain" of the body. The same tissues that make up the central nervous system also comprise the ENS. One hundred million nerve cells exist within the ENS, stretching from the throat to our bottoms. Signals are sent both ways, so if something is going on in the gastrointestinal tract, the ENS sends signals to the central nervous system. Those signals can really influence and shift your mood. The vagus nerve, the longest of all the cranial nerves, plays a large role in modulating the gut-brain axis. This nerve sends signals bidirectionally as it runs from the brain down through the chest and into the abdomen. It is made of 80% afferent and 20% efferent fibers, meaning that information is sent to the mind from the body and from the body to the mind.

Pro-inflammatory states of the gut microbiome, including the imbalance of bacteria, have been related to neurological issues such as Alzheimer's disease and Parkinson's.[7] In addition, research has documented that issues such as depression and anxiety have origins in the gut.[8] What does this all mean for our mental health? It means that we must take extra care in loving and supporting digestive health because it can promote a radical change in mood and wellbeing. This also means that if we take care of our emotional state, it can improve digestion.

GENERAL FOOD REACTIONS

Sometimes, I feel like the guru of food reactions based on my history and story. This section has various suggestions based on my personal experiences.

Always observe how certain foods affect you. If a meal makes you irritable and jittery, recognize that this meal is probably not doing you any favors. This may simply be because the meal is not balanced and is adversely affecting blood sugar levels (discussed in the blood sugar chapter), but it can also mean you are sensitive to this food.

What is "food sensitivity"? We just reviewed why the immune system mounts an attack against a certain food because it is marked as "dangerous." This causes specific sensitivities or food intolerances to develop. It can also be driven by genetics or because the food itself is inflammatory to humans. Some foods have a tendency to be more inflammatory or irritating to all human digestive tracts, such as gluten,[9] while others only affect certain people because of our unique and varying ability to break down certain food compounds. Those who have celiac disease (an autoimmune disease) especially need to avoid gluten, but non-celiac gluten sensitivity also exists.[10] Gluten is just one possible culprit, but other foods can be problematic too depending on the person. For example, my family has a harder time digesting dairy. This can be due to lactose intolerance, which is a digestive issue stemming from the body's inability to process the type of sugar in milk.[11] Lactase is an enzyme that breaks down milk particles.

People may acquire a dairy intolerance as they grow older, or they may not be able to tolerate milk as a child or baby but grow out of it eventually. Certain people argue that we are the only species on the planet that drinks the milk of another species. They assert that our bodies were designed to consume milk only from our own species.

Regardless of the many potential causes of food sensitivities, what is most important is how a food affects YOU, and you should tune into your body for answers. Insight and awareness are key to detecting these seemingly harmless perpetrators. I once again encourage you to turn to your food log. It can be a wonderful thing to keep for several weeks, documenting what you eat and how it affects your mood, focus levels, overall health, energy, and sleep.

Food sensitivities can be mild (such as an occasional digestive inconvenience) or severe (such as crippling brain fog, exhaustion, joint pain, and a racing heart). I experienced both levels when I was at my sickest. Occasionally, I felt utter confusion and debilitating fatigue from a food reaction and had to lie down for two hours before my body cleared it on its own.

When I was an intern, I shadowed a substance abuse therapy group for several months. During that time, I always had mild to moderate reactions after eating my lunch. It was the summer of 2016, and on a typical weekday, I sat in on the afternoon group from one to three. During those groups, I would try so hard to pay attention and remain alert, but it was painfully difficult. I felt disoriented. I felt dizzy, tired, and my vision was hazy. One afternoon, before group began, I took my seat and began a quick conversation with one of the clients. Thirty seconds into the conversation, he said "Do you even listen to anything that I say? I told you that yesterday, remember?" How embarrassing. I felt defeated. I felt like I had let the client down. I had so much shame with these symptoms because they were holding me back from being the best version of myself. They were holding me back from showing how much I cared and how much I wanted to help the people around me. Sometimes I had smaller reactions that included a few hives or feeling itchy; these were also usually accompanied by lower levels of fatigue or brain fog. All of these symptoms were a clear immune response.

If you have experiences such as these, you are not alone. While some reactions take longer to pop up, instant reactions to foods can rapidly highlight what your body is reacting to in that moment. It's also important to note that when the body and immune system are already dysfunctional, severe immune reactions to several foods can be more of a symptom than an entity unto itself. Immune reactions to multiple foods can indicate limbic system impairment, as the limbic system profoundly affects the balanced state of the immune system and can create this exaggerated response. An individual may begin reacting to chemicals or certain foods. Although chemicals and some foods are unhealthy for us, the response is, without question, out of proportion to the stimuli. The body can even begin reacting to healthy foods. This is your ultimate indication that you have leaky gut and limbic system impairment and may explain inexplicable symptoms that are actually autoimmunity in disguise.

AUTOIMMUNITY, LEAKY GUT, AND MOLECULAR MIMICRY

Autoimmunity can play a dramatic role in brain health. Autoimmunity is a complicated topic that is being studied more frequently lately. Autoimmunity happens when the body builds excess antibodies against its own tissues to destroy it, as it would a virus or bacteria. You may have heard of lupus, Crohn's disease, autoimmune thyroid, or rheumatoid arthritis, but did you know that the brain itself can also be affected? This is called neurological autoimmunity. Autoimmune disease has known associations with intestinal permeability,[12] and some research even points to leaky gut as a driver of autoimmunity.[13] Viruses, bacteria, chronic stress, chemical exposure, and traumatic events can cause an overreaction of the immune system. If an individual has elevated antibodies to a specific food, sometimes this can create autoimmunity to tissues. This is due to molecular mimicry. Some foods, viruses, and other pathogens have a structure that is very similar to our own organs. The immune system, which is trying to protect us, can erroneously mix up our organs with a similar-looking food molecule, bacterium, or toxic compound. It then fires an attack. This can occur months or even years before symptoms become evident. When tissue destruction has taken place for long enough, the effects will begin manifesting as various symptoms. Traumatic experiences leave us more vulnerable to autoimmunity because they weaken our immune system and also can create intestinal permeability.[14]

STRESS AND THE IMMUNE SYSTEM

While the immune system has to take care of viruses, bacteria, and other types of pathogens to keep us safe, it has an even bigger enemy. Stress's impact on the immune system cannot be disregarded or overlooked. Stress can suppress the immune system and even open the tight junctions that need to stay predominantly closed for our health and wellbeing. Research has shown that those with PTSD have an increased prevalence of irritable bowel syndrome compared to those without PTSD.[15] Specifically, those with PTSD are three to four times more likely to experience somatic symptoms (such as gastrointestinal issues) compared to those without PTSD.[16] One cause is from a reduction in specific types of beneficial bacteria due to dysregulated hormones such as cortisol and adrenaline.[17] Interestingly, research has also shown that some beneficial bacteria can regulate and alter our cortisol and adrenaline in the body. Stress hormones can wreak havoc when chronic and prolonged, so we are very lucky to have our friendly visitors to help us.[18] I feel lucky to have them. Lastly, when we contemplate the limbic system's role in immune health, it is important to remember that the brain is the control center of the body, so it also controls areas of the immune system. This directly reflects the strong impact of stress on the tight junctions and the gut bacteria.

If you have mental and physical health problems, I want you to again contemplate the emotionally jarring and impactful events you have endured. The connection with stress is so important to your digestive health, limbic system, and immune system. In the chapter on trauma, the reflection helped you explore these issues to acknowledge how strong you are and what you have been through. We must first acknowledge the impacts before we can create a map and plan to move forward and heal. When I look back at my experiences of illness, I recognize that losing my brother was a catastrophically

painful event in my life. It was shocking, frightening, and indescribable. I can say without question that I developed PTSD-like
symptoms from this loss, and that it wore down my body and
immune system, which were already having problems caused by the
medication reactions.

REFLECTION: IMMUNE SYSTEM INFORMATION

Write your answers to each of the following prompts in your journal.
You may need to reread parts of this chapter in order to do so. That
is okay. Reviewing previously read material is a great way to retain
important concepts.

- Write down any insights you gained about the immune system,
  brain health, and whole-body health.

- What symptoms are you currently experiencing that could be
  tied to your immune system?

- How has stress impacted your immune system? Have you
  noticed any specific ways?

- What goals can you set to create a more balanced immune
  system?

    ◦ Identify what you may need more of or less of to take
      better care of your immune system. We have already
      covered a lot of content relevant to this question in
      this book. Stress reduction, nutrition, blood sugar
      regulation, and trauma work can be fantastic starting
      points. Pick one and brainstorm what that category
      would look like for you.

As you can see, our immune system is a powerhouse that can help us radiate health and wellbeing from top to bottom, or it can cripple us without meaning to. The immune system is our protector, our defender. But when it thinks WE are the enemy, things go terribly awry.

The next chapter discusses another factor that affects immune system functioning: toxins. For some people, toxins were the major cause of their autoimmune issues. Toxins can also affect brain health, skin health, and energy production in the body.

15

TOXINS

Toxin exposure is real, has significant impacts, and is sometimes unpredictable. It burdens our immune systems, our
organs, and even our thought processes. We are exposed to
toxins every single day, both in our homes and our travel outside of
the home. They can come at us from the oddest places. Let me give
you an example. Although a fictional character, the Mad Hatter from
Alice's Adventures in Wonderland, shockingly represents real people in
history. During the 1800s, the hat-making industry used mercury
in felt hat production, and hat makers literally went crazy from the
toxicity of the mercury fumes.

Toxin exposure is no joke. Whether in small or large quantities, it
affects our health and wellbeing. We need to use a prevention strategy
as often as possible, in addition to making sure we keep our bodies
detoxifying well. I know we aren't in the 1800s anymore, and you
probably aren't a hat maker. I'm not either. But I have some questions
for you to consider as we think about what can impact the health of
our immune system.

- Have you ever been exposed to toxic mold or lived in an environment (such as very old buildings) with elevated mold?

- Have you tried to "detox" with juice cleanses or supplements, but saw few results?

- Do you eat a lot of fish, in particular those that are very large?

- Do you have your cell phone attached to you 24/7? Even at night?

Toxin exposure can lead to an overactivation of the immune system and drive autoimmunity[1] in addition to allergies[2] and sensitivity to foods, environmental substances, and lesser chemicals such as laundry detergents or perfumes.[3] These incidences can be referred to as a "toxin injury." There is much we can do to protect ourselves and our families. Awareness is the most important thing when it comes to chemicals, what we have around us, and how they can bog us down. A lot of compounds are invisible to the naked eye. Less severe symptoms of toxin buildup can include hormonal imbalances and fatigue.[4] Significant accumulation in the body is detrimental to our immune health and our organs—including the brain.[5] It is SUCH a real thing. We do have many naturally built-in mechanisms for detoxification. When not overloaded, our systems work as a beautiful symphony to cleanse our blood and organs. However, these systems are overwhelmed in a highly toxic environment. They can't get rid of the toxins quickly enough. In this chapter, you will have a chance to consider some simple swaps for a healthier, toxin-free YOU. A version of you that is not being weighed down by mountains of chemicals that can trigger your immune system.

OUR BODY AND DETOXIFICATION

"Are you going in with me?" I grinned at my mother, holding in a burst of laughter with as much force as I could manage. "Are you kidding? Of course!" She replied with just as much enthusiasm, laced with silliness and carefree joy. We waited patiently for our turn while taking in all of the energy around us. At the Paleo f(x) conference in 2018, my mother and I tried out our first infrared sauna tent. The owner of the company motioned for us to enter the two-seater, and we gladly followed his direction. We sat within the confines of a canvas hut, with walls held up by sticks and fastened with a host of infrared lights on one of the walls. After taking a bit of time to look around, we finally rested on the wooden stools and laughed for a long time. I took note of the beautiful orange hue that filled our little tent. It brought a welcomed sense of peace and relaxation, and we remained there until it became too warm—after all, we were fully clothed and in the middle of an expo floor, not at a private spa experience.

I was incredibly curious about the supposed benefits of infrared therapy, which I had read so much about. Relaxation is crucial for good health, and red light therapy tends to do just that for our brains.[6] Research has shown light therapy improves depressive symptoms.[7] As we left the tent, everything outside felt vividly blue and bright. Had the lights in the expo changed, or was it me? Sitting in the infrared sauna no doubt changed how my eyes saw the world outside of the tent for a short period until they readjusted. Being immersed in orange light for even a brief period of time illustrated to me the profound brightness of regular everyday light that I had never noticed before. We were not in the tent long enough to begin sweating, but I can certainly attest to feeling more relaxed while inside. Research on infrared sauna therapy has shown it to be a health-promoting tool, with improvements in heart health and blood pressure,[8] fatigue, and pain.[9] Other types of saunas show similar benefits as well, from immune support[10] to improvements in mental health[11] and blood sugar.[12] Regardless of the type of sauna, most people associate them with releasing toxins, cleansing, or "detoxing."

The word "detox" has become a buzzword recently and shows up in health articles, spas, and beauty products. Protein bars and supplements with the word "detox" on them probably include a combination of herbs and botanicals that support the liver. In addition, many different types of saunas, from dry to steam to infrared, are viewed as vehicles for detoxification. We simply can't avoid every single toxin in this world and live a joyful, happy life of traveling and fun.

While "detox teas," herbs, juice cleanses, and saunas are well advertised in media, magazines, or ads as effective means of detoxification, there's another great secret to detoxing that you might not have guessed. It's something even grander and more effective than the methods just listed. And best of all—it is found within every one of us. It's our dear friend, the limbic system.

Healing and powerful everyday detoxification includes resetting the parasympathetic nervous system and strengthening it. Here is the thing about detox processes—in order to be in tip-top shape, the body needs to be relaxed. Why would your body prioritize effectively clearing toxins if it is on constant alert or in an adrenaline-fueled, fight-flight surge? Why would it spend precious energy on this secondary process when it's trying desperately to keep you alive? It wouldn't. Supplements are great, and spending time in the sauna is one of my favorite things to do, but if you want a magic bullet for improving your detoxing abilities, consider your limbic system and how stressed out, anxious, and fearful you might be right now. It can truly be as simple as that.

In my experience, rewiring the limbic system can be one of the best ways to get your detox pathways running smoothly and efficiently, as they were designed to do. The DNRS program discussed earlier in the book is an excellent resource and tool to learn how to do this. It was most effective for me personally in resetting my parasympathetic nervous system (and brain), so I will also recommend it as a front-line approach to healing detox pathways. Anything that promotes stress reduction and rewires the brain in a positive fashion can also help. Psychotherapy, time in nature, exercise, massage, meditation, and craniosacral therapy are a few examples. Use supplements and detox herbs as complementary approaches to this, if you'd like. This advice is coming from a person who at one point in time probably owned every single supplement on the market. My cabinets were simply bursting full of things that either made me feel worse or didn't do much at all to help me feel better. I am certainly an advocate for taking vitamins and minerals that are tailored to your own nutrition needs. Yet, many supplements and products on the market that claim to assist with "detox" don't live up to their hype. Also, any detox package or program comes to an end eventually, whether it is a juicing package or a special program, and then what? You go back to eating your regular diet. What can you do long-term for efficient detoxing? Heal your limbic system, work on your stress levels, and rewire your brain. There are many different ways to do this, and each person has to find their unique path. What is most important is that you choose a plan that brings your body back into alignment every single day— back into a state where you feel safe and at peace.

Lastly, consider this. The liver has to process all of those supplements, herbal tinctures, and detox teas that you take. That's right. Everything we consume and put in our bodies is filtered by our livers. So even supplements that are healthy for us can be a burden on the liver if we are taking too many. I mentioned this concept earlier in Chapter 10. Therefore, before you get supplement-happy, remember to take only the ones that truly help you and benefit you. Take them as needed or for periods of time. When I was sick, my detoxification capacity was limited because of a rogue limbic system impairment, yet I was loading up on the supplements. Their effects backfired because of this and did little to help me. Even quality supplements that are proven to be effective couldn't help.

Rewiring the limbic system is discussed in the chapter on DNRS (Chapter 5). Relaxing and resetting the stress response just might be a key to shifting your body into being incredibly efficient at detoxification.

PREVENTION

In addition to keeping our detoxification pathways functioning on all cylinders, it is important that we avoid toxin exposure as much as we can (with ease). I'm all for simple actions that feel like effortless habits in the long run and really pay off over time. A lot of chemicals out there are extremely unhealthy for our bodies in both small and large quantities. Chemicals in our water, food, beauty products, homes, cleaning products, air, and even frequencies that come from our technology can burden the body. Sometimes, however, it's easy to get carried away with avoidance, so keep in mind that it is all about balance and doing what you can to make healthy choices MOST of the time while letting your body take care of the rest. Stressing out over every little detail on the following reflection list will only slow down your detox pathways. Let's take a look at what you can do over time (in a manageable way) to lessen your toxin load.

REFLECTION: CLEARING THE TOXINS

Use your journal to complete each of the following activities. You do not have to complete this all in one sitting. It can be something that you tweak and come back to over time (and even check off as you complete your goals). My hope is that this reflection will help you gain awareness of ways to lower your toxin load.

- Take stock of what you put on your body, in your body, and what your environment looks like in a typical day. Write down each of the following bullet points in your journal and put a check next to those that you already do on a daily basis. Then pick one or two items that you would like to work toward this month:

    ○ Filtered drinking water

    ○ Consumption of foods on the Clean Fifteen list and buying organic for foods on the Dirty Dozen list (lists are provided in the Resources section)

    ○ Regular consumption of only low-mercury fish, and rare consumption of fish high in mercury (you can find a list of low-mercury fish online)

    ○ Turning off Wi-Fi at night in the home

    ○ Sleeping with the cell phone in another room or more than six feet away from the bed

    ○ Using "clean" beauty products (discussed in the hormone chapter)

    ○ Living in a healthy home without mold

    ○ Using food containers and cookware that do not leach particles into the food or beverage

- Using GREENGUARD-certified paints in the home
- Using clean laundry detergent and home cleaning products
- Using air filters that remove both allergens and volatile organic compounds (VOCs) from the air
- Effective stress reduction techniques tailored to your personal needs

- What information would you like to learn more about regarding toxins and detoxification? Is it mold? Better cleaning supplies? Electric and magnetic field (EMF) exposure? Write down at least one topic that you would like to research and implement. You can write down what you find in your journal. To learn more about avoiding toxins in everyday life, *Prescriptions for a Healthy House* is a great resource. In addition, Dr. Ann Shippy's work on mold exposure is extensive and can help you take effective action steps if you believe this to be a potential culprit holding you back from optimal wellbeing. Another resource is Dr. Joseph Mercola's recently published book titled *EMF*D*, which teaches about Wi-Fi and cell phone emissions. There are many great resources and books on toxin avoidance and exposure.

- Identify your plan to reduce as much stress as possible and activate the parasympathetic nervous system. How do you currently lessen stress in your life? A stressed body holds on to toxins. A body that is relaxed processes and releases with proficiency. Some ways to activate your parasympathetic nervous system include yoga, other types of exercise, infrared therapy, cold water immersion, meditation, psychotherapy, DNRS, various types of massage, acupuncture, and craniosacral therapy.

A final word on toxins: Two people can be exposed to the same mold, heavy metal, or other toxic substrate and have entirely different reactions. One person may become deathly ill while others feel nothing. This can be due to the different makeup of the person's body and how healthy their mind and body were prior to exposure. Some people have preexisting immune conditions or limbic system impairments that make them more susceptible to toxins. You must rewire your brain and reset your nervous system in order to properly heal from such an exposure. If your limbic system is working well and you are no longer being exposed to the toxin (it has been removed), you can efficiently detox without a ton of fancy supplements or treatments. Lastly, to promote health, prioritizing chemical avoidance to the best of our ability can keep us functioning at our best. In the next chapter, we will learn all about movement and rest, and how a healthy balance is key to prioritizing our wellbeing.

PART THREE

Nurturing Your Body, Mind, and Soul

16

REST AND MOVEMENT

In a world that seems to be spinning faster and faster by the minute, we need more balance. That "always busy" feeling is sometimes invigorating, but it becomes exhausting if not properly balanced with adequate self-care and knowing one's limits. As humans, we are made for a combination of activity and rest, periods of focused productivity followed by well-deserved deep sleep. We were also made to move. We were made to walk long distances and to lift heavy things. We were made to create with our hands. The problem arises when work and being busy take up greater and greater proportions of our days, leaving little time to restore the body and mind.

- Do you feel increasingly exhausted as your week rolls by?

- Do you skimp on sleep in order to meet the requirements of daily life?

- Do you constantly feel like you are on the go throughout the day with little time to relax?

- Does time seem to be in short supply in general, with not enough of it to get everything done?

- Do you find yourself feeling irritable, frustrated, or overwhelmed?

My mother and I have pretty extensive conversations about balance. She has expressed her views and perspective on rest, and how even during the very busy years of raising children, she felt that she always had a little time to read a magazine or lounge. Life seemed to move slower back then. Time and life may appear faster and busier now because of our 24/7 access to technology right at our fingertips. Our ability to check emails from home, order things online, and communicate through more than just a landline phone call can really add up and eat away at our time. Regardless of the source of our increasing busyness, it is important to carve out time to prioritize healing sleep and rest while balancing it with work that brings you purpose and meaning.

In this chapter, I will share the techniques that help me get the most restful sleep possible. For the body and mind to function on all cylinders, they need that healing time to repair tissues and flush the body and lymph of toxins. Our bodies do a significant amount of this work during rest. We'll also talk about life balance and the importance of moving your body for optimal wellbeing.

IT'S TIME TO PRIORITIZE SLEEP

Do you ever wonder why sleep is so beneficial? What does sleep do for us? During sleep, the body repairs our tissues and regulates the immune system.[1] Studies have shown that sleep deprivation can drive inflammation and increase your risk of catching colds.[2] Additionally, lack of sleep can actually make you feel hungrier during the day due to shifts in hunger hormones such as leptin, ghrelin, and insulin.[3] Because of this, sleep (or the lack of sleep) can impact our blood sugar. In addition, sleep deprivation can be detrimental to healthy cortisol levels, which will be reviewed later in this chapter.

Sleep affects the brain itself, too. During sleep, the brain's synapses actually shrink and rest for the night. This is needed in order to prevent these connections from burning out. The brain also shrinks and allows room for waste and buildup to be swiftly removed from the brain by the glymphatic system. The glymphatic system is simply the pathway that clears and filters toxins out of the central nervous system.[4]

We all know someone who needs their sleep or they turn into a cranky monster. Maybe it's your spouse, child, or you. Get enough sleep and you feel refreshed, focused, energized, and positive. Get too little and you feel groggy, irritable, impatient, and suffer from brain fog. I know the sleep-deprived sensation all too well. I know there are people out there in the world who are still a joy to be around, even when they haven't slept. They can work, they can socialize, they're polite and poised human beings. Then, there are people like me. If I don't sleep, I feel significantly different. I feel abandoned by my energy levels, more prone to moodiness and impatience, and significantly less focused and productive. Talk about an impact on wellness! Without adequate sleep, I feel like a slug dragging along the ground, not knowing where to go or what to do. Some people can even begin hallucinating if they become severely sleep deprived.[5] Conversely, my mind is extremely clear on days when I have slept well the night before. I feel calm, articulate my thoughts well, think on my feet, and have the most insightful observations with clients. My mindset is positive, with energy to get me through the whole day and into the evening.

In my clinical practice, I frequently met with a woman over the course of several months to help her work on severe anxiety and depression. Her moods were constantly up and down, and she always felt she had too much to do in a short amount of time. When we began working on stress reduction tools and reviewed her daily schedule, the topic of sleep was addressed. "Elise, at the end of a day, how is sleep for you?" She explained to me how she would put her young daughter to bed around 8 PM or so, then stay up into the wee hours cleaning and getting as much done as she possibly could. Sometimes, she explained, she wouldn't fall asleep until three in the morning, only to wake up to an alarm to get her daughter ready for school three or four hours later. As we discussed the importance of sleep and the connection between her labile moods and sleep, she became more and more willing to put in the effort to get enough sleep. We also explored her need to always have everything done and perfectly in place at home, as these belief systems were truly impacting her life.

At around twenty-three years old, I became a maniac at researching how to improve sleep. I know what it is like to feel absolutely exhausted and toss and turn all night. Even prior to my brother's death, my limbic system loved overfiring at night. This caused me to wake up with my heart pounding followed by not being able to fall back asleep for at least two hours. Sometimes I simply stared at the ceiling. Other times, I would get up and have a snack, try taking a relaxing supplement, or put some lavender on my pillow. These Band-Aid attempts did very little to help me. I struggled with this on and off for three years until my limbic system began relaxing and the inflammation levels in my body lowered. I did, however, discover many tips along the way that helped shift my body into a state of rest at night. These are simple, yet powerful.

GOOD SLEEP HYGIENE

Sleep hygiene may look a little different for each one of us depending on what our body needs. It is a combination of behavioral and environmental habits that we can tweak to improve our sleep.

As you toss and turn in the middle of the night, making yourself fall asleep can feel like an impossible task. But there are several keys to good sleep hygiene that can set you up for success before going to bed.

Using Light to Our Advantage

Our bodies use light (or lack of light) in our environments as a signaling mechanism regarding what "mode" we need to be in. Depending on whether bright light or very little light is sensed, certain hormones and chemical reactions are released. We can use this information to our advantage to improve sleep quality and duration by making changes in our surroundings. A suggestion that may be hard to comply with but is incredibly powerful is to stop using electronics about two hours before bedtime.

Two hormones work in unison to promote sleep: cortisol and melatonin. Ideally, the hormone cortisol is at its highest when you wake up in the morning. It gives you that burst of energy to get up and out of bed. Melatonin is heavily involved in sleep. When your eyes are exposed to blue light (from laptops, TVs, other bright lights from the room, and your cell phone), the body thinks, "Well, it's still light out, so I need to be awake." It then suppresses melatonin production. At ten o'clock at night, suppressing a sleep hormone is not what we want to do, unless we are working the night shift. I get it; watching TV is probably one of your favorite evening pastimes. You may love scrolling social media apps in bed before falling asleep. And wrapping up some work on your laptop from earlier in the day also makes you feel productive before bed. But these seemingly innocent habits are robbing us of deep high-quality sleep.

I enjoy phone time before bed, so I struggled to give it up. I love catching up on emails or hopping on social media. But I experienced a noticeable difference in my sleep quality when I restrict screen time before bed. I fall asleep quicker, stay asleep longer, and wake up with more energy.

Interestingly, our skin has receptors to gauge when it is time for bed based on light exposure. As evening (and bedtime) approaches, be sure to keep lights in the home dim, and if you must work on your computer before bed, use blue-light blocking glasses or install a tint on your computer. This will make your screen a calming orange or yellow color. I own several pairs of blue-light blocking glasses, and although the orange and red varieties appear funny and goofy to friends and family, I really do feel a difference in my body when using them. Since these have become increasingly more mainstream in the last few years, I get a little less roasted by friends when I put them on.

Bright light keeps us from falling asleep, but that means it is a morning ally. Exposing the body and eyes to light first thing in the morning can diminish feelings of drowsiness and improve alertness, mood,[6] and sleep duration.[7]

Bedtime Activities

Do you have a favorite bedtime routine? This can include light stretching, reading a relaxing book, aromatherapy, or meditating. There is no one-size-fits-all approach, so honor what brings you the most peace as you curate a little routine that says to your body "We are getting ready for bed."

One particular activity that many of us find ourselves doing once in a while just doesn't work. That murder mystery or thriller on TV just before bedtime can shoot your cortisol through the roof and make it very difficult to fall asleep (not to mention the nightmares). Once again, I've had to learn from my mistakes the hard way—I love historical fiction and used to read books about WWII before bed. But the poor quality sleep caused by this habit was quite apparent. I would get amped up on adrenaline while reading, and then when it was time for bed, I would end up staring at the ceiling (or thinking about the book) for at least an hour. Keep things calm before bed—your mind will thank you. This suggestion is particularly important if you are a sensitive soul like me who can't handle violent or thriller-oriented entertainment without feeling depleted or on edge.

Food

Yet another factor that affects sleep quality is the amount and type of food you eat during the day, especially dinner. Honoring the uniqueness of your body and your schedule is key. This can take a little experimentation to figure out what works best for you. If you eat an early dinner (say at 5 PM), do you later feel hungry or unsettled before bed? You may need a small snack of protein and healthy fats to keep your blood sugar stable throughout the night. Otherwise, if blood sugar drops too early, you can end up not being able to fall asleep, or waking up and not being able to go back to sleep. This happens because cortisol spikes when blood sugar drops. As we just learned, we want cortisol peaking in the morning, not at night when you are trying to catch some zzzs. It's worth mentioning that limbic system impairment can also cause your blood sugar levels to be very unstable until the impairment is addressed. This may mean your

blood sugar dips at night even if you eat a balanced, substantial dinner that is not prepared and eaten too early.

If you tend to eat a later dinner, in many instances you won't need
a pre-bedtime snack. My magic number is having the dinner meal
two to three hours before bedtime. You may have been advised not
to eat before bed because your body needs to focus on sleep instead
of breaking down food. While it is best to not be bursting full right
before bed, it really depends on the individual and what was eaten at
dinner. Low blood sugar can cause significant sleep disturbances, but
you also don't want a big meal sitting in your stomach while trying
to sleep. Again, play around with when you eat and listen to your
body. Write down the composition and timing details of your dinner
in addition to how the night went for you. Did you struggle to fall
asleep? Did you wake up unable to fall back asleep in the middle
of the night? Did you wake up feeling refreshed, or groggy? These
answers would be excellent additions to your food log.

Next, let's look at the "what" part of dinner. It can be helpful to
include a portion of healthy carbohydrates at dinnertime, as an insulin
release can invoke calm. Balancing the healthy carbohydrates with protein, fiber, and fats at dinnertime ensures that blood sugar will remain
stable. It probably goes without saying that I don't recommend a dinner (or any meal) of just carbs and sugars, even if they are healthy. A
lot of sugar before bed can affect and prevent restful sleep. You may
encounter night sweats, sleeplessness, or feelings of false hunger or nausea from eating a lot of sugar prior to bed. Some healthy carbohydrates
to consider include potatoes, sweet potato, beans and lentils, rice, plan-
tain, squashes, carrots, beets, or yucca, or breads and pastas made from
rice, almond, or cassava flour. Why can carbs be a powerhouse for later
parts of the day? Carbohydrates increase tryptophan levels in the body,
which is an amino acid that promotes relaxation and sleep quality.[8]

Room Tweaks

Beds and bedding accessories are always advertised as having been made for comfort. The softness, silkiness, and plush feeling of bedding and mattresses hook us every time. There are even more ways to cue the cozy than just sheets and pillow toppers. Keeping your bedroom at cooler temperatures in the evening can regulate body temperature and promote more restful sleep.[9] I don't know about you, but having a cooler room during sleeping hours feels pleasant and snug, especially if you have lush bedding as a cocoon to burrow into. Second, darker rooms improve sleep. Electronics with blinking lights may need to be moved into another room or covered with black masking tape. Blackout curtains are helpful if you live near streetlights. I love blackout curtains because they make a room feel like a little cave during the evening hours. You can also purchase a sleep mask for light-blocking power, either for travel-only occasions or for nightly use as needed. My last bedtime routine is a hit-or-miss with other people: I love wearing socks to bed. Putting on socks at bedtime may regulate body temperature, so if this is something you've never tried, I can't recommend it enough! It's a must-do for me.

Some people can sleep easily in rooms with any amount of lightness or dark or temperature, but if you are struggling with having energy throughout the day, this is a great starting point. Sleep is a multifaceted, complex contributor to a good mood, motivated mindset, and positive outlook. We can do many things to promote good sleep, and many of these adjustments are simple and easy to implement in our routine. The reflection section of the chapter will focus on what's holding you back from better sleep.

REFLECTION: SLEEP STRATEGIES

Answer each of the question prompts in your journal. Be as honest as possible, no one is judging. We all have little vices and habits that need to be reined in to support our sleep.

- What lifestyle factors that affect sleep quality might be contributing to your symptoms?

- What foods do you eat for dinner? What time do you eat dinner? How do these factors impact your sleep?

- What changes in sleep hygiene can you begin making today to promote better sleep? Pick one of the following categories and decide which sleep hack you will implement.

  - Using light to your advantage
  - Bedtime activities
  - Food
  - Room tweaks

BALANCING PRODUCTIVITY WITH REST

We all have varying degrees of that go-getter, pack-the-schedule mindset, coupled with a tendency to sit around. Some people tend toward one extreme or the other. To achieve optimal wellness, we need to find the lovely sweet spot between the extremes. Having too much time on our hands and not feeling purposeful can lead to depression and can make life feel as though it lacks meaning. It can keep us in a cycle of low motivation and low energy. And yet, never having downtime can create similar problems. If we feel like we never have a moment to ourselves to stop and rest, or we never have time to do things that we deeply enjoy because the schedule is already full, it can lead to hopelessness, depression, and exhaustion. I invite you to incorporate the mantra first mentioned in Chapter 5 "Rewiring the Brain, DNRS, and Emotional Patterns" regarding this issue:

"I have plenty of time to do all of the things I love, enjoy, and find meaningful."

I created this statement to help remind me that there is no scarcity of time, and that life can support me and provide me with a joyous balance packed with productivity, recreation, and also ample rest. Part of addressing this difficult feat is directing focus to one's thoughts and beliefs. If we believe we have to stay jam-packed busy to be loved or to be good enough, our behaviors will reflect that belief. This attitude can reflect fears of scarcity or missing out. Does your belief system indicate that if you aren't really busy all day, you are lazy? Or a bad friend or family member? You *can* find a satisfying, give-and-take relationship between downtime and on-time. Sound too good to be true? You may not believe it yet, but you can find this balance. The following reflection has some questions designed to prompt insights around this topic.

REFLECTION: HOW DO YOU RELATE TO RELAXING?

Answer each of the following prompts in your journal. Take time to really explore your thoughts, worries, and beliefs about your current schedule.

- Think about your beliefs regarding work and play, on-time and off-time. Jot down those inner beliefs. They can be judgmental or revolve around scarcity. Here are some examples to help get you started:
    - "I am lazy if I take time off."

- "If I took the day off, I would have even more work to catch up on tomorrow."
- "I never have enough time to do anything."
- "If I don't help everyone in my life, I am a bad person."
- "I have to prove myself to show that I am worthwhile as a spouse, parent, employee, or child."

- Is being busy all the time distracting you from pain or difficult emotions or situations that you do not wish to address? How does being busy serve you?

- Do you worry about missing out on fun or deepening your relationships with friends if you don't say yes to every invitation? Do you worry someone will be mad or upset with you if you say no?

- Are you disinclined to fill your day with meaningful activities and service? If you are, what might you be avoiding? What do you believe about yourself and your abilities? Your luck and opportunities? When I was sick I was worried that my body couldn't handle a full day. These thoughts and beliefs sometimes held me back from making even small plans or commitments.

Our subconscious beliefs can sometimes hold us back in this area of our lives, depending on what we think about staying busy or taking time off. But it is crucial that we find a balance between being productive and resting.

EXERCISE AND MOVEMENT

Just like rest, we each have a unique recipe for the types of activity we need to feel our best, and those needs can change over time. I struggled for a long time to accept this. When I was very sick between the ages of twenty-three and twenty-five, I had a very low exercise tolerance. I would get extremely disoriented and dizzy when lifting heavy weights or doing a lot of cardio. And yet, I pushed and pushed and pushed because I held onto a belief that exercise was healthy and promoted healing. I was guided in this direction by books, a handful of well-meaning doctors, and my prior experiences with exercise. During a particular period of physical weakness, one doctor told me I should take up long distance running to help with anxiety. When I finally slowed down and shifted my routine to include walking and bike rides instead of marathon-like training sessions, my nervous system thanked me. The many systems of the body responsible for energy production, including the adrenal glands, began restoring themselves to health. The overtraining had done my body no favors. Because I honored my body's needs and gave it a season of rest and gentle movement, I can now do more intensive activities like long hikes once my body acclimates.

In this section, I do not use the words exercise and movement interchangeably for a reason, for they can be very different things. Exercise involves movement, and most of us associate exercise with movement that takes effort and tires you out. But movement does not require this level of effort. My nervous system still gets a little triggered at the word "exercise" because for two years I couldn't do much without exhausting my whole system for days at a time. Movement, on the other hand, can be as simple as stretching. Movement can mean holding poses. It can mean silly dancing or a gentle unrushed stroll along the beach. When I think of exercise, my mind goes to the gym or exertion or equipment or sweating. Does yours?

Most research uses the word exercise when discussing the positive benefits that it offers. Studies have documented that exercise increases an important growth factor in the brain called brain-derived neurotrophic factor (or BDNF for short). This growth factor improves learning, mood, memory, the preservation of brain cells, and sustainability of the pathways between these cells.[10] Some studies show that exercise improves depression.[11] Exercise is also a powerful antidote for anxiety when used by someone who already has efficient adrenal gland and nervous system functioning.

It is worth noting that when the body is in a constant state of fight or flight, and the nervous system has been chronically overtaxed, the systems that produce our energy and allow us to tolerate high levels of exercise can become fatigued. Our heart rate increases, and blood flows to the extremities in times of extreme psychological and physical stress. From an evolutionary perspective, this is so we can run away from a predator, such as a tiger chasing us, with hopes that we won't end up as his lunch. These are excellent defense mechanisms for survival, but in the case of a stressful day working or a verbal altercation with someone, a chronic overflow of stress hormones breaks down bodily tissues, stalls healing, and can create widespread inflammation.[12] Addressing the limbic system, trauma, and chronic stress can also promote your ability to handle more demanding physical activity and therefore increase exercise tolerance. Physical activity can be a lovely stress reducer and disease preventer if it isn't driving stress hormone production. In many instances it rids the body of excess or elevated cortisol and adrenaline, as addressed in the hormone chapter. So, exercise in varying amounts can be the healer or a perpetuator of fatigue, depending on your body's needs. Focus on the particular season your body is in. Get brutally honest with yourself about how you feel after exercise. If the answer is "amazing" you know what to keep doing. If you feel wiped out, dizzy, disoriented, or inflamed afterward, your routine probably needs tweaking. Find what feels wonderful to your body and give it just that.

Getting exercise does not mean that you are limited to the gym or running for miles on end. While some people find this routine exhilarating and enlivening, I myself could never quite get passionate about going to the gym. Pairing movement with nature such as walking the beach or riding a bike through a beautiful park, trying a new sport such as tennis, or dancing to music are fun ways to change up your routine. The movements in restorative yoga classes can also help reset the body. My mother and I went on a fun girls' trip to Arizona and signed up for rock climbing and an in-pool exercise class. We spent so much time laughing at the instructors' comical enthusiasm we forgot we were even exercising.

Movement and rest are all about balance. We need rest just as much as we need movement to thrive. Doing things throughout the day that you find meaningful, coupled with adequate rest, is a perfect way to create a life full of love and energy.

In the next chapter, we will look at yet another factor in wellness— having fun, getting creative, and never stopping the learning process.

17

FUN, CREATIVITY, AND LEARNING

I have a little life advice for you. And whatever you are struggling with right now, there's a very good chance this advice can help in some way. It consists of two easy, simple words with hidden power behind their meaning. HAVE. FUN. Does this come off as insensitive or confusing at first glance? Have . . . fun? I know what you're probably thinking. "Excuse me, how am I supposed to have fun when I don't feel well? When I have all these physical problems? When I feel depressed, anxious, and exhausted?" I get it. There's no time for fun when so much else is happening in your world. When you feel like you have too much to juggle and no energy for anything else. And yet, this advice is something that helped me much more than I could have ever imagined.

- Do you take the time out of your day to enjoy activities you love?

- Is it difficult identifying things that you like to do for fun?

- Do you find it hard to see the positive side of things?

- Do you laugh a lot? A little? Rarely?

To read the words "Have fun" may feel silly. When I was at my sickest, with all of the physical pain and exhaustion, I can't imagine that I would have taken this advice seriously. Thinking back to that time, fun was something that slowly dropped off my schedule. My mind and day were consumed by managing my health, planning meals that I could eat, taking supplements, attending doctor's appointments, and reading every book on wellness that I could get my hands on. I was constantly researching. I wasn't having any childlike fun. In this chapter, I'm going to tell you my experience with fun. When I invited fun back into my life, I invited along with it a sense of normalcy, more joy, and (surprisingly) quicker healing. Fun, creativity, and learning are good for our brains, and I'll help you find ways to incorporate this powerful trio into your life. You will be SO glad you did!

BECOMING A KID AGAIN

HAVE. FUN. This is exactly what my dad suggested to me when I was at my worst. He didn't tell me to change my diet, go in a sauna, or meditate like some of the books and online resources suggested. He tried to get me to laugh more by watching videos with him of a hilarious comedian named John Pinette. On particularly bad days, he would gently say, "Hey, I have this great video to show you. This guy is pretty funny." Then we would sit on the couch together and watch the comedian on my dad's laptop. The rants about the comedian's less-than-ideal travel experiences, failed attempts at dieting, movie impressions, and singing would leave me gasping for air from laughing so hard. In those moments, the racing thoughts typically present in my head melted away. It was as if someone had clicked the pause button and then flipped to a different channel that was brighter and lighter. My father can always be caught laughing, often just sitting by himself. He always fills at least part of his day with funny videos, movies, jokes, books, and activities, and he often calls people who make him laugh.

Fun is a game-changer. Oxytocin is a chemical released in the body when you experience joy, happiness, and pleasure. This chemical helps heal the brain and body and does quite remarkable things if secreted on a regular basis. Having fun also boosts serotonin and dopamine, leaving you feeling positively wonderful. Norman Cousins embodied the depth and power of this concept. Cousins was diagnosed with ankylosing spondylitis and gave himself unique treatments. In his book, *Anatomy of an Illness*, Cousins discusses how he enjoyed humorous movies, stories, and jokes for an entire month. He even wrote his own jokes and laughed all month long incessantly. When he returned to his practitioner for a checkup, the team was shocked and awed to find that Cousins no longer had any trace of the disease. It truly is remarkable to consider the healing abilities of laughter and lighthearted existence. What's even more eye-opening is the fact that we have always known how to do this, effortlessly and subconsciously—children instinctually embody this type of energy.

THE THERAPEUTIC VALUE OF FUN AND CREATIVITY

Children's play is beautiful and inspiring. Their free expression is a fundamental part of what they do, and is important for processing emotions. Yet as we age, we drop much of our play and spend more time on academics, work, and responsibilities. Do you remember how you had fun as a child? Did you paint, or draw, or make up stories or plays? How did you play? I remember childhood fun. I enjoyed creating stories and casting my family members in different roles. One evening, I decided that I would be a princess, my father was the king, and my brother and mother were the staff members of the castle who took care of us. My eldest brother, who at the time was probably fifteen or so, refused to participate. I arranged two chairs next to each other to serve as the royal throne. Wearing a crown and holding a magnificent plastic wand complete with a sparkly star at the tip, I ordered the staff members around and asked them to prepare a bountiful feast (the plastic apples, oranges, and other items from my kitchen set). Other times my brother and I would make home movies featuring our stuffed animals. Some were the "good guys," and others were the "bad guys." We took turns doing the voice-overs. What a comical sight that must have been to witness.

As we get deeper into adulthood, there is less time for creativity. Our schedules fill with many, many other things. However, creativity is fundamental for good mental health. Research has shown that engaging in play and creative projects facilitate the healthy expression of emotion, processing of emotion, and promotion of insight.[1]

I worked with a high-spirited seven-year-old girl who was having a lot of outbursts and irritability at school and at home. Whenever she didn't get her way or was surprised by something, her parents would brace themselves for the explosions that followed like clockwork. In therapy, I allowed Maddy to choose whichever toys she wished to play with. I sat with her on the ground and often played along when invited. Maddy loved creating her own stories about the Playmobil figures, the castle, and the house that she picked out each session. However, many of these stories shared similar themes. It revolved around the (plastic) children being alone without parents, who were always at work. Maddy did not have a sister, but in her stories, she made one, and she assigned that role to me. Maddy decided that she and her sister lived together in the castle by themselves, but they had each other.

Maddy's play demonstrated that she had some ideas about what was happening at home and what she thought would resolve it. She also exhibited controlling behavior and would demand that I do certain things for her while playing. In this safe play space, she could finally feel in control of her environment and express her emotional needs.

When was the last time you allowed yourself to create? To make something? To use your imagination? Expressions of creativity can take many different forms; try to find your own. Writing is a form of creativity, whether it be through journaling, creating poems, or stories. Writing this book was a form of creative expression for me. Painting, crafting, dancing, singing, and making music are other forms of creative expression that can help you open your heart and share how you feel.

ENGAGING ACTIVITIES AND LEARNING

Let's talk about fun activities from a research perspective. Things that we find pleasurable, enjoyable, exciting, or interesting are often good for our health. Things that grab our attention and hold it for long periods of time can improve focus, activate the prefrontal cortex, and turn on executive functioning. Stimulating the prefrontal cortex dampens and quiets downs limbic system activation.[2] DNRS teaches and promotes the principles of elevating mood throughout the day (through fun and creativity) and learning new things because both are important efforts to rehabilitate the brain from limbic system impairment.[3]

The concept of doing things that excite us will be discussed more in Chapter 19. Time moves quickly when we are in a state of joy and complete focus. Neurologically speaking, since depression decreases the firing of the frontal lobe, then things that activate the frontal lobe can be helpful for boosting mood and wellbeing.[4]

The brain's growing and changing capabilities were once thought to be quite limited once we reached a certain age. However, new and exciting research in the field of neuroscience has made these old ideas obsolete. The brain is capable of change throughout our lifetimes, a concept called neuroplasticity, which was mentioned in the DNRS (Chapter 5.)[5] In fact, the brain is constantly changing based on our everyday experiences and activities, whether wonderful or negative. The brain is able to create new connections between brain cells and can hop over damaged cells if needed. This is wonderful news for mental health and wellness, as we now know that we can change the current state of our brains, move toward optimal health, and change how we are feeling. It also reminds us that our experiences can impact us on a physiological level in negative ways, too.

When we try new activities or learn new things, we increase the brain's capacity for neuroplasticity and the creation of new pathways. If an old pathway is not used, it will slowly shrink away. It becomes a path in the forest covered in overgrown bushes, trees, and grasses. It is no longer the highway of choice for the brain's split-second uses. What you feed, grows.

So, what will you choose to learn? What new thing will you try today? As you embark on something new for the first time, keep in mind that you may not be a "natural." You may struggle a little or become irritated. If this is a new activity, patience goes a long way. It's also helpful to avoid setting unreachable goals for yourself with a new hobby. One week of piano lessons won't make you Beethoven. I was one of those people who believed otherwise. I wanted to be able to play everything under the sun within a week or two. To my disappointment, I could barely play a simple child's nursery rhyme after my first week. One week of shooting hoops won't make you Michael Jordan.

In the book *Flow: The Psychology of Optimal Experience*, Mihaly Csikszentmihalyi describes the principles of an engaging hobby or interest. He explains that in his study, people most enjoyed the activities that were well matched with their capabilities. He states, "a piece of music that is too simple relative to one's listening skills will be boring, while music that is too complex will be frustrating. Enjoyment appears at the boundary between boredom and anxiety."[6] In order to get the most enjoyment out of the activities you partake in, you must have balance between the two. We want challenge that invigorates us, not something so complicated it exhausts us.

This topic reminds me of a client I worked with when I provided home and school visits in 2018. I was providing therapy to a little boy who had been diagnosed by another professional with a delay in his developmental milestones and learning. When I first visited him at school, I brought some LEGO car kits to build with him. The recommended age for the kits matched his chronological age at "six and up." After what felt like just moments, he grew irritable, frustrated, and stormed out of the room. However, when I replaced the LEGOs with a puzzle that suited his actual learning level, he was absolutely thrilled to be able to complete it. After he solved it once, he wanted to do the puzzle again and again and again. And he invited me to celebrate with him each time and would scream in delight. This exemplifies the concept of the "boundary between boredom and anxiety," as Csikszentmihalyi puts it.

The next reflection includes questions to help you identify enjoyable or delightfully challenging activities. When I ask clients what hobbies they really enjoy, many say, "That's a great question" or "I don't really know anymore." If this is you, rest assured that sometimes life gets in the way, and it is completely normal not to know. We also change over time, and some things we used to like are no longer exciting. If you find yourself getting stuck, have patience. Take some time to answer the prompts and reflect on how you can have more fun, get creative, and learn. You may just find your next favorite hobby or flow experience.

REFLECTION: IMPROVING YOUR PLAY PLAN

In this reflection, use your journal to answer the following questions. You can list them one by one, answer in paragraph form, or draw pictures. Use coloring supplies to add some fun to it!

- What things grab your attention and make time fly by?

- What topics or activities do you find most interesting? Pick one to research or learn more about this week.

- What is something you have always wanted to try? New things are exciting to the brain and can increase memory.

- How can you include more uplifting, silly, or funny activities into your day? Could you skip the murder mystery or thriller and let yourself have a good laugh from a comedy or some funny YouTube videos? I have included some in the Resources section. Or consider listening to music and dancing or writing down happy thoughts, jokes, and memories.

- Create a bucket list of hobbies or activities. Remember that when you try something new, it can be a little challenging or frustrating at first. This is COMMON when we don't practice these activities on a regular basis. A little patience gives our brains time to rewire that area.

For the final part of the reflection, read through the following exercise and take a bit of time with it.

- Close your eyes and picture yourself in the happiest place you can think of. You see yourself with a huge smile on your face. Pause and feel this. Then, notice who is around you. Where are you?

- Write down what came to mind. What did you visualize? Did it create any shift in your mood? A shift in how your body feels?

Remember that you can conjure up tidbits of happiness from thinking back to a lovely past memory or thinking about your future self having a great time. Isn't that interesting? When the mind is visualizing an image or a scene, the neural pathways and brain chemicals used are the same as if you were actually experiencing the event. Thus, even though we may want Disney World ASAP, our brains can benefit from simply imagining the castle, the Mickey balloons, or the characters from a favorite ride.

Having fun, getting creative, and learning may seem like obvious and simple ways to boost wellness. But often in the busyness of life these activities are pushed aside to make room for big priorities and responsibilities. Many of my clients cannot identify which hobbies they enjoy on an intake sheet because they are out of touch with the need to play and be in the flow. Severe stress, whether from physical illness or psychological pain and strain, takes away our desire for and joy in the simple art of play. Stress makes us forget our passions and what we love to do most. It can make us listless. Neuroplasticity tells us we can regenerate our excitement for learning, trying new things, and enjoying our recreational time. Bit by bit, the brain will change.

We will continue to reflect on what we need more of in the next chapter, on meaningful relationships and connections. This ongoing dialogue with ourselves is one of the most profound ways to improve our health.

18

MEANINGFUL RELATIONSHIPS AND CONNECTION

Humans are meant for connection—we are social beings. John Bowlby said, "Attachment theory regards the propensity to make strong emotional bonds to particular individuals as a basic component of human nature."[1] If you've been feeling anxious or depressed lately, or much of your life, I am certain that your desire to socialize has probably been impacted or affected along the way. Who wants to see people when you don't feel like talking? When you feel sad or just want to isolate? Relationships can also be really stressful.

- Do you resist reaching out to others for help?

- Do you find it hard to trust people?

- Do you feel that others won't understand what you are going through?

- Is it often easier to isolate than to try connecting with people?

- Do you find that people in your social circle don't really "get you"?

I'm not saying that taking some alone time is a bad thing, because it can be wonderful to have a day to yourself for self-care, journaling, relaxing, and peace. But sometimes the things that we don't want to do the most are the things that will really help us. One of them can be spending time with positive, loving, caring people who are there for you. Notice I did not specify "friends" or "family" because for some people, certain family members can be harsh or unsupportive. In addition, you may have friends who don't take time to listen to you and really be there for you. What you need during your low points is to have a handful of people you can reach out to and know that they will comfort you and hear you. People you can connect with. They may not always know just what to say, but they give you their undivided attention, and you can feel it. You feel safe. You can really be authentic in their presence. And they hold a container and space for you.

The quality of social relationships deeply impacts one's mental health for better or for worse.[2] Relationships that are supportive and caring can help reduce stress and foster a greater sense of meaning and purpose in life.[3] Having a strong, loving support system also promotes our physical health. Research has shown that healthy social supports can regulate stress hormones and reduce blood pressure.[4] Do you have some people in your life who offer peace and reassurance simply by being themselves? Are there others who make your blood boil or your anxiety go through the roof? This chapter focuses on our crucial need for healthy, **life-giving relationships** with others. Our environment and social circles have a profound impact on mental and physical wellbeing.

FINDING YOUR "PEOPLE"

My mother and I first visited Austin, Texas, in April 2016. I had heard about a yearly health conference called Paleo f(x) from several health authors I followed on social media. They had shared several posts about the conference that immediately piqued my interest. A health conference filled with many doctors, health coaches, and resources was just the thing I needed in that moment. I was starving for more information about my own health and ideas to help me get back on track. My mother and I both decided it was a great idea to attend the event. And yet, we both showed some hesitation about the trip. By that point, I had tried everything I could think of to get my health back on track. Would I really get anything new out of the trip? Would it be a waste of time and money? Could someone share something new with me, something that could change my life? We really did not know what to expect or predict. Looking back, it's quite comical that I thought I had tried everything at that point. A whole world was out there for me to discover, and I was just about to encounter it.

We booked our flight, purchased tickets to the event, and off we went. I remember walking to the conference from our hotel for the first time. I had on a pair of sneakers and comfortable athletic wear that morning, and I was enjoying the beautiful walk with flowers all along the path and Lady Bird Lake to the right. People were running, doing yoga, and stretching all around us. The air felt so warm and inviting. The weather was sunny, and a lovely light breeze filled the air. We walked into the convention center, signed in, and moved toward the front door. Looking in at the convention hall, I could see rows and rows of tables lined up and filled with food samples, supplements, and health-care products. Our adrenaline surged, and we practically skipped down each aisle, trying many tasty (and healthy) snacks and learning more about the latest gadgets and products for wellness. But this was only the beginning. Throughout each day there were many presentations to choose from, conducted by medical doctors, seasoned health coaches, chiropractors, and authors about many interesting topics. It was very hard to choose which presentations to sit in on and we looked at the schedule often to strategize. When I sat down for the first presentation and heard the speaker begin, I felt an overwhelming lightness and energy like I hadn't before. "This person understands me," I thought. "They really get me." It was the sensation of putting a hand in a "just-right"–fitting glove. It felt like a warm embrace. My nervous system was completely calm and at peace.

The rest of that weekend was filled with similar feelings and thoughts. I kept meeting people on the convention floor who knew so much about health struggles because of their own challenges. I felt incredibly validated—my experiences were known and familiar. Many presenters had ideas, suggestions, and stories about how they surmounted their own challenges. The most important aspect of the convention for me was an undeniable sense of community and the sense that I was not alone in my struggles. Many, many people had overcome something that I was in the midst of trying to solve. It felt like coming home to people who understood me. They did not doubt or question my truth. They looked at me with sympathy, compassion, and kindness and, unforgettably, with the strength that comes only from overcoming. We spent the whole weekend asking speakers many questions, mingling and laughing among the doctors and naturopaths at the booths, and riding camels (yes, this convention had camels). What started out as a trip to gain more information became a yearly tradition and a way for us to connect with community, like-minded thinkers, researchers, and resources. We do this because it is fun, because it lights something up deep down within us. We find passion and excitement and profound joy. We feel a lightness there among the others.

In the midst of my problems, I found that having a supportive community was invaluable. Being invalidated and judged feels like someone is smacking you across the face and ostracizing you from social connections, which can be painfully damaging to a person's hopefulness and positive outlook on their mental or physical illness. You need people who understand, who care about you and validate all of your experiences. You need people who make you feel heard and known, someone to say, "I get it." This can be in the form of a support group, a Bible study, an online group, or another type of group or community. The core goal is for you to connect with others who have encountered similar experiences and have moved or are moving through them. Follow inspiring people on social media who have overcome suffering or pain. Pick up an invigorating book on someone's amazing story. Finding this health conference and attending it for the first time gave me the most profound hope. It propelled me forward and kept me going.

It is important for you to know that you can overcome your own struggles and that there are many people out there to lean on for support. I also find that connecting with people who understand you profoundly lessens the blow when you encounter those who do not.

I had very similar experiences when I met several functional medicine doctors, coaches, and healers, and when I found DNRS. These individuals and DNRS gave me the validation I needed. Everything that I reported, including my stories of feeling so sick, were believed and seen fully. Not only that, each of these people gave me the gift of hope and connection because they had some real and genuine explanations for what I was going through. And they also reassured me that I was not crazy. I was also told that it was not my fault. I had carried around that guilt, that shame, and that confusion before I was given a thorough explanation for the biological and psychological underpinnings of my struggles. I had finally experienced the absolute glory of the disconfirming experience. When I met these individuals and joined the DNRS community and in-person seminar, I finally felt connected again. These people were on the same page as I was, and I felt held and safe. I stopped believing that everyone thought I was crazy. The hopelessness stopped. I stopped believing that I had to carry all of this by myself. I finally could believe that it was safe to share and that I was worthy of receiving answers and healing.

Whatever you're going through right now, I am certain there is a space and community out there for YOU. A space that can offer you hope and help you connect with people. People out there can help you through whatever it is that you are suffering from. I want you to know that you are not alone in your suffering. You are not alone in your pain. I believe your story, and I believe that you are strong and a fighter. We all need help sometimes. The biggest step is identifying what the right help is for you. What type of support do you need? The first thing I needed was people who believed me and empathized with me. I also needed someone who could explain why I felt the way that I did. I got a whole lot of that and more from all of the doctors and communities that I found. I searched until I found what I needed. It is okay to try something and decide that it does not resonate with you. That is simply part of the process and exploration. You will know when you find what works for you.

Imagine what it would feel like to be surrounded by people in your inner circle who really supported you in all of the ways you needed them to? What if they were able to meet your needs and hopes within a relationship? What if you felt loved, celebrated, and cared for every single day? Can you imagine how powerful that could be for your mental health and life? You'd probably feel like you could take on anything. Before envisioning and creating the relationships we dream of, we must place a high value on ourselves and our beauti-ful uniqueness first. In order for others to love and support you in all the ways that you deserve, you must first learn how to treat yourself this way. It may sound cliché or cheesy to "love yourself," but within these words lie deep and true meaning. To honor yourself. To respect and stick up for yourself. To know your importance. Because you are important. You are valuable to others. You have so much to offer and so much to give. You are a blessing.

I once saw a meme on social media that said, "People often go to therapy to deal with the people in their lives who won't go to ther-apy." I instantly laughed—it struck a chord of truth within me. I work with people who suffer through so much relationship discord in my clinical practice. I often work with clients on their personal relationships and assess whether those people are supporting the client's best self or creating stress, pain, or frustration for them. Our environments can either support us by creating great mental health and wellbeing or be a toxic sludge through which we can't move, like quicksand. People in our lives can help keep us stay regulated and on track, and they can also derail us. It's important to acknowledge who we choose to surround ourselves with. Tony Robbins suggests that the five people we hang around with most can tell us a lot about ourselves. Now, I'm not implying that our problems are the fault of the people around us. It is up to us to make healthy, productive decisions for ourselves because it's our life. We are in control of it—therefore WE get to decide who we spend our time and energy with. WE get to decide whether we need to remove ourselves from a toxic environment.

THE LOVE OF A GRANDMOTHER

There may be no greater energetic love than that of an Albanian grandmother. When I visit mine, she always has a very special way of making me feel loved. As soon as her front door opens, the initial look she gives me says it all. It is a look of complete and utter acceptance. It says "I cherish all of you" with an energy that permeates walls. In that moment, I feel like I'm everything. I feel loved. I feel wanted. I feel SEEN and known and celebrated all at once. She gives me a massive, giggly grin, followed by a profoundly affectionate embrace. She wraps her arms around me completely. She strokes my hair. I can feel the love permeate my being. When she gives her love, she gives freely. She embodies love. You feel it in her presence, and you feel it with her every move. I've felt this way about her since I was a small child. My mother describes her grandmother in this same way.

At our very core, this is all any of us want in life. To feel like we matter to someone and to feel like we can be ourselves and still feel safe. Everyone in their life should have people in it who make them feel this way. I am more than certain that if every person on the planet had at least one relationship, one human being who gave them this reassurance of emotional safety and support, of validation, our world would look very different. It can be family, but it certainly doesn't have to be. It can be family of choice and friends. This type of connection can be, without question, one of the most healing things for us. Healing from trauma, healing the physical body, and healing to the soul. To have someone look at you with pure love and kindness fosters feelings of being profoundly celebrated and cherished. Those feelings can't be easily replaced within our nervous systems. We are social beings. Much of our trauma is from our social relationships. To HEAL, to be resilient and still see the world overall as a positive place of love, we have to have the evidence before us—in relationships that we feel safe in.

◆

REFLECTION: EXAMINING YOUR INNER CIRCLE

In this reflection, you will have the opportunity to deeply explore your current social relationships and examine what you may need more of from them. You will also review how to expand your social circle. We ALL have the need to be loved, cared about, and surrounded by support. I use these exact prompts with clients in private practice to help them identify safe people in their lives as well as what they need out of relationships.

Qualities and Characteristics of Your Ideal Social Circle

First, in your journal make a list of all the things you look for in a strong, healthy relationship. This can be any relationship—neighbors, someone from work, family, friends, a doctor, therapist, coach, teacher, et cetera. This can even include the qualities of a pet. You can make categories such as "in a friend," "in a romantic partner," in "family members" or you can simply use one list. Come up with at least ten qualities or characteristics. If you don't really know what qualities you like or admire in relationships, that it is perfectly okay and normal. You may need a bit more time and space to really challenge yourself to come up with a list. I have included a list of nouns to help you get started. Here are some prompts to get the list going:

- What are relational **behaviors** that you appreciate in friends and family? Do they demonstrate loyalty? Do they make thoughtful gestures such as bringing you coffee? Do they make you laugh? Do they keep their word? These are just examples.

- What kinds of **attitudes** do you value in a friend? Positivity? Warmth? Kindness? Validation of you?

- How do you want to **feel** with them? As a characteristic, you may write, "They help me feel . . . (calm, accepted, confident, strong, loved)."

- How do you **benefit** from the relationship with this person? You may write, "They help me with/by . . . (self-esteem building, providing emotional support, skill building, et cetera)."

- What do you **need** from people? From community? This can include any of the preceding categories, such as behaviors they exhibit, attitudes they hold, ways that they make you feel, and what benefits they bring to the relationship.

CHARACTERISTICS AND QUALITIES REFLECTION SUGGESTIONS:

- Love
- Support
- Compliments
- Kindness
- Joy
- Thoughtfulness
- Compromise
- Excitement
- Reliability
- Commitment
- Learning
- Validation
- Humility
- Help

- Compassion
- Independence
- Challenge
- Consistency
- Coping Skills
- Loyalty
- Dedication
- Communication
- Honesty
- Trust
- Positive Regard
- Acceptance
- Appreciation
- Celebration

- Authenticity
- Comfort
- Relaxation
- Forgiveness
- Companionship
- Fun
- Humor
- Growth
- Freedom
- Confidence
- Respect
- Safety
- Quality Time

How Does Your Social Circle Add Up?

Once you have created a list of qualities that you value in a relationship, it is time to reflect on your current relationships and how they compare to this list. It is important to understand that you are worthy of friendships and relationships with people who naturally have all of these wonderful and lovely qualities. In your journal, answer the following questions:

- How do my current relationships compare to this list? Do they embody some or many of these characteristics?

- If your answer to the preceding question is "no" or "sometimes," here is a follow-up: What would it be like to have a circle of people in my life who have a lot of these qualities? Focus on the feelings, then write them down. Would you feel loved? Supported? Held? Included? Cared for? If it is difficult to come up with feelings, picture yourself surrounded by people who collectively have all of the qualities and characteristics on your list. They could have their arm around you, clapping for you, spending time with you, celebrating you, et cetera.

Creating a Life-Giving Social Circle

Lastly, we need to think about how you can receive more of what you listed in your life by adding and subtracting. Having this list and a better understanding of exactly what you want and need from relationships can be a first step in the right direction, and you're already there. Maybe we need to add a little more support to our lives by finding a greater sense of community and increasing social connections. In your journal, answer these prompts:

- Where can you find people who believe in what you believe in and value similar things? In thinking about this, reflect on what you are deeply passionate about. What do you value?

- Do you know at least one person who has similar values, passions, or interests? Make a note to reach out to them about making contacts with others who hold similar goals. Where there is one, there is a link to more.

- Write down (and brainstorm) ideas regarding where you can find out about gatherings, conferences, webinars, social media pages, courses, local clubs, and local activities within your community.

We also need to reevaluate our current relationships, taking note of what changes need to be made and which relationships may no longer serve us. This can provide great insights about why some current relationships don't feel fulfilling. In this instance, there are three primary choices. Take a moment to read each one carefully as you think about some of your more difficult relationships. You can:

- Accept that a relationship can't give you a lot of what you need AND be okay with it.

- Decide that you need more and try asking for what you need from this person IF they are receptive to it.

- Make the choice to no longer keep the person in your life because the relationship is not healthy or is not serving you. This can be a difficult choice but is often necessary if the preceding two bulleted items don't work for you. You deserve to surround yourself with people who support your highest self.

Are there any relationships for which you need to pick one of these options? Write them down in your journal. Even if you make a decision within the pages of your journal, it can take time to act on these ideas. That is perfectly okay. This exercise simply helps you become more aware of your relationships.

One important concept regarding this topic and reflection is that each person offers something special and different within their relationships. One friend may provide a listening, loving ear, while another is someone you have a lot of fun with. One person does not have to meet every single one of your relationship needs. That is the beauty of having a social CIRCLE of people to turn to for different types of support. That is also the beauty of celebrating individuals for who they are. We are human. None of us have every positive quality out there. What is important is that you identify what it is that you really need from others. Figuring this out can do wonders for your mental health and relationships.

Creating a life for yourself that includes meaningful relationships and loving, positive support is essential for your wellbeing as a human. We were not created to be alone or isolated. And yet, trauma and feeling unwell can cause us to remove ourselves socially and lose our trust and hope in people. By identifying safe relationships and figuring out what your social and emotional needs are, you can construct a solid foundation for connecting with others.

In the next chapter, we will visit the effects caused by a lack of purpose in life. Participating in purposeful work and service are essential to good health and helps us maintain an attitude of optimism, vibrance, and excitement for all that we are offered in this world.

19

FINDING PURPOSE

Many people spend some portion of their day dissociated. We've all been there. We move from place to place, perform duties and responsibilities as if on autopilot, and then do it all over again the next day. When we arrive at work after our commute, we often (many times) can't recall it. We experience a lack of meaning, spark, and true connection to what is being accomplished each day. To the present. Sometimes a sense of living on autopilot can be the result of inflammation, brain fog, or depression. Nothing is pleasurable. Nothing seems meaningful. The prefrontal cortex of the brain is not firing as strongly as it used to.[1] It can be the result of not living on purpose.

- How do you feel about your day-to-day experiences?
- Do you feel a sense of dread about going to work? About upcoming projects or something that you are in the process of working on?

- Do you feel a lack of passion about what you do or what you are going to school for?

- Do you feel a sense of ambiguity or confusion about what you are good at and what you enjoy doing?

We all get into funks sometimes. We forget what we like to do. We focus on our long to-do list and try to get everything done that is required of us. As my mom likes to say, sometimes "we're just trying to survive." In this chapter, we will learn about connecting to the profound joy, excitement, and passion for life that is our birthright. We don't have to live on autopilot. We can break free. I'll review research, present encouraging stories and examples about purpose, and review ways in which you can reconnect with and find yours. We all have things that light us up, that make us feel passionate, that give us intrinsic motivation from within. Life doesn't have to feel so hard.

TURN OFF AUTOPILOT

One of the best and most intriguing strategies that we can do to improve our mental and physical health is to connect ourselves to things that spark joy. Things that we haven't made time for in a long time. Things that weren't on the to-do list or the priority list, because they were recreational or "just for fun." Those get moved off our schedule quickly when we have a lot of other things on our plate.

I observed a tremendous gain in my health when I began moving toward goals that I was passionate about. I've found that tapping into my passions and gifts brought me out of feeling down or low.

Doing things that we are passionate about actually produces those much-needed pops of serotonin and dopamine in the brain. It helps us to feel alive, motivated, and much more prone to purposeful behaviors. It helps us get up in the morning every day with something to look forward to, something to live for.

Many studies have been conducted on purpose and health. One study examining sleep quality showed that a sense of purpose in life was correlated with lower incidences of sleep disturbances.[2] Research has shown that those with a stronger purpose in life also have a reduced risk of developing depression and anxiety.[3] Living with purpose can even protect us from the negative effects of stressful events.[4] A sense of purpose has been linked to a lower risk of cardiovascular disease and Alzheimer's.[5] We need purpose. Every human being does—for both our emotional and physical wellbeing. If we do not feel purposeful, if we are not doing things that help honor our unique talents and gifts, we can fall flat. Stress is inevitable in life, but living on purpose can affect how we perceive and process stress.

I remember the days when I did not feel a sense of purpose. This state began toward the end of my undergraduate degree around age twenty-two. I wanted to finish school, and that included goals such as attending class, completing papers, and reviewing notes for tests. But the purpose and fiery passion were not there. I had not connected to my sense of purpose yet. I hadn't found it. It is a hard thing to do if you are not feeling well. I felt like a bobber floating aimlessly in the water. Like a blob. I was completing things just to complete them, so I could check them off the list. It was exhausting. I was an exhausted bobber-blob floating around in the water; I didn't have the spark or intensity that I once had when I was younger. My eyes lacked sparkle, and I was not motivated to create things or do things. Health and purpose feed off each other. Good health provides you with the ability to connect with your purpose and have energy to put into it. Simultaneously, purpose is an incredible source of energy and power than can reignite a tired, depleted soul.

If you can tap into your unique purpose that God has created you for, and sent you here for, it is like plugging yourself into an abundant, powerful source of energy, engagement, and excitement for life. It took some time for me to find my purpose. It did not come to me in a lightning bolt as a fully formed thought one day. I was not asking myself the right questions. I was focused entirely on my health, somewhat on school, and lastly on getting those menial chores done that needed to be completed.

No matter how you are feeling, know that it is possible to find your purpose, manifest it, enjoy it, and live it. In my doctoral program, I picked up the book *Flow* by Mihaly Csikszentmihalyi for an assignment on optimal wellbeing. Flow is a state of consciousness in which we become so involved, so intimately focused, that nothing else around us seems to matter. It is simply that enjoyable. Doing something just because it's fun? Now that's impressive. Not because "I have to" but because "I want to." This can be a profound shift in our internal dialogue. As I read the book and prepared a presentation on the premises of the book, I was stunned by an example of a seventy-six-year-old woman who found it difficult to differentiate free time from her working hours in the Italian Alps. She was asked about her daily activities and what she would enjoy doing if she was rich in resources and time. Notably, this inspiring woman named the very same list of things, a mirror image of her current activities. When I think about purpose, I often wonder about that woman and whether somehow, in some way, the general population is seriously missing something. If you don't enjoy your "on" hours working, what is really being accomplished? Are you gaining anything beneficial for yourself other than a paycheck and financial stability? We can create a better way of life, find a way to enjoy each day and feel fulfilled and full of drive and passion. We can do this by putting more of the things we love doing into our daily life. Can work and purpose be strenuous? Sure they can. But as Csikszentmihalyi points out, "It may always have to be hard, or at least harder than doing nothing at all. But there is ample evidence that work can be enjoyable, and that indeed, it is often the most enjoyable part of life."[6]

CHOOSE YOU

Living your purpose is when you are living in authenticity with yourself, with the energetic current that is uniquely yours and only yours. It is recognizable as simply YOU. We each have our own energetic current, which shines brilliantly when we embrace it, when we live deeply in it and tap into it fiercely and freely. When we are aligned within ourselves, we can share our God-given gifts and passions with others and make a deep impact in this world. When we don't live in them, life gets a little muddled. Fuzzy. Cloudy.

I have spent a portion of my life trying to live in the energy of other people. Family. Friends. Relationships. I did this by trying to please others. I did this by trying to make them happy so they could be content. But that life was not mine. This kind of life is partly the result of codependency, which was reviewed in the Family of Origin chapter. One cause is trying to fit in, like many young teens do, and even adults. It can also be the result of simply trying to survive. Living this way clouds your inner knowing; it dulls your intuition and your ability to think for yourself and know exactly who you are as a person. It obscures your ability to know what you want, and why. Even though my choices over this portion of my life were not necessarily bad, or poor, or catastrophic, they were not authentically mine. I was making choices based on other people's goals, dreams, and desires. And when those choices began piling up and I couldn't digest what I had chosen, well, then I physically couldn't seem to digest anything. I could not digest my choices. I could not process my food. This is when physical exhaustion set in and my immune system tanked.

You may be wondering whether I am referring to big decisions in life, such as career choices or where to live. On the contrary, I am actually referring to the smaller everyday decisions about how to live my life, my outlook, how to feel about myself, how to treat myself, and how to look at the world. It can be incredibly difficult sometimes to choose YOU and for YOU when you don't know how. When you don't know what it feels like to stand up for yourself, what you believe in, and what matters to you. To self-activate. But deep down somewhere, you do know. You know exactly what that brilliant current of energy that is you feels like. The hardest part is putting aside other people's wants, needs, desires, and demands and connecting to what your heart calls for.

I urge you not to believe that your ideas and joys must be confined within a box of what the world and others tell you it should be. A box restricting what happiness looks like, or how your day or a job should look. Life is full of opportunities and possibilities for us to create a life that we adore. This includes choosing purposeful, deeply meaningful activities that match our gifts, talents, excitement, and unique flow of energy. You will know when you find it because you will have more flow states. You will know when you find it because life will feel lighter, freer, and more focused. Your brilliant energy will be channeled, and you will move gracefully. That feeling is not easily replaced or missed.

MY DISCOVERIES

How do we figure out what our gifts and talents are? How do we tap into our passions? Ben Greenfield, health and wellness speaker, author, and coach, offered several techniques during his talk at the Paleo f(x) wellness event that can help get the ball rolling.

We can first ask ourselves what we enjoyed doing in our childhood. How simple! When I thought back to what I loved doing most as a child, well, I quickly thought of the Florida Keys and swimming in pools (a common theme for children, of course). But my number one thing? When I was alone, I would line up all of my dolls one by one and sit them in front of an easel. I would teach them math and how to write the alphabet. Then they would "take tests" and I would grade them. I was doing this as early as five years old. When I first heard this question from Ben Greenfield at the conference, it hit me square between the eyes. I like to teach. I also used to sit in the back of my mother's van as she drove my two brothers to soccer practice, karate, school, et cetera, and I would just read. All. The. Time. I can also get into deep flow when I write. These are the things I am doing when I am most connected to God and feel aligned with him and feel immeasurable joy.

Ben also pointed out the utility of reflecting on what struggles are currently happening, what struggles have been overcome, and what has piqued deep curiosity within. Answering this question brings me right to the topic of this book and its purpose. As you know by now, I had some rough years with my physical health and mental health. I did a lot of reading and research. I am now on the other side of that struggle and continue my journey toward better health every day. I can look back and see how all of those challenges prepared me for something far greater: helping others with similar challenges, cheering them on, supporting them, and sharing my heart that is literally bursting with compassion for anyone who is suffering. And what profoundly has piqued my interest? All the vast research about health, an interest that was driven by my suffering.

But something else made me quite curious at a younger age.

When I was in high school, and possibly even middle school, I was always stumped by why some people did what they did. In my mind, a lot of things that the people around me did just did not seem logical from any standpoint I could wrap my head around. I would think "Why is she so mean?" or "Why did this person act like that?" Little Katy, completely baffled by the complexities of the human mind and behaviors. Dumbfounded. You can see plainly now why I picked psychology as an eighteen-year-old starting my undergraduate degree.

The next reflection is intended to get you thinking about your own energy and how to begin embodying your purpose. Keep your journal close by to record responses.

REFLECTION: YOUR PLAN FOR PURPOSE

Read each of the following questions out loud before circling back to answer them. Use lists, paragraphs, or pictures to answer. Pictures and drawings are a fun way to tap into the creative, childlike part of ourselves. You don't have to answer the questions in words.

- When I am (or was) incredibly happy, what am I (or was I) doing?
- As a child, what did you enjoy doing the most? What did you have simply the best time doing?
- What struggles have you overcome in your life? What are you struggling with right now?
- Has anything happened in your life that deeply piqued your interest and curiosity?

Your answers can lead you to many different ideas for finding meaningful work, activities, and even career choices. This is simply a starting point for you to look at on paper on ponder. You'll be surprised by the ideas that emerge. Give yourself room to explore these questions. Bring yourself back to those perfect, special moments—moments where all was well in the world and you felt a stillness within. You can come up with as many answers as you wish to each question.

For the last part of the reflection, you will consider what you need MORE of in your life to feel more joyous and purposeful. Identifying your needs is of paramount importance. You will also brainstorm ways to add these experiences into your daily schedule.

- When have you experienced flow? Think about when you have felt joy, peace, stillness, serenity, and connection—when the world stands still and you are in sync with the present. Create a list of activities that bring you this gift.

- What do you need in your life right now to receive and experience more of what you authentically need? From the list you just created, what one or two things can you add into your schedule this week? What tweaks to your daily routine might you need to make?

- When can you squeeze in the joy this week? Pick a time and day, even if it's for just an hour, and do something fun.

- How can you limit or manage the obligations or responsibilities that don't bring you as much joy, in order to make more room for all that does? How can you create balance?

- Do you ever feel like you can't have needs? That you can't do things that you love and enjoy right now? Does it feel selfish to you? It is important to identify whether this is a reason why you may shy away from giving yourself more of what you love.

You do not have to feel guilty for choosing something that you love doing and limiting things that don't bring as much joy. We all have responsibilities in life. We all have varying degrees of obligation.

We also deserve to be happy. The point is that you can and should make room to give yourself purposeful, joyful experiences as often as possible. They will make you the absolute best version of yourself—the best parent, partner, friend, and employee. Participating in purpose-driven acts gives us more patience for those obligations and responsibilities. Happy and purposeful people are more positive. They are fun to be around and more relaxed. They are more loving and helpful.

Although it may initially feel selfish, reflecting on your own personal needs is nowhere near the same ballpark as selfishness or ignoring other people's wants or needs. It is not about being narcissistic, impulsive, or not taking care of your priorities or commitments. It is simply living authentically. It is doing what you love and enjoy and spending time with people and things that you love and enjoy. Limit, place boundaries around, or say goodbye to what you do not love and enjoy. Yes, it truly is possible. You can have this kind of life. A life of purpose. A life that is yours. If you need permission to do so, I give you that permission.

In the next chapter, I share one of the most incredible steps in my journey to health and wellness—something that impacts the entire body. It was one of the last gifts I received in my healing process, and I constantly receive its benefits. This gift is spirituality.

20

SPIRITUALITY

When things are going well, we can't help but feel blessed. Everything is in order, luck is on our side, and we feel relaxed and at peace with how life is going. We feel like we've been dealt a good hand, with hardly any inconveniences along the way. When things aren't going so well, it can be so challenging to hear the well-meaning friend or family member who says, "It'll get better" or "You'll be okay, don't worry. Pray about it." We forget about the blessings, we lose faith in others, and sometimes we begin to lose faith in God.

- Has the idea of religion and spirituality been something that you've struggled to define for yourself?

- Do you often feel alone, confused, or lost in the hard times, asking "Why?"

- Is it hard to believe that you are being healed or guided when things are not going the way you want them to?

Research has documented an intricate relationship between spirituality and mental health. Some studies have shown a connection between resiliency in the face of life's stressors and an individual's degree of spiritual beliefs.[1] A spiritual life has also been associated with higher rates of health,[2] positivity,[3] and lower rates of depression and anxiety.[4]

What exactly is spirituality? And how is it related to religion? The definitions of spirituality and religion are unique to each individual, but in general, they are understood as a set of beliefs and attitudes concerning purpose and connectedness to others, the self, and to something sacred or important. Religion and spirituality are intertwined but not identical. The term "religion" typically incorporates a worship practice that may be part of a formal institution and typically includes an outward expression of one's faith practice. Spirituality is typically understood as more of an inward expression of such beliefs and faith. After reflecting on spirituality and religion, ask yourself, "Do I feel drawn toward this type of community, practice, or relationship in my life?" and "What does spirituality look like to me?"

A spiritual practice, believing in something much bigger than ourselves and that all of this around us is not an accident, gives us hope. In this chapter, you will learn about my own spiritual journey and have the opportunity to reflect on your own.

THE DEEPEST CONNECTION OF ALL

I am a Christian, and viewing my spirituality through a Christian lens has been incredibly influential on me throughout my life. I experience spirituality through my relationship with God. I encourage you to honor your own spiritual and religious experiences and how you authentically connect within these relationships in your life. We each have a beautifully unique spiritual journey and experience, and my hope is that you embrace your own fully.

In August 2019, I had the pleasure of visiting Peru with my family. I was hesitant about my degree of readiness for this level of activity, as we would have three days in a row of hiking the Andes mountains. In Chapter 8, "Honoring the Body's Innate Wisdom," I told you about how, back in 2015, if I tried to sprint, I would get incredibly dizzy and nauseated. A one-hour exercise class would wipe me out for a few days. I knew I had come a very long way since then, but the defeating memories lingered in my nervous system and mind. Exactly how far had I come? And was it enough to conquer these steep, high-altitude hikes? There was only one way to find out. The morning of August 12th at around 5:30 AM, we left for the drop-off point to climb to Machu Picchu. We walked over the Urubamba River on a large, sturdy bridge and heard the rushing water below, awed by its immense power and beauty. Our climb began with intense and long inclines, pockets of chilly and very welcomed shade, periods of beautiful sunshine and bright blue skies, and many short declines. The clouds were wispy—so magical and angelic. At times, my heart would pound out of my chest, and I had to call a break for our group. Other times I pressed on and tried utilizing DNRS techniques to propel myself forward. I noticed the bright purple orchids growing on the mountainsides. I placed my hands on the bedrock to feel its strength and coolness, and I stared in awe at the vivid green and orange fungi growing on rocks and the walls of the mountainside. I grounded myself in that place and in the moment. I took in all of the gorgeous sights and sounds—trickling water, a waterfall, our footsteps, and our voices.

We had a wonderful tour guide with a contagious laugh. His English was excellent, and he never tired of my relentless questions and curiosity about his country. He taught me to lean forward and use my hands to climb up the steepest inclines; this made them much easier to bear. After a long while, we took a lunch break to enjoy the food packed by the tour company. Homemade potato chips (potato is a HUGE staple for Peruvians—lucky me), an orange, chicken, and quinoa with vegetables. Peru has the best quinoa I have ever consumed in my entire life. It is absolutely delightful.

After wrapping up lunch, we finished our last portion of the hike: the road to the sun gate and the site of Machu Picchu. When we finally arrived at the site, I looked out to my right and saw the tops of many, many mountains with hues of deep blue and dark green. I stared in wonder and amazement. I had never seen anything like it before in my entire life. My eyes could not take in, and my brain could not fully absorb, all of the beauty.

I recall that scene often, and if I hold it long enough, I tear up every single time. It was a moment of magic, of incredible beauty, of awe, and of the realization that the world is full of abundance. Looking over the site itself, with its remnants of ancient buildings, homes, and sacred spaces, I could feel the presence of the Divine. The flood of peace within me was too great to think otherwise. When I think back to that moment, my heart wants to dive into the colors, the nature, the tranquility, and the stillness of the site. That day was an intensely spiritual and personal moment for me. God was there. Right there in the midst of it all. I felt an indescribable intense lightness. The presence of angels. The Holy Spirit, and perhaps the Blessed Mother. Through the entire day's journey, I was divinely guided and assisted so I could see this view and feel this joy. I was guided so that I could be shown that my old limitations were simply illusions now. I had come so far. I cried on the bus ride back down, later in the day. I cried because of victory. I cried because

I had completely overcome and reset my belief systems about my physical abilities to THRIVE.

Spirituality is a deeply personal experience, and every individual's perspective on their own spirituality is valid. It is important to understand that you are never alone—I believe there is something far greater than us that is constantly guiding, assisting, helping, and healing every single one of us if we are open to the work and to the surrender. I believe that this guiding love comprehends exactly what we need, even if we are not able to know that for ourselves. Something you wish for dearly may look like the perfect fit from the outside—a dream home, a dream job, a dream partner. But sometimes we are limited in our understanding of what will make us the happiest or best serve our greater good. You may have a lot of goals, plans, ideas. But surrendering the end goal to God—now that is another thing entirely. It is beautiful and healthy to hold desires and goals for your future and life, and I encourage that, but understand that what God has planned for you, what is being moved in your life, what you are learning and how it is changing you is much larger than your own wants and wishes. You are being shaped into something far greater than anything you can conceive or imagine. I fully believe this for you, and I will hold the thought and energy for you, even if you don't yet believe all of that is possible for you. It can be painfully, and I mean PAINFULLY hard to surrender to this idea sometimes when things are completely wrecked; I know that.

I have a strong spiritual and religious practice that has deepened throughout the years and throughout my life. As hard as it may be to admit, the events and circumstances that shaped my beliefs were also the most painful and profound events in my life. One was my severe medication reaction and having to crawl out of the hole of physical, emotional, and psychological pain and suffering. Another was the sudden and tragic loss of my beloved brother, Bert. Many times, I begged for guidance and answers from God regarding my personal health challenges and my family's loss. Sometimes I got answers, and it was incredibly clear what I needed to do next. Other times I felt like I was floating in a hopeless sea with no real direction. The waves were thrashing me about and almost swallowing me whole. But if I hadn't been in that sea, doing my best to stay afloat, I never would have discovered what that experience feels like. I wouldn't have been able to empathize as well as I do now, and I'm not sure how much I would have been able to help others. I learned so much along the way that has allowed me to give back to others. I never would have been able to share with others what helped me so much or be able to say, "I deeply empathize with what you're going through." I'm able to provide direction to others now on topics in which I had no direction myself until I went through it, met wonderful people along the road, and researched. When I see how my suffering has led to others' healing, it all ends up making sense. And the reward and payoff are indescribable in those moments.

The experience of illness moved me into my purpose and higher calling in life. I now have clarity about why I am here and why I was made. I did not see it then, but looking back it is profoundly obvious. Know that whatever you are going through right now, there is a purpose behind the suffering. It is to grow you into a deeper version of yourself. To make you a better person, to give you more compassion for others, to strengthen your will to live, your will to keep going. When bad things happen, you will be shocked at the amount of strength that comes from within you that helps you keep going. You might be thinking, "How can I find purpose from THIS?" It is hard to imagine now, but you will. I asked myself and God "Why?" a thousand times. The answer only came later. Eventually, you will see the strength that you never thought you had.

Make a greater connection to God and surrender your plans. Surrender your need for control. God will provide. Many experiences brought me to my knees, but God picked me back up again as a changed person, a better person with more wisdom and a bigger heart to give to others. You will receive blessings and people to help you. You will be sent moments of peace and calm. The important thing is to look for it, then wait. To expect that things will arise and show up to help you. They may look entirely different than what you expect and hope for. That's part of the deal, working with God. But know that help is coming. And although it will be exactly what you need, it may or may not be what you want. Let's pause and contemplate these deep, complex topics together.

REFLECTION: HELP IS ALWAYS COMING

Answer each of the following prompts in your journal. Take as much time as you need and answer honestly. There are no wrong answers.

- What does spirituality mean to you? Do you consider yourself someone who is spiritual, religious, both, or neither?

- When you read the statement "You are not alone," in regard to spirituality and God, how does it make you feel? Do you believe it? Did you believe this statement at one point but aren't so sure now? Do you feel abandoned or confused about why you are having to struggle so much right now?

- Have you encountered any difficult situations that affected you deeply or from which you gained something positive? If so, what good came from the pain? How did it help you?

- Can you think of a time when you felt deeply connected to something greater than yourself? Write down the experience. Who was with you? How did you feel? Did you gain any insights or messages? Were prayers or hopes answered? How can you create more experiences like this in your life?

In the remaining sections of this chapter, I will share more about my personal experiences with spirituality and my thoughts on why we experience hard things in life. I hope these experiences encourage you as you seek spirituality in your own way.

SERVING OUR GREATER GOOD

In the book, *The Universe Always Has a Plan,* author and spiritual guide Matt Kahn outlines several steps to becoming unlocked from feeling stuck. Matt explains that all experiences serve a unique and divine purpose intended to help you in some way. This probably prompted you to think of a few difficult circumstances, and you can't help but think, "How did that possibly help me? How could that possibly help?" I know the feeling. But this is not so much about the event itself as it is how the event changes you and causes you to evolve into a different person—someone with more compassion for others, more empathy. If you can look at things from the standpoint of "everything is here to help me," as Matt explains, you may feel a curious expansion taking place.

I also understand and feel deep sympathy for you if the statement makes you frustrated or angry. Sometimes it can be challenging to look at hardships that way. Inconveniences may find a place in there, such as mustering patience when you get a flat tire or are facing a delayed flight. A minor health issue or storm that knocks out the electricity may bring a deeper appreciation for what you have. But what happens when the bomb hits? You know exactly what I am talking about. The bad ones. What happens then? The bigger it is, the more you are being shaken to change your ways, to evolve, to become who you were made to be. To advocate. To make change in the world. These big challenges are not simple taps on the shoulder. My health crisis was a full-blown wrecking ball caused by my decision to continually ignore the smaller issues that kept popping up.

ACCEPTANCE AND FAITH

When I began writing this chapter, I wanted it to be meaningful and impactful for those reading it. I set aside time to ask for guidance from my guides—the Holy Spirit, the Lord, and Jesus, wondering what it was that I needed to say the most and what needed to be heard for healing and transformation.

In my healing journey, and in my life, I didn't develop a deep spiritual relationship and practice until I was in college. It took root during my childhood and adolescence, but the personal relationship, one where I felt truly known and truly connected, did not come until I was older.

When difficult things began happening around me, I needed the stable ground of God to feel secure. I needed forgiveness. I needed guidance from him. And I intuitively felt a deep need to receive protection from him and Archangel Michael. I sensed the need for wisdom from the Holy Spirit, the love and peace of Mother Mary, and the gentleness, the kindness, and mercy that Jesus Christ represents to me. As I grew older and experienced the changes of life, my connections with each of them deepened. And in the midst of my suffering, in the midst of my healing crisis, I came to know them on a completely new level. It was as if my eyes began to open for the first time, the fog cleared, and the invisible wall that I had built between us began coming down. The wall was built on low self-esteem, on people pleasing, on not being true to my needs, my values, and who I really am. My suffering dismantled this wall brick by brick. The burdens. The pain. It shattered my old reality and brought me into who I was made to be. I came to know God differently as a result of my journey. It is from this viewpoint that I provide my suggestions for greater healing on all levels, whether mental or physical.

First, it is important to be genuine when you ask for help and look to see what comes. This is paramount for strengthening your relationship with God. Second, it may be difficult to maintain this at first, but accept that you are SO deeply loved, uniquely made, and intentionally created for a deep purpose. The message that "You are loved" came to me in a car ride one day when I was reflecting on what needed to be learned. I hope this statement permeates every cell of your body and brings you the peace and love only God can bring.

I was also given a message of providing forgiveness. We have all heard the saying that holding a grudge is like drinking poison and hoping that it affects the other person. Not forgiving someone does just that. It keeps us stuck in the pain and suffering of the past, of what was done to us, and it keeps us in a cage labeled "victim." Whatever has happened in your life, whatever choices others made or you made that ended poorly and deeply affected you, know that finding a way to release the charged energy surrounding the events and circumstances can bring you a profound sense of peace. This may need to be worked through in therapy or in creative ways unique to you. This can include forgiving yourself, too. Know that you did the best you could with the tools you had in that moment and time. And know that people who hurt people may have been embroiled in their own emotional turmoil. This does not excuse the behavior that was carried out, or the pain caused, but it can allow a softening of the anger and the hurt. In the movie and book *The Shack,* the Holy Spirit reveals to

Mack that his own father who physically abused him was abused as a child terribly by his own father.

People cannot give love if they were not shown love. They can only do what they know, and what they were taught. For yourself, your wellbeing, and your health, I hope you will learn your own way to let go of the resentment, the anger, and the sorrow of what happened and forgive it in the name of God. Ask for help in whatever way you see fit, and ask to be released from the anger, from the emotional charge of it all. The past only exists in your mind, and although you may not forget, forgiveness is an essential component to taking back your mental health and wellbeing and moving to the light and all that God is ready to bless you with, instead of looking at the dark. If you can reframe the situation and what you learned from it, how you grew from it, and how you can help others because of it, you can achieve freedom.

FILL YOUR CUP

When someone is sick physically and mentally, they may feel depleted. And it is hard to give from an empty cup. In order to give freely of your time, your energy, your love, it feels best and most authentic when it is from a full cup. It is important to take care of yourself and prioritize your health and needs and show yourself the love and care that you have been denying yourself for so long. When you give, it must be for the right reasons, not to please other people or so someone doesn't get angry with you. When you begin prioritizing yourself, and your cup begins to fill, come back to this chapter and review how you can give to the world and to others AUTHENTICALLY. In a way that makes you feel full of life.

You can give your time to others. This can be through charity events and drives, or by providing a listening ear to a neighbor or friend. It can be through praying for someone who deeply needs it. It can be providing your gifts of encouragement, of love, of validation and acceptance. Every human on this planet needs to receive these gifts. They are vital to our sense of safety in the world, of not feeling alone.

You can also give empathy to others. This relates to validation, encouragement, and love. You will be amazed at your sense of vitality and renewed energy when you give of yourself from these viewpoints. You do not need to fix everyone's problems and every single thing, but to give to others and to yourself love, acceptance, prayer, and encouragement is to give fully and abundantly. You may be drawn to a specific type of charity that fills your heart and is meaningful to you. You feel this way because you are called to serve and meant to share your gifts and blessings in this way. Understand that this urge is a calling and a sign and enjoy giving freely, as a devotion of love and kindness to others and to yourself.

I felt this way on my trip to Haiti in 2018. We lived simply while visiting and sometimes slept outside in tents under the beautiful stars and still night air. I remember falling in love with the people, the children. Hugging them and talking with them. Asking them about their lives, and encouraging them. Donating time and money to help them access better education or healthier living conditions. I saw God everywhere I looked. It meant the world to me, and helping the people of Haiti is a cause I continue to support and hold near and dear to my heart.

REFLECTION: EXPLORING YOUR SPIRITUALITY

Using your journal, contemplate each of the following questions. Read them slowly as you ponder. These are incredibly deep and personal questions, and there are no wrong or right answers. I hope that your answers give you some insight and clarity into your own relationship with and views of spirituality.

- How does the phrase "Everything is here to help you" feel? Is it confusing? Frustrating? Outrageous? Does it make you feel curious?

- Do you have a special relationship with any spiritual guides? Do they have a name? What do you feel from them? Is it compassion? Love? Protection? Guidance? How can you create an even deeper relationship with them?

- Who is someone in your life you need to forgive? Do you need to forgive yourself? How does the information that people who hurt others are often in deep emotional pain affect your view of forgiveness?

- When you think about giving fully and authentically of your time and energy, what types of activities come to mind? If you are or were involved in charity work or service, what is/was gained?

Spirituality and religion are unique, personal choices and experiences for each of us. Having faith and hope that you are supported in ways much larger than yourself can promote a positive outlook in both the good times and the difficult moments. It also expands our meaningful relationships and connection.

This book concludes with a final chapter: "With Me All Along," where I share more about my experiences, my brother, and coming full circle in my health journey.

21

"WITH ME ALL ALONG"

Our "work" on ourselves is never truly done. To feel peaceful, joyous, and at our clearest and best we must put in the work to maintain a high level of wellbeing and vibrancy. It all begins with identifying our true needs, as discussed in the book. What are your unique needs? Are they nutrition-related? Relationship-oriented? Spiritual in nature? Do you need to change a habit? Try something new? Stand up for yourself? Learn to love all the magnificence that is you? I hope I have pointed you in the right direction to discover your own answers. Once you understand your needs, you can make daily changes to address them.

Motivational speaker and functional life coach Mastin Kipp describes doing this type of work as the equivalent of taking a shower every day. We can't just take a shower once and expect to stay clean for the entire year. It is the same with doing the emotional work. We need to be consistent and intentional about daily self-care. My "work" is different from your work, which is different from our friends' work, spouse's work, parents' work, and boss's work. Make your work a priority.

WHAT IS THE "MIRACLE CURE"?

This book covered many aspects of what helped me get well. Although I incorporated information from every single chapter of this book in my healing, some concepts offered more payoff than others. One of the biggest improvements came from the DNRS program. I believe that physically, emotionally, and cognitively, it had one of the largest impacts on my health. First, it provided me with a real and true explanation of what I was actually experiencing: limbic system impairment. When you are feeling sick, trying to figure out the real problem can be confusing and frustrating. Having a lot of symptoms with no arrow to point you in the right direction feels really scary. You go down rabbit holes with no light at the end of the tunnel. DNRS shined a light on this diagnosis for me—it accounted for so many symptoms that no other theory could encompass. It accounted for the exercise intolerance, the reason many supplements made me feel worse, and my light and sound sensitivities. It helped me understand why changing my diet and lifestyle didn't help like I had hoped. It also explained the root cause: how bacterial infections, fungal infections, medication reactions, and emotional trauma pushed my body into physical and cognitive dysfunction. I experienced the most amazing and profound feelings when I was gifted with these explanations. Second, the active practices and components of DNRS helped rehabilitate my brain and health.

Other pillars of my recovery included connecting to myself and honoring exactly what I needed. This took place in many ways over time. It looked like: a diet that fit my needs, balancing my blood sugar, moving my body on my own terms (in nature), knowing how my genetics affect my body, and giving myself adequate rest. It also included allowing myself to have more fun, and having only loving, safe relationships in my innermost circle of support. It meant the addition of more deeply meaningful experiences: a career where I could feel a profound sense of purpose, learn, and grow; cherished time spent with people I care about; and sacred alone time to spend with God and myself. It meant connecting to my grief and my brother in new ways. Lastly, it meant gaining awareness into subconscious motivations and behaviors, reviewing my thought processes and deeply held beliefs about the world and people around me. I learned from some of the best life coaches and therapists. I learned through certain programs, therapies, and workshops that those beliefs and patterns come from our experiences and the experiences of our family. It is essential that the patterns are reflected on and healed. I became profoundly more spiritual through all of this, and that made the healing not only easier but even more worth it. I became connected to God in a way I never thought possible. I believe it is because I decided to become closer to myself.

HOW DO YOU KNOW WHEN YOU'VE HEALED?

During my sickest moments and even after I had made considerable improvements in my mental and physical health, I experienced a sense of not being able to fully delight in life's gifts and connections, both large and small. I didn't want to run into people. Even the thought of being at a big gathering exhausted me, and when I did go, I would fantasize about being home alone in bed. In peace. When I think back to this period of time, I get honest with myself and acknowledge that this wasn't just me craving some me time. This was a sneaky, subtle symptom of depression and listlessness. It was an indicator of my limbic system dysfunction, and it had been staring me right in the face. When the body's energy production is low, we have less motivation and less energy to enjoy life's joys. We focus only on survival, immediacy, and priority. I didn't fully come to terms with this until my best friend's wedding. That was one of the handful of days I knew for certain "I am really healing, and this is on an entirely different level than expected."

There I was, at my best friend's wedding, dancing with friends when a thought entered my brain: "I am in the present moment." Then another: "I am having the best time," followed by "I am so thankful for these people." I did not have an overwhelming urge to leave. I was laughing. I was free. I was not tired. I was PRESENT. And do you know what else? I was GRATEFUL. I was acknowledging and honoring the moment that I was in. It was profound. It happened again at my own wedding. I looked around and thought, "I love all of these people so much. I am so thankful they are here today." I was elated and excited and delighted all at once. I had finally crossed over into the space and time of the present. It felt like I had shifted into a different reality. That is when I knew I had healed.

That's the funny thing about healing. We focus on a laundry list of things we want to be better, but we are often blind to other things that need to change to live our best life. When our bodies heal, the nervous system doesn't scan the "need to fix" list and check things off. No, our bodies heal on levels that we couldn't have imagined or created. It heals things we didn't even know were an issue.

I had lost myself for a while. My head felt like it was in a gray cloud of dissociation married to apathy and indifference during my health challenges and loss of my dear brother. Have you ever felt like you've lost yourself? That the things you used to like don't make you happy, and that you are just on autopilot trying to get through life? Life is meant to be LIVED. Life is about having fun with ease and grace. It is meant to be met with gratitude. I know what it is like to not feel this way. And yet, I can tell you how mind blowing and marvelous it is when you are healing and are able to be in the present moment. You tap back into gratitude for the beauty in your life. The people. The friends, the relationships, the love. All the magnificence that is life. It happens so slowly and subtly sometimes that you don't even realize how far you've come until you are miles past the finish line, looking back, thinking WOW. When did this happen? You are capable of this experience. We all are. When we uncover the right tools, when we tap into the innate wisdom of our bodies, and when we reconnect to our inner voice and direction, we will find that our answers were always with us, waiting to be uncovered. Our faith, our knowledge and knowing, our capacity to heal, our joy, God, and those that we thought we lost have been here all along.

MY BROTHER'S INSIGHT

Bert and I both lived in the same big city where I attended college for four years, and we met often for church or dinner. He could see me slowly breaking down with each visit. From stress, from school, from lack of sleep, from being on the go so much. And most importantly, from not being in alignment with the core of myself. He could already see the handwriting on the wall. One weekend in the spring semester of my freshman year, we both decided to visit home. I had gotten really, really sick with a cold that week and couldn't seem to shake it no matter how hard I tried. I remember sitting across the table from him at a family gathering, with everyone around us lost in their own conversations. I was just nineteen years old. He said, "Kates, please slow down. You need to slow down." The look he gave me was incredibly serious. It was as if Bert already knew what was coming, what I was about to go through. In hindsight, I could see it in his wise, analytical eyes. I could tell he wanted to say more, but my dismissive look and comments stifled his pleadings.

Bert was still with us in 2014, in the early stages of my health confusions, and he badly wanted to help me. He had done quite a bit of research for his own health, and he had hoped to offer his resources to his baby sister. He was passionate about proper alignment in the back and neck, and he also knew about specific pressure and reflexology points. One particular rough day when my back pain was out of control, I lay on the floor in my bedroom and he touched the side of my ankle. Somehow, he knew this was a pressure point that needed to be relieved, but it hurt SO BADLY. I screamed in even more pain. In that moment, he said something I will never forget. First, he said, "Sometimes in order to truly learn, you have to suffer." Then, while I groaned, he explained that in order to heal, you had to move through pain. You had to move through suffering.

I hope that by sharing my journey I can help you move through your own pain and find your own healing path. I hope that while you are in the thickest parts, the mysteries, the confusion, that you never forget the stories and lessons I've shared.

The rough periods in one's life serve a purpose. They are here to shift you (sometimes aggressively) into the vibrant core and energy that is your best self, the person you were meant to be. The hard times are here so that you can help others in some way. Although I do not know the precise reason or purpose for what you are going through, I do hope that it will be made fully known to you, and that you embrace it.

A PROMISE, KEPT

Bert had his own health challenges, many of which he kept to himself. One day in early 2014 I was walking with him at a golf tournament trying to find the rest of our family among the crowds of people. He wasn't feeling very well that day; neither of us were. Oddly, I remember being in that moment and cherishing our time walking around, just the two of us. It reminded me of when we were younger. I looked at him and said, "I promise you with my whole heart that I will find out exactly what's wrong with both of us, and one day we will both be healthy." I was robbed of the ability to fully honor the promise because I wasn't given enough time to do so for him. My brother left us far too soon, just a year and a half later. But I did keep half of the bargain. I found out how to heal ME. And I know it's because I had his help. I thought I was going to be able to figure it out all on my own, but I needed him. I needed his guidance.

I learned many things from Bert. He started me on this path of better health, better nutrition, but most of all, of finding MYSELF when I felt like I didn't know who I was anymore. He taught me that I needed to slow down. I needed to take care of myself. I needed to deeply ponder the people, places, things, and choices in my life and whether they were serving me or not. Bert wasn't about wasting time. He was about action and right choices. His inspiring view propelled me to keep going and to never give up on myself—but also, to give up everything else. Things that didn't matter. Things that kept me sick.

WHERE AM I NOW?

I am a professor, a counselor, a newlywed, a new aunt. I nourish my body with the foods it does well on, and I take one or two supplements on a daily basis. I do not experience food reactions, tightness in the chest, abdominal pain, or brain fog after eating. My days are filled with things I love and enjoy doing, and I have the energy to do them. I love, laugh hysterically with my family and friends, and I have so much fun. I LIVE. And it was all because I uncovered the answers

I needed. I uncovered clarity. This is what life is all about. It's also about having incredibly loving people in your life with whom you feel safe. People who support you and value your heart and soul. It's about having a fiery passion in your heart to do what you love and serving the world in your own way. It's about connecting deeply to yourself and to God. It's about gratitude and abundance in blessings and joy. Life is bursting full of these possibilities. Of fulfillment. Of play and creativity and wonder. Trauma and illness blunted these feelings and experiences for me for far too long. But I found out how to get to the root of it all, how to heal, and how to make my way back to my authentic, true self. A self that is full of personality, laughter, strength, kindness, and meaning.

When I reflect back on those early days filled with stacks of blood-work, shelves of supplements, and lists of saved health website tabs, I'm astounded at how far I've come. I can focus for significant periods of time on things that I love and enjoy. I love to read. I adore writing. I consider myself a generally happy, hopeful, and loving person. My sense of humor, wit, and silliness has returned, full throttle. I have felt myself return. My self-esteem. My self-love. My self-encouragement. My drive for life and my love for people. Along with it has come a deep passion for living, for my family, nature, traveling, projects, creating, discovering, and purpose. I feel things deeply and experience color and the world around me intensely. I absolutely adore what I do as a profession, and I am full of energy on my best days.

And yet, I get anxious sometimes. I doubt myself. I get tired. I am human. For many individuals, like myself, doubts, fatigue, mental health issues, and physical health symptoms fade immensely after doing the work and as you continue doing the work. The symptoms become an occasional visitor who pops in to tell you when and if you've been working too hard or are shifting out of your own unique and brilliant energy. Sometimes challenges pop in because you are ready to move into your next level of personal growth. And yes, there are days that I still feel deep grief in my heart. It is because we love those people who have gone. And love that deep never goes away.

It is your turn now, dear readers. It is your turn to move into the light that has always been yours. It is your turn to know and experience what it is like to be in complete and full alignment with yourself and your soul. It is your turn to have and claim abundant wellbeing, joy, and purpose. Remember that all of the wisdom and healing potential of the world exists inside of you. You may need to implement certain tools and skills learned along the way, but your capacity to heal is limitless and it never left you or abandoned you for one second. It has been with you all along.

AFTERWORD PARABLE

One day, a girl began a vast journey alone through a forest and mountain range. The trails were long and winding, and she had no direction or guidance, aside from an arrow pointing forward. On her back she carried a large bag full of dark and bulky rocks. These rocks were heavy, and sometimes painful to carry around. They made the girl grow weary and tired. Sometimes her knees would buckle and shake under the weight of the pack. Still, she pressed on. With dark bags under her eyes, her hair wiry and disheveled, she clung to the handles of the pack with great determination. As she journeyed through the forest and mountains, one day she neared a clearing and noticed the pack did not feel quite so bulky. The next day the pack seemed to lighten even more. Finally, she decided to stop and open up the pack, wondering what had happened. The rocks were all still there, completely unchanged. The rocks had not changed. She had. Her journey brought her to her true strength.

ACKNOWLEDGMENTS

I am eternally grateful to my wonderful support team that has made this book possible. This team includes those that were my cheerleaders during illness and healing, in addition to those who helped in the creation and completion of the book. To my husband Tim; Thank you for your patience, love, and peaceful, accepting nature throughout this entire process as I healed and brought this book to life. You have helped me reset my nervous system. To my mother, Cyndie Bosso; Thank you for equipping me with tireless resiliency, encouragement, and your unwavering compassion from start to finish on the journey. Thank you for believing in me. To my father, Billy Bosso; Thank you for your positive attitude, outlook, and fantastic sense of humor. It has gotten me through so much in my life and helped me rewire my brain. To my brother, Bou Bosso; Thank you for the amazing inspiration to do what I love, follow my intuition, and take bold chances. You have always led by example in making your own way in the world, on your terms. It has been incredible to witness. Thank you to my grandparents, Virginia Sandy, James Sandy, Luisa Bosso, and William Bosso, Sr. Each of you have deeply inspired me in your own unique ways and helped me to believe in my abilities and worthiness. To my entire extended family, including my amazing aunts, uncles, cousins, and in-laws, thank you for creating a strong and grounded foundation that has allowed me to not only access but live as my authentic self.

I am so thankful for all of my wonderful life-long friends who have been so thoughtful as I healed and wrote this book these last several years. Your loving interest in my writing and health have fueled my heart and soul. I thank too my writer's group: Anne, Becca, Becky, Ernesto, and Reija. You have given me a sacred place to discuss many ideas that I have had for a long time. Your mentorship and friendship has changed my life. I thank many mentors that I have had throughout this time, including doctors, healers, therapists, professors, supervisors, and coaches. This book had a strong rock of people and experiences to be built on. Special thanks to Annie Hopper and the DNRS team of coaches for providing the world a groundbreaking program through which miracles occur. I am thankful for my team of editors and designers at Greenleaf Book Group and Jennifer Kubiak of KN Literary who tirelessly worked to make this book the best that it could be. Lastly, I thank God for the opportunities, lessons, and blessings that have brought me to this point. This is not only humbling to reflect on, but also a moment that is full of awe and gratitude.

RESOURCES

RECOMMENDED BOOKS

The Body Keeps the Score, Bessel van der Kolk

Brain Maker, David Perlmutter

Breaking the Habit of Being Yourself, Joe Dispenza

Boundless, Ben Greenfield

Change Your Brain Change Your Life, Daniel G. Amen

Claim Your Power, Mastin Kipp

Clinical Applications of the Polyvagal Theory, Stephen Porges

Codependent No More, Melody Beattie

Dirty Genes, Ben Lynch

Easy to Love, Difficult to Discipline, Becky Bailey

Food & Behavior, Barbara Reed Stitt

Full Catastrophe Living, Jon Kabat-Zinn

Go to Bed, Sarah Ballantyne

How to Do the Work, Nicole LePera

In an Unspoken Voice, Peter Levine

A Mind of Your Own, Kelly Brogan

Prescriptions for a Healthy House, Paula Baker-Laporte, Erica Elliott, and John Banta

The Autoimmune Paleo Cookbook, Mickey Trescott

The Healing Kitchen, Alaena Haber and Sarah Ballantyne

The Hormone Cure, Sara Gottfried

The Tapping Solution, Nick Ortner

The Universe Always Has a Plan, Matt Kahn

Why Isn't My Brain Working?, Datis Kharrazian

Wired for Healing, Annie Hopper

You Can Heal Your Life, Louise Hay

RECOMMENDED WEBSITES

ACE Questionnaire: https://cdn2.sportngin.com/attachments/document/0129/7914/ACEs___Resilience_Questionnaire-McMillan_.pdf

DefenderPad EMF Blocker: https://www.defendershield.com

Dr. Axe: https://Draxe.com

Dynamic Neural Retraining System (DNRS): Retrainingthebrain.com

Headspace: headspace.com

The Institute for Functional Medicine: ifm.org

"SIBO: Start Looking to the Brain for Solutions" video of Dr. Randall Gates and Dr. Martin Rutherford talking about the trauma-digestion connection, minutes 19 to 22: https://youtu.be/Mhs2LNOmb-I

Funny

John Pinette, "I Say Nay, Nay,": https://www.youtube.com/
watch?v=VqluUUtI9hQ

"Laughing Quadruplet Babies": https://www.youtube.com/
watch?v=qBay1HrK8WU

RECOMMENDED CLEAN SNACK BRANDS

Boulder Canyon Avocado Oil Chips, https://bouldercanyon.com

Bread SRSLY (bread), https://breadsrsly.com

Culina (plant-based yogurt), http://www.culinayogurt.com/

Epic Provisions (jerky), https://epicprovisions.com

GT's Living Foods (yogurt and Kombucha), https://gtslivingfoods.com/

Honey Mama's (chocolate bars), http://www.honeymamas.com/

Hu Kitchen (snacks), https://hukitchen.com/

Jack's Paleo Kitchen, https://www.jackfrancisfoods.com/

Lesser Evil (snacks), https://lesserevil.com

Lovebird (cereal), https://lovebirdfoods.com

Paleo Angel (power balls), https://paleoangel.com

Purely Pecans (pecan butter), https://purelypecans.com

Siete, https://sietefoods.com

Simple Mills (snacks and baking products), https://simplemills.com

SuperFat (nut butters), www.superfat.com

RECOMMENDED SUPPLEMENT BRANDS

Apex Energetics

Microbiome Labs

Moon Juice

Seeking Health

RECOMMENDED PERSONAL CARE PRODUCTS

All of these products can be found online, and some may be on the shelves at your local natural grocery store, depending on where you live.

Body

100% Pure

ACURE

Alaffia

milk + honey

Pacha Soap Co.

Primally Pure

The Seaweed Bath Co.

Dental

JĀSÖN

Redmond's Earthpaste

Face

ACURE

Alba Botanica

Annmarie Skin Care

Beuti Skincare

cocokind

Dr. Woods

Herbivore

Kinship

pai

Face (cont.)

Primally Pure

Odacité

OSEA

Tata Harper

Truth Treatment Systems

Haircare

100% Pure

ACURE

Desert Essence

Morocco Method

The Seaweed Bath Co.

Makeup

100% Pure

ILIA

Pacifica

Sun Care

100% Pure

Alba Botanica

AUCTIV

cocokind

RECOMMENDED FOOD CONTAINERS AND FOODS

Food Containers

Bee's Wrap

Hydro Flask

LunchBots

stasher

Paper, stainless steel, and glass containers

Foods: The Clean Fifteen, from the Environmental Working Group

1. avocado
2. sweet corn
3. pineapple
4. onion
5. papaya
6. frozen peas
7. eggplant
8. asparagus
9. cauliflower
10. cantaloupe
11. broccoli
12. mushroom
13. cabbage
14. honeydew melon
15. kiwi

Foods: The Dirty Dozen, from the Environmental Working Group

1. strawberries
2. spinach
3. kale
4. nectarines
5. apples
6. grapes
7. peaches
8. cherries
9. pears
10. tomatoes
11. celery
12. potatoes

NOTES

CHAPTER 1

1. *Diagnostic and Statistical Manual of Mental Disorders,* 5th ed. (American Psychiatric Association, 2013), 20, https://doi.org/10.1176/appi.books.9780890425596.

2. "Mental Health Information," *National Institute of Mental Health.* Accessed January 2022. https://www.nimh.nih.gov/health/statistics/mental-illness.

3. R. Kinscherff et al. *Promoting Positive Outcomes for Justice-Involved Youth: Implications for Policy, Systems, and Practice,* Judge Baker Children's Center, Harvard Medical School, 2019. https://jbcc.harvard.edu/sites/default/files/jbcc_juvenile_justice_policy_brief_interactive_spread_version.pdf?msclkid+f9f573bdc25811ecbf810dcd76bd8f72.

4. "Statistics," *National Institute of Mental Health.* Accessed January 2022. https://www.nimh.nih.gov/health/statistics.

5. Daniel Whitney and Mark Peterson, "US National and State Level Prevalence of Mental Health Disorders and Disparities of Mental Health Care Use in Children," *JAMA Pediatrics* 173, no. 4 (2019): 389–391, https://doi.org/10.1001/jamapediatrics.2018.5399; Sheryl Kataoka, Lily Zhang, and Kenneth Wells, "Unmet Need for Mental Health Care among U.S. Children: Variation by Ethnicity and Insurance Status," *American Journal of Psychiatry* 159, no. 9 (2002): 1548–1555, https://doi.org/10.1176/appi.ajp.159.9.1548.

6. Shahram Heshmat, "What Is Confirmation Bias? People Are Prone to Believe What They Want to Believe," *Psychology Today*, April 23, 2015, https://www.psychologytoday.com/intl/blog/science-choice/201504/what-is-confirmation-bias#; Deborah Fried, "Corrective Emotional Experience," in *Encyclopedia of Psychotherapy* (Academic Press, 2002), 551–555.

CHAPTER 2

1. Garry Landreth, *Play Therapy: The Art of the Relationship*, 3rd ed. (Routledge, 2012), 10.

2. Melissa Merrick et al. "Vital Signs: Estimated Proportion of Adult Health Problems Attributable to Adverse Childhood Experiences and Implications for Preventions--25 States, 2015–2017," *Morbidity and Mortality Weekly Report* 68, no. 44 (November 8, 2019): 999–1005, https://doi.org/10.15585/mmwr.mm6844e1.

3. John Bowlby, *A Secure Base: Parent-Child Attachment and Healthy Human Development* (Routledge, 1988), 30.

4. Sue Johnson, *Hold Me Tight: Seven Conversations for a Lifetime of Love* (Little, Brown, 2008), 17.

5. Amir Levine and Rachel Heller, *Attached: The New Science of Adult Attachment and How it Can Help You Find—and Keep—Love* (Tarcher Perigee, 2011), 8.

6. K. Bartholomew and L. M. Horowitz, "Attachment Styles among Young Adults: A Test of a Four-Category Model," *Journal of Personality and Social Psychology* 61, no. 2 (1991): 226–244, https://doi.org/10.1037/0022-3514.61.2.226.

7. M. Gerard Fromm, ed., *Lost in Transmission: Studies of Trauma across Generations* (Routledge, 2012).

8. Melody Beattie, *Codependent No More: How to Stop Controlling Others and Start Caring for Yourself* (Hazelden Publishing, 1992), 1.

CHAPTER 3

1. Stephen Porges, "Connectedness As a Biological Imperative: Understanding Trauma through the Lens of the Polyvagal Theory." Presented at the New England Society for Trauma and Dissociation, December 6, 2014; Stephen Porges, *The Polyvagal Theory: Neurophysiological Foundations of Emotions, Attachment, Communication, and Self-regulation* (W. W. Norton, 2011), loc. 368, Kindle.

2. Bessel van der Kolk, *The Body Keeps the Score: Brain, Mind, and Body in the Healing of Trauma* (Viking, 2014).

3. van der Kolk, *The Body Keeps the Score.*

4. Eric Kandel et al. *Principles of Neural Science*, 5th ed. (McGraw-Hill, 2013).

5. *Diagnostic and Statistical Manual of Mental Disorders,* 5th ed. (American Psychiatric Association, 2013), 271, https://doi.org/10.1176/appi.books.9780890425596.

6. Rosenthal, *Your Life after Trauma.*

CHAPTER 4

1. John James and Russell Friedman, *The Grief Recovery Handbook: The Action Program for Moving Beyond Death, Divorce, and Other Losses* (William Morrow, 2017).

2. https://www.goodreads.com/quotes/9657488-grief-i-ve-learned-is-really-just-love-it-s-all-the.

CHAPTER 5

1. Annie Hopper, *Wired for Healing: Remapping the Brain to Recover from Chronic and Mystery Illnesses* (The Dynamic Neural Retraining System, 2014).

2. Jon Kabat-Zinn, *Full Catastrophe Living: Using the Wisdom of Your Body and Mind to Face Stress, Pain, and Illness* (Bantam Books, 2013).

CHAPTER 6

1. Christina Spinelli, Melanie Wisener, and Bassam Khoury, "Mindfulness Training for Healthcare Professionals and Trainees: A Meta-Analysis of Randomized Controlled Trials," *Journal of Psychosomatic Research* 120 (2019): 29–39.

2. Louise Champion, Marcos Economides, and Chris Chandler, "The Effectiveness of a Brief App-Based Mindfulness Intervention on Psychosocial Outcomes in Healthy Adults: A Pilot Randomized Controlled Trial," *PLOS ONE* 13, no. 12 (2018): 1–20.

3. Rongxiang Tang, Karl Friston, and Yi-Yuan Tang, "Brief Mindfulness Meditation Induces Gray Matter Changes in a Brain Hub," *Neural Plasticity* (2020), https://doi.org/10.1155/2020/8830005.

4. Adrienne Taren, J. David Creswell, and Peter Gianaros, "Dispositional Mindfulness Co-varies with Small Amygdala and Caudate Volumes in Community Adults," *PLOS ONE* 8, no. 5 (2013), https://doi.org/10.1371/journal.pone.0064574.

5. J. Douglas Bremner, "Effects of Traumatic Stress on Brain Structure and Function: Relevance to Early Responses to Trauma," *Journal of Trauma & Dissociation*, 6, no. 2 (2002): 51–68, https://doi.org/10.1300/J229v06n02_06.

6. Tammi R. A. Kral et al. "Impact of Short- and Long-Term Mindfulness Meditation Training on Amygdala Reactivity to Emotional Stimuli," *Neuroimage* (2018): 181, https://doi.org/10.1016/j.neuroimage.2018.07.013.

7. Anna Lardone et al. "Mindfulness Meditation is Related to Long-Lasting Changes in Hippocampal Functional Topology during Resting State: A Magnetoencaphalography Study," *Journal of Neural Transplantation & Plasticity* (2018): 5340717–5340719, https://doi.org/10.1155/2018/5340717.

8. Habib Yaribeygi et al. "The Impact of Stress on Body Function: A Review," *EXCLI Journal* (2017): 16, http://dx.doi.org/10.17179/excli2017-480.

CHAPTER 7

1. Qing Li, "Effect of Forest Bathing Trips on Human Immune Function," *Environmental Health and Preventative Medicine* (2010): 15, https://doi.org/10.1007/s12199-008-0068-3.

2. Akemi Furuyashiki et al. "A Comparative Study of the Physiological and Psychological Effects of Forest Bathing (Shinrin Yoku) on Working Age People with and without Depressive Tendencies," *Environmental Health and Preventive Medicine* 24, no. 1 (2019): 46–46, https://doi.org/10.1186/s12199-019-0800-1.

3. Andrea Faber Tayor and Frances E. Kuo, "Children with Attention Deficits Concentrate Better after a Walk in the Park," *Journal of Attention Disorders* 12, no. 5 (2009), https://doi.org/10.1177/1087054708323000.

4. Gregory Bratman et al. "The Benefits of Nature Experience: Improved Affect and Cognition," *Landscape and Urban Planning* 138 (2015): 41–50, https://doi.org/10.1016/j.landurbplan.2015.02.005.

5. Bratman et al. "The Benefits of Nature Experience."

6. Owen Wong et al. "Does Gratitude Writing Improve the Mental Health of Psychotherapy Clients? Evidence from a Randomized Controlled Trial," *Psychotherapy Research* 28, no. 2 (2018): 192–202, https://doi.org/10.1080/10503307.2016.1169332.

7. Natasha Loi and Di Helen Ng, "The Relationship between Gratitude, Wellbeing, Spirituality, and Experiencing Meaningful Work," *Psych* 3, no. 2 (2021): 85–95, https://doi.org/10.3390/psych3020009.

8. Ernest Bohlmeijer et al. "Promoting Gratitude as a Resource for Sustainable Mental Health: Results of a 3-Armed Randomized Controlled Trial Up to 6 Months Follow-Up," *Journal of Happiness Studies* 22, no. 3 (2020): 1011–1032, https://doi.org/10.1007/s10902-020-00261-5.

9. Greg Siegle et al. "Increased Amygdala and Decreased Dorsolateral Prefrontal BOLD Responses in Unipolar Depression: Related and Independent Features," *Biological Psychiatry* 61, no. 2 (2007): 198–209, https://doi.org/10.1016/j.biopsych.2006.05.048.

CHAPTER 9

1.   Datis Kharrazian, *Why Isn't My Brain Working? A Revolutionary Understanding of Brain Decline and Effective Strategies to Recover Your Brain's Health* (Elephant Press, 2013).

2.   "How to Treat Low Blood Sugar," *Centers for Disease Control and Prevention*, Accessed March 25, 2021). https://www.cdc.gov/diabetes/basics/low-blood-sugar-treatment.html.

3.   Chris Kresser, "How to Prevent Diabetes and Heart Disease for $16," *Chris Kresser* (blog), March 17, 2019. https://chriskresser.com/how-to-prevent-diabetes-and-heart-disease-for-16/.

4.   Chris Kresser, "Why Your 'Normal' Isn't Normal (Part 2)," *Chris Kresser* (blog), November 18, 2010. http://chriskresser.com/when-your-"normal"-blood-sugar-isn't-normal-part-2/.

5.   P. J. Lustman et al. "Depression and Poor Glycemic Control: A Meta-Analytic Review of the Literature," *Diabetes Care* 23, no. 7 (2000), https://doi.org/10.2337/diacare.23.7.934; Andrew Green, Kathleen Fox, and Susan Grandy, "Self-Reported Hypoglycemia and Impact on Quality of Life and Depression among Adults with Type 2 Diabetes Mellitus," *Diabetes Research in Clinical Practice* 96, no. 3 (2012), https://doi.org/10.1016/j.diabres.2012.01.002; Kate Beecher et al. "Long-Term Overconsumption of Sugar Starting at Adolescence Produces Persistent Hyperactivity and Neurocognitive Deficits in Adulthood," *Frontiers in Neuroscience* 15 (2021), http://dx.doi.org/10.3389/fnins.2021.670430.

CHAPTER 10

1.   Julia Bird et al. "Risk of Deficiency in Multiple Concurrent Micronutrients in Children and Adults," *Nutrients* 9, no. 7 (2017), https://doi.org/10.3390/nu9070655; Chris Kresser, "Well Fed but Undernourished: An American Epidemic," *Chris Kresser* (blog), April 28, 2018. https://kresserinstitute.com/well-fed-but-undernourished-an-american-epidemic/.

2. Ian Darnton-Hill, "Public Health Aspects in the Prevention and Control of Vitamin Deficiencies," *Current Developments in Nutrition* 3, no. 9 (2019), https://doi.org/10.1093/cdn/nzz075.

3. Aditi Hazra et al. (2008), "Common Variants of FUT2 Are Associated with Plasma Vitamin B12 Levels," *Nature Genetics* 40, no. 10 (2008): 1160–1162, https://doi.org/10.1038/ng.210; Patrick Broel and Charles Desmarchelier, "Genetic Variations Associated with Vitamin A Status and Vitamin A Bioavailability," *Nutrients* 9, no. 3 (2017), https://doi.org/10.3390/nu9030246; Keith Keene et al. "Genetic Associations with Plasma B12, B6, and Folate Levels in an Ischemic Stroke Population from the Vitamin Intervention for Stroke Prevention (VISP) Trial," *Frontiers in Public Health* 2 (2014): 112–112, https://doi.org/10.3389/fpubh.2014.00112.

4. James DiNicolantonio, James O'Keefe, and William Wilson, "Sugar Addiction: Is It Real? A Narrative Review," *British Journal of Sports Medicine* 52, no. 14 (2018): 910–913, https://doi.org/10.1136/bjsports-2017-097971.

5. Erica Schulte, Nicole Avena, and Ashley Gearhardt, "Which Foods May Be Addictive? The Roles of Processing, Fat Content, and Glycemic Load," *PLOS ONE* 10, no. 2 (2015), https://doi.org/10.1371/journal.pone.0117959.

CHAPTER 11

1. Shima Azizzadeph-Roodpish, Max Garzon, and Sambriddhi Mainali, "Classifying Single Nucleotide Polymorphisms in Humans," *Molecular Genetics and Genomics* 296, no. 5 (2021), https://doi.org/10.1007/s00438-021-01805-x.

2. Pingyuan Gong et al "Revisiting the Impact of OXTR rs53576 on Empathy: A Population-Based Study and a Meta Analysis," *Psychoneuroendocrinology* 80 (2017): 131–136, https://doi.org/10.1016/j.psyneuen.2017.03.005.

3. Laura Maintz and Natalija Novak, "Histamine and Histamine Intolerance," *American Journal of Clinical Nutrition* 85, no. 5 (2007): 1185–1196, https://doi.org/10.1093/ajcn/85.5.1185.

4. Amanda Schlueter and Carol Johnston, "Vitamin C: Overview and Update," *Journal of Evidence-Based Integrative Medicine* (2011), https://doi.org/10.1177/1533210110392951.

5. Traci Stein, "A Genetic Mutation That Can Affect Mental & Physical Health," *Psychology Today*, September 5, 2014. https://www.psychologytoday.com/us/blog/the-integrationist/201409/genetic-mutation-can-affect-mental-physical-health.

6. Lin Wan et al. "Methylenetetrahydrofolate Reductase and Psychiatric Diseases," *Translational Psychiatry* 8, no. 1 (2018): 242, https://doi.org/10.1038/s41398-018-0276-6; Kevin Krull et al. "Folate Pathway Genetic Polymorphisms Are Related to Attention Disorders in Childhood Leukemia Survivors," *The Journal of Pediatrics* (2008), https://doi.org/10.1016/j.jpeds.2007.05.047.

7. "MTHFR," Public Health Genomics and Precision Health Knowledge Base, *Centers for Disease Control and Prevention*, Accessed March 7, 2022. https://phgkb.cdc.gov/PHGKB/huGEPedia. action?firstQuery=MTHFR&geneID=4524&typeSubmit=GO&check=y&typeOption=gene&which=2&pubOrderType=pubD.

8. Ben Lynch, *Dirty Genes: A Breakthrough Program to Treat the Root Cause of Illness and Optimize Your Health* (HarperCollins, 2018).

CHAPTER 12

1. *Merriam-Webster*, s.v. "Hormone (*n.*)," Accessed April 22, 2022. https://www.merriam-webster.com/dictionary/hormone.

2. Stephen Nussey and Saffron Whitehead, *Endocrinology: An Integrated Approach* (Oxford: BIOS Scientific Publishers 2001).

3. Maggie Armstrong, Edinen Asuka, and Abbey Fingeret, "Physiology, Thyroid Function," in *National Library of Medicine*, March 23, 2021, https://www.ncbi.nlm.nih.gov/books/NBK537039/.

4. Mariusz Stasiolek, "Neurological Symptoms and Signs in Thyroid Disease," *Thyroid Research* (2015): 8, https://doi.org/ 10.1186/1756-6614-8-S1-A25.

5. "General Information/Press Room," *American Thyroid Association*, https://www.thyroid.org/media-main/press-room/.

6. Datis Kharrazian, *Why Do I Still Have Thyroid Symptoms when My Labs Are Normal?* (Elephant Press, 2010).

7. Layal Chaker et al. "Hypothyroidism," *Lancet* 390, no. 10101 (2017): 1550–1562, https://doi.org/10.1016/S0140-6736(17)30703-1.

8. "Hyperthyroidsim (Overactive Thyroid)," *Mayo Clinic*. Accessed November 14, 2020. https://www.mayoclinic. org/diseases-conditions/hyperthyroidism/symptoms-causes/ syc-20373659.

9. Amy Arnsten, "Stress Signalling Pathways That Impair Prefrontal Cortex Structure and Function," *Nature Reviews Neuroscience* 10, no. 6 (2009): 410–422, https://doi.org/10.1038/nrn2648; Hyo Jung Kang et al. "Decreased Expression of Synapse-Related Genes and Loss of Synapses in Major Depressive Disorder," *Nature Medicine* 18, no. 9 (2012): 1413–1417, https://doi.org/10.1038/nm.2886.

10. Michael van der Kooij et al. "Role for MMP-9 in Stress-Induced Downregulation of Nectin-3 in Hippocampal CA1 and Associated Behavioural Alterations," *Nature Communications* 5, no. 1 (2014): 4995–4995, https://doi.org/10.1038/ncomms5995.

11. J. Tintera, *Hypocortisolism*, 8th ed. (Adrenal Metabolic Research Society, Hypoglycemic Foundation Inc., 1974); James Wilson, "Clinical Perspectives on Stress, Cortison, and Adrenal Fatigue," *Advances in Integrative Medicine* 1, no. 2 (2014): 93–96, https:// doi.org/10.1016/j.aimed.2014.05.002.

12. Pai-Cheng Lin et al. "Insomnia, Inattention and Fatigue Symptoms of Women with Premenstrual Dysphoric Disorder," *International Journal of Environmental Research and Public Health* 18, no. 12 (2021): 6192, https://doi.org/10.3390/ijerph18126192; Stephanie Collins Reed, Frances Levin, and Suzette Evans, "Changes in Mood,

Cognitive Performance and Appetite in the Late Luteal and Follicular Phases of the Menstrual Cycle in Women with and without PMDD (Premenstrual Dysphoric Disorder)," *Hormones and Behavior* 54, no. 1 (2008): 185–193, https://doi.org/10.1016/j.yhbeh.2008.02.018.

13. Yaelim Lee and Eun-Ok Im, "Stress and Premenstrual Symptoms in Reproductive-Aged Women," *Health Care for Women International* 37, no. 6 (2016): 646–670, https://doi.org/10.1080/07399332.2015.1049352.

14. Walter Crinnion, "Toxic Effects of the Easily Avoidable Phthalates and Parabens," *Alternative Medicine Review* 15, no. 3 (2010): 190–196.

15. Cynthia Metz, "Bisphenol A," *Workplace Health & Safety* 64, no. 1 (2016): 28–36, https://doi.org/10.1177/2165079915623790.

16. Sara Gottfried, *The Hormone Reset Diet: Heal Your Metabolism to Lose Up to 15 Pounds in 21 Days* (HarperOne, 2016).

17. Datis Kharrazian, *Why Isn't My Brain Working? A Revolutionary Understanding of Brain Decline and Effective Strategies to Recover Your Brain's Health* (Elephant Press, 2013).

18. "PCOS (Polycystic Ovary Syndrome) and Diabetes," Centers for Disease Control and Prevention. Accessed March 24, 2020. https://www.cdc.gov/diabetes/basics/pcos.html.

19. Kharrazian, *Why Isn't My Brain Working?*

CHAPTER 13

1. Herbert Dupont et al. "The Intestinal Microbiome in Human Health and Disease," *Transactions of the American Clinical and Climatological Association* 131 (2020): 191.

2. Melinda Engevik et al. "Microbial Metabolic Capacity for Intestinal Folate Production and Modulation of Host Folate Receptors," *Frontiers in Microbiology* 10 (2019): 2305, https://doi.org/10.3389/fmicb.2019.02305.

3. Siri Carpenter, "That Gut Feeling," *Monitor on Psychology* 43, no. 8 (2012), https://www.apa.org/monitor/2012/09/gut-feeling.

4. Hui Duan et al. "Antibiotic-Induced Gut Dysbiosis and Barrier Disruption and the Potential Protective Strategies," *Critical Reviews in Food Science and Nutrition* 62, no. 6 (2022): 1427–1452, https://doi.org/10.1080/10408398.2020.1843396.

5. Batian Seelbinder et al. "Antibiotics Create a Shift from Mutualism to Competition in Human Gut Communities with a Longer Lasting Impact on Fungi than Bacteria," *Microbiome* 8 no. 1 (2020): 133, https://doi.org/10.1186/s40168-020-00899-6.

6. Michael Maes, Marta Kubera, and Jean-Claude Leunis, "The Gut-Brain Barrier in Major Depression: Intestinal Mucosal Dysfunction with an Increased Translocation of LPS from Gram-Negative Enterobacteria (Leaky Gut) Plays a Role in the Inflammatory Pathophysiology of Depression," *Neuro Endocrinology Letters* 29 (2008): 117–124.

7. Giampaolo Perna et al. "Are Anxiety Disorders Associated with Accelerated Aging? A Focus on Neuroprogression," *Neural Plasticity* (2016): 1–19. https://doi.org/10.1155/2016/8457612.

8. Hai-yin Jiang et al. "Altered Gut Microbiota Profile in Patients with Generalized Anxiety Disorder," *Journal of Psychiatric Research* 104 (2018): 130–136, https://doi.org/10.1016/j.jpsychires.2018.07.007.

9. Michal Werbner et al. "Social-Stress-Responsive Microbiota Induces Stimulation of Self-Reactive Effector T Helper Cells," *mSystems* 4, no. 4 (2019), https://doi.org/10.1128/mSystems.00292-18.

10. Datis Kharrazian, *Why Isn't My Brain Working? A Revolutionary Understanding of Brain Decline and Effective Strategies to Recover Your Brain's Health* (Elephant Press, 2013), 164.

CHAPTER 14

1. Lars Hanson et al. "The Transfer of Immunity from Mother to Child," *Annals of the New York Academy of Sciences* 987, no. 1 (2003): 199–206, https://doi.org/10.1111/j.1749-6632.2003.tb06049.x.

2. Herbert Renz-Polster et al. "Caesarean Section Delivery and the Risk of Allergic Disorders in Childhood," *Clinical* *and Experimental Allergy* 35, no. 11 (2005), https://doi.org/10.1111/j.1365-2222.2005.02356.x.

3. Selma Wiertsema et al. "The Interplay between the Gut Microbiome and the Immune System in the Context of Infectious Diseases throughout Life and the Role of Nutrition in Optimizing Treatment Strategies," *Nutrients* 13, no. 2 (2021), https://doi.org/10.3390/nu13030886.

4. Ashwin Skelly et al. "Mining the Microbiota for Microbial and Metabolite Based Immunotherapies," *Nature Reviews Immunology* 19, no. 5 (2019): 305–323, https://doi.org/10.1038/s41577-019-0144-5; Dana Kadosh and Naama Geva-Zatorsky, "How Do Gut Bacteria Regulate Our Immune System" *Frontiers for Young Minds*, July 15, 2021, https://doi.org/10.3389/frym.2021.721325.

5. Stefani Lobionda et al. "The Role of Gut Microbiota in Intestinal Inflammation with Respect to Diet and Extrinsic Stressors," *Microorganisms* 7, no. 8 (2019), https://doi.org/10.3390/microorganisms7080271.

6. Eleanor Busby et al. "Mood Disorders and Gluten: It's Not All in Your Mind! A Systematic Review with Meta-Analysis," *Nutrients* 10, no. 11 (2018): 1708, https://doi.org/10.3390/nu10111708; Verena Ly et al. "Elimination Diets' Efficacy and Mechanisms in Attention Deficit Hyperactivity Disorder and Autism Spectrum Disorder," *European Child & Adolescent Psychiatry* 26, no. 9 (2017): 1067–1079, https://doi.org/10.1007/s00787-017-0959-1.

7. Yijing Chen, Jinying Xu, and Yu Chen, "Regulation of Neurotransmitters by the Gut Microbiota and Effects on Cognition in Neurological Disorders," *Nutrients* 13, no. 6 (2021), https://doi.org/10.3390/nu13062099.

8. Michael Maes et al. "Increased IgA and IgM Responses against Gut Commensals in Chronic Depression: Further Evidence for Increased Bacterial Translocation or Leaky Gut," *Journal of Affective Disorders* 141, no. 1 (2012): 55–62, https://doi.org/10.1016/j.jad.2012.02.023; Megan Clapp et al. "Gut Microbiota's Effect on Mental Health: The Gut Brain Axis," *Clinics and Practice* 7, no. 4 (2017): 131–136, https://doi.org/10.4081/cp.2017.987.

9. D. Bernardo et al. "Is Gliadin Really Safe for Non-Coeliac Individuals? Production of Interleukin 15 in Biopsy Culture from Non-Coeliac Individuals Challenged with Gliadin Peptides," *Gut* 56, no. 6 (2007): 889–890: https://doi.org/10.1136/gut.2006.118265.

10. Sylvia Cruchet et al. "Truths, Myths and Needs of Special Diets: Attention-Deficit/Hyperactivity Disorder, Autism, Non-Celiac Gluten Sensitivity, and Vegetarianism," *Annals of Nutrition and Metabolism* 68, no. 1 (2016): 43–50, https://doi.org/10.1159/000445393.

11. "Lactose Intolerance," *Mayo Clinic.* Accessed March 5, 2022. https://www.mayoclinic.org/diseases-conditions/lactose-intolerance/symptoms-causes/syc-20374232.

12. Mehrnaz Nouri et al. "Intestinal Barrier Dysfunction Develops at the Onset of Experimental Autoimmune Encaphlomyelitis, and Can Be Induced By Adoptive Transfer of Auto-Reactive," *PLOS ONE* 9, no. 9 (2014): e106335, https://doi.org/10.1371/journal.pone.0106335; Alessio Fasano, "Leaky Gut and Autoimmune Diseases," *Clinical Reviews in Allergy & Immunology* 42 (2012): 71–78, https://doi.org/10.1007/s12016-011-8291-x.

13. Bilal Ahmad Paray et al. "Leaky Gut and Autoimmunity: An Intricate Balance in Individuals Health and Diseased State," *International Journal of Molecular Sciences* 21 (2020), https://doi.org/10.3390/ijms21249770.

14. Isobel Leake, "Is There a Link between Stress and Autoimmunity?," *Nature Reviews Rheumatology* 14, no. 8 (2018): 442, https://doi.org/10.1038/s41584-018-0053-1; G. Zheng et al. "Corticosterone Mediates Stress-Related Increased Intestinal Permeability in a Region-Specific Manner," *Neurogastroenterology and Motility* 25, no. 2 (2013): e127–e139, https://doi.org/10.1111/nmo.12066.

15. Qin Xiang Ng et al. "Systematic Review with Meta-Analysis: The Association between Post-Traumatic Stress Disorder and Irritable Bowl Syndrome," *Journal of Gastroenterology and Hepatology* 34 (2018): 68–73, https://doi.org/10.1111/jgh.14446.

16.   Patricia Andreski, Howard Chilcoat, and Naomi Breslau, "Post-Traumatic Stress Disorder and Somatization Symptoms: A Prospective Study," *Psychiatry Research* 79, no. 2 (1998): 131–138, https://doi.org/10.1016/s0165-1781(98)00026-2.

17.   Annelise Madison and Janice Kiecolt-Glaser, "Stress, Depression, Diet, and the Gut Microbiota: Human Bacteria Interactions at the Core of Phsychoneuroimmunology and Nutrition," *Current Opinion in Behavioral Sciences* 28 (2019): 105–110, https://doi.org/10.1016/j.cobeha.2019.01.011.

18.   Timothy Dinan and John Cryan, "Regulation of the Stress Response by the Gut Microbiota: Implications for Psychoneuroendocrinology," *Psychoneuroendocrinology (2012)*, https://doi.org/10.1016/j.psyneuen.2012.03.007.

CHAPTER 15

1.   David D'Cruz, "Autoimmune Diseases Associated with Drugs, Chemicals, and Environmental Factors," *Toxicology Letters* 112 (2000): 421–432, https://doi.org/10.1016/S0378-4274(99)00220-9; Lifeng Wang, Fu-Sheng Wang, and M. Eric Gershwin, "Human Autoimmune Diseases: A Comprehensive Update," *Journal of Internal Medicine* 278, no. 4 (2015): 369–395, https://doi-org.proxy.pba.edu/10.1111/joim.12395; Sarah Ballantyne, *The Paleo Approach: Reverse Autoimmune Disease and Heal Your Body* (Victory Belt, 2013), 48–29.

2.   San-Nan Yang et al. "The Effects of Environmental Toxins on Allergic Inflammation," *Allergy, Asthma & Immunology Research* 6, no. 6 (2014): 478–484, https://doi.org/10.4168/aair.2014.6.6.478.

3.   Stephen Genuis, "Sensitivity-Related Illness: The Escalating Pandemic of Allergy, Food Intolerance and Chemical Sensitivity," *The Science of the Total Environment* 408, no. 24 (2010): 6047–6061, https://doi.org/10.1016/j.scitotenv.2010.08.047.

4.   Aleksandra Buha Djordjevic et al. "Endocrine-Disrupting Mechanisms of Polychlorinated Biphenyls," *Current Opinion in Toxicology* 19 (2020): 42–49, https://doi.org/10.1016/j.cotox.2019.10.006.

5. J. Medlin, "Environmental Toxins and the Brain," *Environmental Health Perspectives* 104, no. 8 (1996): 822–823, https://doi.org/10.1289/ehp.96104822.

6. Agnes Chan et al. "Photobiomodulation Improves the Frontal Cognitive Function of Older Adults," *International Journal of Geriatric Psychiatry* 34 no. 2 (2019): 369–377, https://doi.org/10.1002/gps.5039.

7. P. Cassano, "Transcranial Photobiomodulation with Near-Infrared Light for Major Depressive Disorder: Efficacy and Tolerability Analyses from the ELATED 2 Pilot Trial," *Brain Stimulation* 12, no. 2 (2019): 453–453, https://doi.org/10.1016/j.brs.2018.12.471.

8. Richard Beever, "Do Far-Infrared Saunas have Cardiovascular Benefits in People with Type 2 Diabetes," *Canadian Journal of Diabetes* 34, no. 2 (2010): 113–118, https://doi.org/10.1016/S1499-2671(10)42007-9.

9. Fredrikus Oosterveld et al. "Infrared Sauna in Patients with Rheumatoid Arthritis and Ankylosing Spondylitis: A Pilot Study Showing Good Tolerance, Short-Term Improvement of Pain and Stiffness, and a Trend Towards Long-Term Beneficial Effects," *Clinical Rheumatology* 28 (2009): 29–34, https://doi.org/10.1007/s10067-008-0977-y.

10. Wanda Pilch et al. "Effect of a Single Finish Sauna Session on White Blood Cell Profile and Cortsol Levels in Athletes and Non-Athletes," *Journal of Human Kinetics* 39 (2013), https://doi.org/10.2478/hukin-2013-0075.

11. Akinori Masuda et al. "Repeated Thermal Therapy Diminishes Appetite Loss and Subjective Complaints in Mildly Depressed Patients," *Psychosomatic Medicine* 67 (2005), https://doi.org/10.1097/01.psy.0000171812.67767.8f.

12. Mark McCarty, Jorge Barroso-Aranda, and Francisco Contreras, "Regular Thermal Therapy May Promote Insulin Sensitivity while Boosting Expression of Endothelial Nitric Oxide Synthase-Effects Comparable to Those of Exercise Training," *Medical Hypotheses* 73 (2009), https://doi.org/ 10.1016/j.mehy.2008.12.020.

CHAPTER 16

1. Maria Guadalupe Rico-Rosillo and Gloria Bertha Vega-Robledo, "Sleep and Immune System," *Revista Alergia Mexico* 65, no. 2 (2018): 160–170, https://doi.org/10.29262/ram.v65i2.359.

2. Aric Prather et al. "Behaviorally Assessed Sleep and Susceptibility to the Common Cold," *Sleep* 38, no. 9 (2015): 1353–1359, https://doi.org/10.5665/sleep.4968.

3. Jianfei Lin et al. "Associations of Short Sleep Duration with Appetite Regulating Hormones and Adikopines: A Systematic Review and Meta-Analysis," *Obesity Reviews* 21, no. 11 (2020): e13051, https://doi.org/10.1111/obr.13051.

4. Lulu Xie et al. "Sleep Drives Metabolite Clearance from the Adult Brain," *Science* 342, no. 6156 (2013): 373–377, https://doi.org/10.1126/science.1241224.

5. Flavie Waters et al. "Severe Sleep Deprivation Causes Hallucinations and a Gradual Progression Toward Psychosis with Increasing Time Awake," *Frontiers in Psychiatry* 9 (2018): 303–303, https://doi.org/10.3389/fpsyt.2018.00303.

6. Kyungah Choi et al. "Awakening Effects of Blue-Enriched Morning Light Exposure on University Students' Physiological and Subjective Responses," *Scientific Reports* 9, no. 1 (2019): 345–345, https://doi.org/10.1038/s41598-018-36791-5.

7. William Killgore et al. "0884 Morning Blue Light Exposure Improves Sleep and Fear Extinction Recall," *Sleep* 42, no. Supplement_1 (2019): A355–A356, https://doi.org/10.1093/sleep/zsz067.882.

8. C. R. Markus, "Effects of Carbohydrates on Brain Tryptophan Availability and Stress Performance," *Biological Psychology 76, no. 1–2* (2007): 83–90, https://doi.org/10.1016/j.biopsycho.2007.06.003.

9. Kazue Okamoto-Mizuno and Koh Mizuno, (2012). Effects of Thermal Environment on Sleep and Circadian Rhythm. *Journal of Physiological Anthropology* 31, no. 14 (2012), https://doi.org/10.1186/1880-6805-31-14.

10. Devin Binder and Helen Scharfman, "Brain-Derived Neurotrophic Factor," *Growth Factors* 22, no. 3 (2004): 123–131, https://doi.org/10.1080/08977190410001723308; Krisztina Marosi and Mark Mattson, "BDNF Mediates Adaptive Brain and Body Responses to Energetic Challenges," *Trend in Endocrinology and Metabolism* 25, no. 2 (2014): 89–98, https://doi.org/10.1016/j.tem.2013.10.006.

11. Siri Kvam et al. "Exercise as a Treatment for Depression: A Meta-Analysis," *Journal of Affective Disorders* 202 (2016): 67–86, https://doi.org/10.1016/j.jad.2016.03.063.

12. Yun-Zi Liu, Yun-Xia Wang, and Chun-Lei Jiang, "Inflammation: The Common Pathway of Stress-Related Diseases," *Frontiers in Human Neuroscience* 11 (2017): 316–316, https://doi.org/10.3389/fnhum.2017.00316.

CHAPTER 17

1. Heather Stuckey and Jeremy Nobel, "The Connection between Art, Healing, and Public Health: A Review of Current Literature," *American Journal of Public Health* 100, no. 2 (2010): 254–263, https://doi.org/10.2105/AJPH.2008.156497.

2. Maria Ironside et al. "Effect of Prefrontal Cortex Stimulation on Regulation of Amygdala Response to Threat in Individuals with Trait Anxiety: A Randomized Clinical Trial," *JAMA Psychiatry* 76, no. 1 (2019): 71–78, https://doi.org/10.1001/jamapsychiatry.2018.2172.

3. *Dynamic Neural Retraining System Student Manual: Seminar Version* (Dynamic Neural Retraining System, 2008–2019).

4. Greg Siegle et al. "Increased Amygdala and Decreased Dorsolateral Prefrontal BOLD Responses in Unipolar Depression: Related and Independent Features," *Biological Psychiatry* 61, no. 2 (2007): 198–209, https://doi.org/10.1016/j.biopsych.2006.05.048.

5. Kelly Lambert et al. "Optimizing Brain Performance: Identifying Mechanisms of Adaptive Neurobiological Plasticity," *Neuroscience and Biobehavioral Reviews* 105 (2019): 60–71, https://doi.org/10.1016/j.neubiorev.2019.06.033.

6. Mihaly Csikszentmihalyi, *Flow: The Psychology of Optimal Experience* (HarperCollins, 1990), 145.

CHAPTER 18

1. John Bowlby, *A Secure Base: Parent-Child Attachment and Healthy Human Development* (Routledge, 1988), 162.

2. Debra Umberson and Jennifer Karas Montez, "Social Relationships and Health: A Flashpoint for Health Policy," *Journal of Health and Social Behavior* (2010): 51, https://doi.org/10.1177/0022146510383501.

3. Sheldon Cohen, "Social Relationships and Health," *American Psychologist* 5, no. 8 (2004): 676–684, https://doi.org/10.1037/0003-066X.59.8.676.

4. Bert Uchino, *Social Support & Physical Health: Understanding the Health Consequences of Relationships* (Yale University Press, 2004).

CHAPTER 19

1. Greg Siegle et al. "Increased Amygdala and Decreased Dorsolateral Prefrontal BOLD Responses in Unipolar Depression: Related and Independent Features," *Biological Psychiatry* 61, no. 2 (2007): 198–209, https://doi.org/10.1016/j.biopsych.2006.05.048.

2. Eric Kim, Shelley Hershner, and Victor Strecher, "Purpose in Life and Incidence of Sleep Disturbances," *Journal of Behavioral Medicine* 38 (2015), https://doi.org/10.1007/s10865-015-9635-4.

3. Børge Sivertsen et al. "The Bidirectional Association between Depression and Insomnia: The HUNT Study," *Psychosomatic Medicine* 74, no. 7 (2012): 758–765, https://doi.org/10.1097/PSY.0b013e3182648619.

4. Stacey Schaefer et al. "Purpose in Life Predicts Better Emotional Recovery from Negative Stimuli," *PLOS ONE* 8, no. 11 (2013): e80329–e80329, https://doi.org/10.1371/journal.pone.0080329; Carien van Reekum et al. "Individual Differences in Amygdala and Ventromedial Prefrontal Cortex Activity are Associated with

Evaluation Speed and Psychological Well-Being," *Journal of Cognitive Neuroscience* 19, no. 2 (2007): 237–248, https://doi.org/10.1162/jocn.2007.19.2.237.

5. Eric Kim et al. "Purpose in Life and Reduced Incidence of Stroke in Older Adults,'" *Journal of Psychosomatic Research* 74, no. 5 (2013): 427–432, https://doi.org/10.1016/j.jpsychores.2013.01.013; Eric Kim et al. "Association between Purpose in Life and Objective Measures of Function in Older Adults," *JAMA Psychiatry* 74, no. 10 (2017), https://doi.org/10.1001/jamapsychiatry.2017.2145.

6. Mihaly Csikszentmihalyi, *Flow: The Psychology of Optimal Experience* (HarperCollins, 1990), 145.

CHAPTER 20

1. Fábio Duarte Schwalm et al. "Is There a Relationship between Spirituality/Religiosity and Resilience? A Systematic Review and Meta-Analysis of Observational Studies," *Journal of Health Psychology* 27, no. 5 (2022): 1218–1232, https://doi.org/10.1177/1359105320984537.

2. Harold Koenig, "Religion, Spirituality, and Health: The Research and Clinical Implications," *ISRN Psychiatry* (2012): 278730–278733, https://doi.org/10.5402/2012/278730.

3. Brenda Whitehead and Cindy Bergeman, "Coping with Daily Stress: Differential Role of Spiritual Experience on Daily Positive and Negative Affect," *The Journals of Gerontology: Series B* 67, no. 4 (2012): 456–459, https://doi.org/10.1093/geronb/gbr136.

4. J. Gonçalves et al. "Religious and Spiritual Interventions in Mental Health Care: A Systematic Review and Meta-Analysis of Randomized Clinical Trials," *Psychological Medicine* 45, no. 14 (2015), https://doi.org/10.1017/S0033291715001166; Emile Abou Chaar et al. "Evaluating the Impact of Spirituality on the Quality of Life, Anxiety, and Depression among Patients with Cancer: An Observational Transversal Study," *Support Care in Cancer* 26, no. 8 (2018): 2581–2590, https://doi.org/10.1007/s00520-018-4089-1.

ABOUT THE AUTHOR

KATY BOSSO is a professor of counseling and a licensed mental health counselor in the state of Florida in private practice. She holds a doctorate in counselor education and works with clients to overcome anxiety, depression, and relationship issues by helping them connect to their most authentic selves. Katy specializes in wellness, the mind-body connection, and how both help individuals thrive.